The Text and Contexts of Ignatius Loyola's
"Autobiography"

The Text and Contexts of Ignatius Loyola's "Autobiography"

John M. McManamon, S.J.

FORDHAM UNIVERSITY PRESS
New York   2013

Fordham University Press has no responsibility for the persistence
or accuracy of URLs for external or third-party Internet websites
referred to in this publication and does not guarantee that any
content on such websites is, or will remain, accurate or appropriate.

Fordham University Press also publishes its books in a variety of
electronic formats. Some content that appears in print may not be
available in electronic books.

Library of Congress Cataloging-in-Publication Data

McManamon, John M.
    The text and contexts of Ignatius Loyola's autobiography / John
M. McManamon.
        p. cm.
    Includes bibliographical references and index.
    ISBN 978-0-8232-4504-8 (cloth : alk. paper)—
ISBN 978-0-8232-4505-5 (pbk. : alk. paper)
    1. Ignatius, of Loyola, Saint, 1491–1556.   2. Christian saints—
Spain—Biography.   3. Ignatius, of Loyola, Saint, 1491–1556.
Autobiografia.   I. Title.
    BX4700.L7.M56 2013
    271'.5302—dc23
    [B]

                                                2012028211

Printed in the United States of America

15 14 13   5 4 3 2 1

First edition

For Roland and Frank, Clare and Mark

Contents

Preface

I would be the first to admit that this is a somewhat atypical book, synthetic in part and original, I believe, in its emphasis on the Lukan paradigm that guides the spiritual geography of Ignatius Loyola. I also believe that the premises for the book are sound and the need for the book bona fide. Ignatius Loyola consciously intended his narrative of God's activity in his life, properly titled *Acta*, as a way to assist his companions. Therefore, Jesuits of any era and those who collaborate in Jesuit apostolates or have interest in Jesuit spirituality will benefit by studying his *Acta*. In the immediate aftermath of a Thirty-Fifth General Congregation of the Society of Jesus and in a historical moment when issues of Jesuit identity feature on many agendas, it is appropriate to give that seminal text another look. In what follows, a rereading of Ignatius's text is facilitated by refracting its content through the lens of recent scholarship on the text itself, the beginnings of the Society of Jesus, and the Lukan New Testament writings. When paraphrasing the narrative of the *Acta*, I use the historical present to alert the reader to that fact. This book seeks to appeal to specialists and a more general audience, without insulting the intelligence of either. Jesuit history has enjoyed a renaissance of late, and Ignatius has featured prominently in that scholarship. I have used the notes to assist interested readers in finding relevant publications on key issues of historical context.[1]

For recent historical study of the so-called autobiography of Ignatius Loyola, two scholarly works have broken new ground. Marjorie O'Rourke Boyle dedicated a monograph to Ignatius's *Acta* that was published by the University of California Press in 1997. Throughout, O'Rourke Boyle emphasized that the text constitutes a "mirror of vainglory" as typical vice in the heart of Ignatius and a paean of praise for God's accomplishments in his heart. O'Rourke Boyle properly argued that the text is not an autobiography, an account of the entire life of Ignatius that Ignatius himself wrote. The existing text does not cover Ignatius's entire life, and he did not write it, strictly speaking. Moreover, since Ignatius did not intend the work to be an autobiography, he never used the first person pronoun when referring to himself. Readers have long known that Ignatius designates himself "the pilgrim" or "the prisoner," but they have often failed to appreciate the implications of that choice for genre and message. Ignatius would say that readers who call the work his autobiography have not "seen clearly" why he narrated as he did.

Jerónimo Nadal (1507–80), Ignatius's trusted collaborator and frequent traveler for official Jesuit business, did see clearly when he argued that the text was best titled *Acta*, in the sense that the word is used in the Acts of the Apostles: a celebration of "all that God had done with them" (Acts 14:27, 15:4). The title reflects a major emphasis of that book, its activism, well encapsulated in the question that Ignatius posed to himself midway through the narrative: "What should he do?" (*Quid agendum*).[2] Jesuits see God's Spirit acting in the hearts of believers, and Jesuits realize their vocation by doing. As O'Rourke Boyle noted, Ignatius asserted in the Principle and Foundation of his *Spiritual Exercises* that human beings exist, in the first place, "to praise God." She used her insight to propose a stringent hermeneutic for the entire text: when the narrative blames the sinner, it is Ignatius speaking, and when the narrative praises the saint, it is Gonçalves da Câmara editorializing.[3] Marjorie O'Rourke Boyle is a proven scholar with masterful knowledge of early modern sources. She supplies helpful information on the literary and religious world in which Ignatius's narrative was born. The text of Ignatius's *Acta* may add still one more reason for utilizing her scholarship as a way to understand his *Acta* better. In Ignatius's thirst for substantive spiritual conversation, he often consulted women.

John W. O'Malley, in turn, emphasized Ignatius's *Acta* as a narrative offering contextualized meaning for what it is to be a Jesuit. All Jesuits, to a greater or lesser degree, will share the spiritual experience of Ignatius that unwound in stages: from interior repentance for sinfulness to a decision to help souls to pursuit of an education as vital for that service to harassment and persecution in that service. O'Malley's book *The First Jesuits* helps to fill the gap in years between the dictation of Ignatius's narrative from 1553 to 1555 and the narrative's ending in 1538.[4] In the years from 1538 to 1553, the Society of Jesus came into existence, and Ignatius gained vital experience as leader of the organization.

Years of crisis for the nascent Society supply the immediate backdrop for the project. Internally, Ignatius confronted the troubling rebelliousness of Simâo Rodrigues (1510–79) and Nicolás Bobadilla (1509–90), among his earliest companions, and the regressive efforts of Jesuit novices, intent on transforming the Society into a traditional monastic order. Externally, Ignatius faced attacks on his *Spiritual Exercises* in Spain and on the Society's Institute in France. When Ignatius stopped dictating because of the heat of the summer of 1555, he referred to Rome's renowned daytime temperatures. At that moment, Ignatius also was experiencing the figurative heat generated by friction with a clear antagonist in Pope Paul IV, who, as a bishop and a cardinal, had already sparred with Ignatius. O'Malley's scholarship adds a second critical dimension: the *Acta* as a mirror of vainglory and a mirror of apostolic religious life. The opposition that Ignatius was experiencing from elements in the church suspicious of his apostolic order may have focused his memories. The number and detail of passages in the *Acta* that Ignatius dictated about his encounters with church inquisitors are greater than the passages he dictated about his mystical visions.

Opposition and persecution also play a fundamental role in Luke's Acts of the Apostles. This study principally argues that an appreciation of the two New Testament writings ascribed to Luke, his Gospel and Acts, helps interpret the theological perspectives of Ignatius in his *Acta*. Ignatian spirituality draws on the richer stream of all four Gospels. This book, however, contends that the specific geography of Luke's two writings and the theology that undergirds Luke's redactional innovation assisted Ignatius in remembering and understanding the crucial acts of God in his own life. Consequently, Lukan spirituality can renew and enrich Ignatian spirituality. That does not mean that only Luke's writings are relevant to Ignatian spirituality. It does mean that Luke's writings are especially helpful in appreciating the narrative of the *Acta*. As Louis Beirnaert observed, the overall trajectory of Ignatius's narrative moves from a traditional pilgrimage to Jerusalem to an apostolic mission to the entire world.[5] Though Beirnaert did not make the connection, that is the precise trajectory of Luke's writings. In discerning a religious vocation of active service to his urban world, Ignatius could find one source of inspiration in Luke's description of apostolic ministries in Acts. Even the odd choice of the name for Ignatius's religious order may have found partial inspiration in passages such as Acts 4:13, where Peter and John are recognized as "those who were with Jesus" (Vulgate *quoniam cum Iesu fuerant*) or, following the New Revised Standard Version's translation of the Greek text, as "companions of Jesus." Those ordinary men act boldly in the Spirit and do amazing things "in the name of Jesus" (Acts 4:18). There is only one thing those men cannot do: not share the gift of what they have seen and heard.

Some may object that Ignatius was not a scholar and lacked sufficient knowledge of Luke's writings to make such applications. It is true that Ignatius was not a scholar, but he was university trained. Roland Barthes and Marjorie O'Rourke Boyle were right to question the image of Ignatius as unlettered, an image that owes much to obscurantist hagiography.[6] Ignatius's most effective tool for communicating his spirituality, the *Spiritual Exercises*, breaks up the Gospel accounts of the life of Jesus into individual contemplations spread across Weeks Two, Three, and Four of that spiritual retreat. He began that series of contemplations with Luke's account of the Annunciation and ended with Luke's account of the Ascension. In between, there were passages from the evangelists, including Luke, that Ignatius would review every time that he guided someone in making the *Exercises*. Moreover, we know that Ignatius valued education as essential to his apostolic goals. We know that Ignatius switched universities and colleges within universities to obtain an education suited to his goals. And we know that Ignatius embraced education as an evangelical ministry.

In addition to conversance with the Gospels through university study and spiritual direction, Ignatius had the scriptures mediated to him through the art and ritual of his day. Paintings of the Annunciation, recorded only in Luke, became ubiquitous in Italy during the fifteenth and sixteenth centuries. Luke's account of the meeting of the two disciples with Jesus on the road to Emmaus had, in its traditional medieval interpretation, a matrix of pilgrimage. The Emmaus text was read as the Gospel at the liturgy on Easter Monday, the day on which the event occurred in Luke's Gospel. And the Emmaus narrative supplied the basis for a liturgical drama regularly enacted in Catholic lands at vespers on that same Easter Monday. The drama interpreted the two disciples as representing the Old and New Testament: the named disciple Cleopas was portrayed by an elderly actor to symbolize the Old Testament, and the unnamed disciple, logically considered to be Luke, was portrayed by a young actor as representative of the New Testament. Evidence from a pilgrim's guidebook indicates that the Franciscan guide at the presumed site of Emmaus would enlist medieval pilgrims to recite the story in situ. That Lukan passage portrayed a conversion that involved education of the ignorant (Vulgate *stulti*) and a deep-seated change of heart (Vulgate *tardi corde ad credendum*).[7] Ignatius had an academic knowledge of the scriptures sufficient for ordination to the priesthood and a lived knowledge of the scriptures mediated through art, ritual, drama, and his own *Exercises*.

The meaning of Ignatius's *Acta* is best appreciated in the context of the language that he dictated, the events that he chose to include or not include, and the cultures that helped to shape his expression and understanding. One appreciates those cultures by moving forward to Ignatius and his times through the Renaissance, not by viewing backward through the lens of the Counter-Reformation, which distorts our understanding. The early Jesuits themselves, as we shall see, contributed to that distortion by suppressing the *Acta* in favor of official biographies composed by Jesuits with impeccable counterreforming credentials. For example, Ignatius has been characterized as a former soldier who endowed the Society of Jesus with a quasi-military discipline, reflected in his choice of *compañia / societas* as the official designation for his new religious order. Yet, early in the *Acta*, Ignatius made clear his distaste for misguided military heroics and aristocratic crusading fervor.

Moreover, the Castilian term *compañia* had other relevant meanings in Ignatius's day. His Basque homeland had a flourishing shipbuilding industry based on extensive reserves of timber and iron. Basques were the only accomplished seafarers in medieval Europe between Scandinavia to the north and the Mediterranean to the south and east. They dominated shipbuilding and transport in the northwestern Atlantic and early on reached the Americas in search of new fishing and whaling grounds. Among Basque and Iberian sailors of the sixteenth century, a spirit of sharing in the risks and rewards of the undertaking still predominated. As a portion of their pay, those sailors accepted shares in the venture, and to emphasize their collaborative engagement, they called themselves a *compañia* and called each other *compañero*. If Ignatius was influenced by that vital industry of his homeland and that peculiar approach of coparticipation, then *compañia*, as applied to his new religious order, takes on resonances of partners in a common venture and distinguishes his Society from the rigid hierarchy and often violent discipline of every military society. The sacred rituals on board Iberian vessels offer a further clue for possible influence of the culture of seafaring. The most important religious ritual on those vessels in the time of Ignatius was not the Mass, given the rarity of a chaplain, but a solemn singing of *Salve Regina* followed by litanies on Saturday evenings.[8]

I may well suffer from vainglory, and I am sure that I struggle with pugnaciousness and impatience. I therefore beg the reader's pardon for any remaining inaccuracies or overly aggressive criticisms on my part. I would like to express my gratitude to John Padberg, S.J., Richard Blake, S.J., and the other members of the National Seminar on Jesuit Spirituality, among whom the idea for this research was born. A number of Jesuit friends encouraged me to continue this research when I was not altogether sure where it was leading. They include Steve Corder, Jack Benz, Phil Chmielewski, Rob McChesney, Mike Engh, Rob Scholla, Mike Pastizzo, Tom Tobin, Mike Scully, Jim Siwicki, Dan Hartnett, Alejandro Olayo, and Pat Douglas. I would like to thank two special friends who read portions of this study prior to its publication and graciously offered suggestions for improving it: Dr. (in an academic sense) David Keene and Dr. (in a medical sense) Myles Sheehan, S.J.

I thank Daniel Bornstein, erudite professor at Washington University in Saint Louis, and Raymond Schroth, S.J., distinguished editor of *America* magazine in New York City, for their careful scrutiny of the manuscript on behalf of Fordham University Press and for their helpful suggestions to improve it. From the day that I emailed Will Cerbone with a prospectus of this book, I have found him a most gracious and supportive editor. I thank Will and all at Fordham University Press for their generous commitment to publishing scholarship on Ignatian history and spirituality. I would be remiss not to acknowledge the probing questions and helpful revisions that Julie Palmer-Hoffman contributed. I would finally like to thank Loyola University Chicago and the Center for Medieval and Renaissance Studies at UCLA for awarding me summer grants in support of this research, and I thank my brother Dave, unofficial mayor of Venice Beach, for supplying me a most congenial place to do much of the writing.

Last, I would like to dedicate this book to four erudite and inspirational friends. Two of the four are now deceased: Roland Murphy, O.Carm., with whom I had the privilege to live during doctoral studies and from whom I learned to appreciate the myriad good things that God has done for us through the gift of the scriptures, and F. X. Martin, O.S.A., from whom I learned to prize the gift of my Irish heritage and in whom I always cherished a combination of intelligence and wit that epitomized his committed life of scholarly activity. The living members of this venerable quartet are Clare O'Reilly, who quietly exemplifies the dogged dedication of the text scholar and graciously makes "Killakee" (County Dublin) so welcoming and hospitable, and Mark Henninger, S.J., who carries on the research and teaching of Scholastic philosophy from his endowed chair at Georgetown University and does so with his characteristic insight, common sense, and integrity.

The Text and Contexts of Ignatius Loyola's "Autobiography"

The *Acta* as Privileged and New Source

In Lent of 1548, only eight years into the experiment, the Society of Jesus that Ignatius Loyola had founded came in for severe criticism when Melchor Cano (1509–60), a learned Spanish Dominican, preached against the Jesuits. Cano subsequently structured his criticisms according to the pastoral advice offered in 2 Timothy 3:1–6, seeing in the Jesuits the manifestation of those evil ways that will make the last days such "distressing times." Cano shared the millennial perspectives of many of his Spanish contemporaries. Those perspectives exponentially increased the perceived dangers of sinful behavior.[1] Inspired by the author of that pastoral letter, Cano took it upon himself to make the folly of the Jesuit way of proceeding apparent to everyone. Cano accurately characterized the novel features of Jesuit religious life: Jesuits walk down the streets of cities, eat like everyone else, and eschew mortification in keeping with a comfortable lifestyle. They have become the latest fad in spirituality, but one should not misconstrue their true intentions. The Jesuits' easy accommodation with the world has put credulous women at risk everywhere: "[A]mong them are those who make their way into households and captivate silly women, overwhelmed by their sins and swayed by all kinds of desires" (2 Timothy 3:6).

For the rest of his life, Cano remained an eloquent and ardent opponent of the Jesuits. In Cano's estimation, with only the coarseness of their theological training as preparation, Jesuits preached a watered-down Christian spirituality. Cano's personal dislike for Ignatius himself fueled his antagonism toward the Jesuit order. Cano had met Ignatius on at least three different occasions. The Dominican friar attacked the spiritual teachings of Ignatius, especially as Ignatius proposed them through his *Spiritual Exercises*. Because Ignatius posited the direct guidance of the Holy Spirit in every believer's heart, Cano felt that he had embraced the heretical positions of the Spanish *alumbrados*. Moreover, the Ignatian teachings on indifference and on modes of contemplation accessible to all would have dangerous social consequences, leading many to abandon their daily duties at work and in the home and turn to hours of personal prayer. For Cano, it was not surprising that Ignatius would evangelize in that dangerous way, for the founder of the Jesuits was anything but holy. Cano claimed that Ignatius had fled from the Inquisition in Spain when he sensed that the tribunal would judge against him. The Basque renegade had no integrity but did have much vanity. In the words of 2 Timothy, Ignatius was one of those "lovers of himself," a boaster and one swollen with conceit. Cano had grown weary of Ignatius's vain posturing, his penchant for touting his visions and brandishing his titles. Cano reminded his audience that vainglory was one of the devil's most effective tricks, for vainglory made evil persons seem to be good. What made Cano such a formidable opponent was the quality of key elements in his analysis. While categorically rejecting Cano's assertions that he was teaching the heretical positions of the *alumbrados* and had fled the Inquisition, Ignatius would admit that vainglory was the most serious flaw in his character. He confessed as much in his *Acta*.[2]

Genesis of Ignatius's *Acta*

In fact, the work came to be because Ignatius took vainglory so seriously. When close Jesuit friends requested that Ignatius leave them an account of his spiritual life, they put him in a quandary. To honor their request might well lead Ignatius to practice vainglory, which by that time he had come to acknowledge as the foremost vice of his life. Vainglory is defined as excessive or ostentatious conceit, especially in one's achievements. The vice has a strong quotient of visibility and feeds off acquiring fame. Christian spiritual writers actually detected a subtle difference between pride and vainglory and rated vainglory the most difficult vice to uproot from the soul.[3] In the words of Matthew's Gospel (6:1), vainglorious believers practice their "piety before others in order to be seen by them." There is something fundamentally hypocritical about disciples who sound a trumpet before giving alms or stand in synagogues when praying or look dismal while fasting.

Despite Ignatius's reticence to give such an account, his Jesuit friends pestered him to provide one. For his intimate associate, Jerónimo Nadal, Ignatius's account would constitute nothing less than the "authentic founding of the Society [of Jesus]." Nadal was convinced that a narrative of the ways in which the Lord had educated Ignatius would supply "paternal education" for his spiritual sons.[4] Ignatius alone could provide a mirror for Jesuit apostolic service. But Ignatius feared that were he to do so he would fall once again into the vice of vainglory, which troubled him from the feckless days of his youth.

Nonetheless, Ignatius did acquiesce, and the preface to his narration explains how he resolved his dilemma.[5] The memory of that resolution was so clear that the protagonists could supply an exact time and place for it: Friday morning, 4 August 1553, the vigil of Our Lady of the Snows, in the garden of the Duke's residence in Rome.[6] Ignatius overcame his reservations thanks to a conversation about spiritual matters with another Jesuit, Luis Gonçalves da Câmara. Ignatius discovered that Gonçalves da Câmara was also struggling with vainglory. As a remedy for that spiritual illness, Ignatius recommended that his fellow Jesuit acknowledge all the blessings of his life as a gift from God and be grateful to such a generous Lord. Ignatius's advice worked, for the tears that streamed down Gonçalves da Câmara's face indicated to Ignatius a change in interior disposition. The conversation convinced Ignatius that he could use his account as a way to help Jesuits. He should supply Jesuits with a mirror of vainglory because his principal vice might be theirs as well: apostolic religious life appealed to the vainglorious. At the same time, he could offer a mirror of the apostolic vocation by showing that the Lord had inspired him to repent for his sins and to help souls through various ministries. Scholars today generally concur that the narrative is not an autobiography. The text does, however, have distinct elements of the Ignatian examination of conscience writ large, as it reviews the actions of God in the life of Ignatius until he settled in Rome in 1538.[7] And the preface anticipates important themes in the account that follows: Ignatius's lifelong desire for substantive spiritual conversation, his simple and eloquent characterization of the apostolate as helping souls, and his trust in tears as a generally reliable indicator of a change of heart. Ignatius wanted Gonçalves da Câmara to take his dictation because, at that point in their lives, they both needed to reflect seriously on the vice of vainglory.[8]

The entire project, however, made halting progress, which reflects Ignatius's struggle to handle vainglory properly. Gonçalves da Câmara, in his preface, quotes Ignatius as remembering that he had sought healing for his vanity over the two years he spent in travel from Loyola to Jerusalem. When Ignatius stopped narrating for significant blocks of time, he acquired a persuasive note of integrity, what rhetoricians call ethos. He really did fear giving in to the temptation to celebrate his accomplishments.[9] Ignatius also had other reasons to interrupt the project: he was often ill and had much to do as superior-general of the Society of Jesus. Nonetheless, beginning in September of 1553, he communicated a first portion of the story, dealing with his "youthful escapades." Some commentators think that we no longer have that account, given that the published text has no record of any sexual liaisons. They may be right, but it may also be the case that Ignatius had a different preoccupation from our own. There are two issues involved: What qualify as youthful episodes, and what does "youthful" mean in the mid-sixteenth century? Because Ignatius was more concerned with vainglory, he emphasized those "youthful escapades" that illustrated his struggle with that vice, particularly during the arc of time from his wounding at Pamplona to his departing from Jerusalem. In Ignatius's day, a male's youth lasted until he had attained knighthood, married, and inherited his father's property. Classical theorists contended that adolescence lasted well into one's twenties or even thirties. In Alcalá in late 1526, a Father Hernando Rubio, O.F.M., when giving a deposition for the Inquisition, twice called Ignatius a youth (*mancebo*) and estimated that Ignatius was around twenty years old when he was actually around thirty-five.[10]

For over a year, illness and business interrupted the dictation of the narrative. When Nadal sent Gonçalves da Câmara to press Ignatius to begin again, their collective pleading failed. Only in March 1555 did Ignatius find time to resume dictating, but he was soon interrupted by a rapid succession of papal deaths and elections, from Julius III to Marcellus II to Paul IV. After Paul's election in May, the summer heat descended on Rome and again forced a delay. By 21 September 1555, Ignatius was willing to start anew but then delayed the dictation again, this time because Gonçalves da Câmara kept trying to get a close look at Ignatius's face as he spoke.[11] Such absorption with the exterior, rather than the interior, revived the reservations Ignatius felt for the entire undertaking. Nonetheless, after urging Gonçalves da Câmara to obey the order's rule about modesty when looking at another, Ignatius resumed narrating and managed to finish in late October, just as Gonçalves da Câmara was to depart for Spain. The written text had a lengthy and difficult gestation, evolving from Gonçalves da Câmara's memorization of Ignatius's verbal account, to written notes that served as the basis for dictation to secretaries, to a completed text written in Spanish for most of the narrative and switching to Italian for its final segment.

Granting the complicated process of composition, there are still at least three reasons to consider the text a valuable source for Ignatius's thinking. First, Gonçalves da Câmara characterized Ignatius as a "vivid describer," whose account was easy to memorize.[12] That would fit Ignatius well, who consistently utilized a norm of "seeing clearly" when he sought to discern the inspiration of God at crucial moments in his life. There are three occasions in the prefatory material and twelve occasions in the text of the *Acta* where the Spanish words *claro* (clear) and *claridad* (clarity) are used, and there are two occasions in the text where the Italian adverb *chiaramente* (clearly) is used.[13] Following the path of his pilgrimage from Azpeitia to Jerusalem to Rome allowed Ignatius to search his inventory of mental images and find those relevant to his account of God's dealings with him.[14] Second, as the account came to a close, Gonçalves da Câmara remembered that Ignatius was in especially good humor. Ignatius felt that he had supplied a straightforward narrative of God's action in his life. Ignatius acknowledged that he had continued to struggle with vices even after he had dedicated himself to serving the Lord, though he was confident that none of his sins had been mortal. Contrary to the opinion of his adversaries, Ignatius did know the difference between a mortal and a venial sin.[15] Finally, the text was completed in Ignatius's lifetime, and he did not object to its circulation. Nadal, too, was pleased with the results. "The whole life of the Society is contained in germ and expressed in Ignatius's story."[16]

Removal of Ignatius's *Acta*

The *Acta* accurately reflect the historical reality that Ignatius alone founded the Society of Jesus. The founding was not the collective venture that Nicolás Bobadilla or Simâo Rodrigues later imagined.[17] The precise elements of that story also reflect conscious decisions on the part of Ignatius as his thinking matured over time. He had extensive opportunity to consider what he would share with his fellow Jesuits. What he chose to narrate and what he chose not to narrate indicate his discerned priorities. Once Ignatius published his considered narrative, the book ironically had a brief shelf life beyond his death in 1556. For long periods of time, Jesuits and other interested readers could not consult Ignatius's *Acta*.

In effect, the *Acta* constitute a relatively new historical source, for within fifteen years of the book's completion, all copies had been removed from circulation. It was not until the mid-eighteenth century that the Bollandists first published a Latin translation of the text in the seventh volume of *Acta sanctorum*. Ignatius's narrative was critically edited from the surviving vernacular manuscripts and published only in 1904, and the two versions, vernacular original and Latin translation, were published side by side in 1943. The lag in publishing a critical edition occurred because Jesuit leadership in the sixteenth century decided to confiscate all existing copies of the book. During his term as superior-general, Francisco de Borja (1510–72) locked up those copies of the *Acta* in the Jesuit archives. The letters that Borja and Pedro de Ribadeneira (1526–1611) exchanged with their fellow Jesuit, Jerónimo Nadal, furnish the bare details of that operation.[18]

On 8 January 1567, Borja first wrote to Nadal, then traveling in central Europe, to ask that Nadal send documents to Rome relevant to the research that Borja had commissioned on the life of Ignatius. Borja indicated a special concern for the autograph manuscript of Ignatius's writings on devotional and spiritual movements, his *Spiritual Diary*. Borja also requested any documents that Nadal had pertaining to Ignatius, whether the writings of Ignatius himself or notes that Nadal or others had made about Ignatius or documents related to the founding of the Jesuits, and he explicitly stipulated the *Acta* that Gonçalves da Câmara had dictated to Jesuit secretaries and the *Acta* that Ribadeneira had written on the life of Ignatius. Nadal responded to Borja on 20 February and assured the superior-general that Father Diego Jiménez was busy copying the documents that Nadal, in response to Borja's request, had found. Nadal admitted that he had located little beyond two works involving Gonçalves da Câmara, the *Acta* of Ignatius and the *Memoriale* of Gonçalves da Câmara while minister in Rome, and one work of Ribadeneira, the *Acta*. Nadal informed Borja that he gave the autograph copy of Ignatius's *Spiritual Diary* to Diego Laínez (1512–65), among the first companions of Ignatius and the Jesuits' second superior-general. Nadal suspected that Laínez, prior to his death, had passed that copy to Alfonso Salmerón (1515–85), another of Ignatius's first companions. Nadal did have a copy of the work in the event that Borja could not track down the autograph. Nadal complimented Borja on his support for historical research and encouraged him to pursue the project. On 24 March, though convinced that copies of almost all the important documents were available in Rome, Nadal sent the materials that Jiménez had copied. He promised to continue looking for anything that would be of assistance, including a Spanish copy of the *Spiritual Exercises* that had autograph notes by Ignatius.

When Nadal next heard from Rome, the news came from Ribadeneira, who wrote on 29 June 1567, the feast, as Ribadeneira noted, of his patron, Saint Peter. That subtle note of authority reflects the demanding tenor of the letter. Ribadeneira used his missive to explain the research project more carefully and inform Nadal that he had misunderstood the superior-general's purpose. Borja had asked Ribadeneira to compose a biography of Ignatius, and Ribadeneira had moved from Rome to Frascati, where he had nearly finished a draft of the first of the four parts he envisioned for the work. He hoped by summer's end to complete a draft of the second part as well. He asked Nadal to do two things to assist him: write down his own detailed account of the thoughts and words of Ignatius and do a better job executing Borja's instructions, which the superior-general had recently sent to all Jesuit provincials as well. Nadal had interpreted the instructions to relate to a research project where copies of the original documents would serve the purpose. But because Ribadeneira was writing a sanctioned biography of Ignatius, as he now informed Nadal, all existing copies of the *Acta* would need to be collected so that the work could no longer circulate and Jesuits no longer read it. Ribadeneira claimed that Ignatius's *Acta* did not fully cover his life (*cosa imperfecta*) and might obstruct or undermine faith in the fuller account, which he was composing. To avoid fostering rumors, Nadal should act with speed and prudence. A sinister note had crept into the project.

In a letter of 15 July, Borja confirmed the course he had chosen. Given the steady progress that Ribadeneira had made in writing his biography, Borja wished to remove from circulation all written materials bearing on that subject in every province of the Society (*mi pare si levino di mano tutti li trattati di cose simili in tutte le provincie*). Wherever Nadal traveled, he was to attend to this matter. Borja supplied the reasons for his decision. He emphasized that he wanted to ensure a consistent interpretation of the life of Ignatius, especially in the case of some matters not fully researched (*acciochè si levi la varietà et forsi alcune cose manco bene essaminate*). Nadal seemed surprised by the new instructions and decided to delay in fulfilling them. On 14 August, he wrote to Borja to inform him that the Jesuits who had materials relating to Ignatius's life preferred to keep them until they had seen Ribadeneira's biography. Once they had a chance to compare the two, they would comply immediately with the superior-general's wishes. Nadal decided not to force the issue with those Jesuits he had already visited and interpreted Borja's instructions to refer to the provinces he would visit in the future.

Though Borja and Ribadeneira were not pleased with Nadal's independent direction, they apparently decided to wait and discuss the matter with him personally upon his return to Rome. On 9 October, Borja briefly informed Nadal that Ribadeneira had completed the draft of the first two parts of his biography. A few weeks later, on 24 October, Ribadeneira sent to Nadal a much longer account of the project's status. Given the progress Ribadeneira had made, he obtained permission from Borja to take a leave of absence from his administrative duties at the Roman colleges and continue his writing. The two had decided to quicken the pace of the work. Ribadeneira expressed his hope of completing a first draft of the entire biography by the time that Nadal returned to Rome. At that point, Nadal could personally offer his comments and corrections. Ribadeneira admitted that writer's block and a lack of documents had slowed his progress. Juan Alfonso de Polanco (1517–76), longtime secretary to the superior-general, was searching for key documents back in Rome. Ribadeneira supplied Nadal with the fullest explanation yet of the decision to remove Ignatius's *Acta* from circulation. Borja reached the decision only after consulting the appropriate Jesuits living in Rome, and they all agreed on its wisdom. Ribadeneira's biography was to have official status and eliminate diversity of opinion on matters related to the life of Ignatius. Because Ignatius himself had dictated his *Acta*, the work had the potential to counteract a biography by another author. Though Ribadeneira granted that the *Acta* were faithful to the substance of Ignatius's life, it lacked important details and, in his view, reflected the weakness of Ignatius's memory when past sixty years of age. Although Ribadeneira indicated his conviction that Borja's instructions were the safest course of action, he suggested that Nadal hold on to any materials he had found until he returned to Rome. Once back home, Nadal could take up any difference of opinion directly with Borja.

Pierre-Antoine Fabre has suggested that the preface Nadal wrote for the *Acta* may be his last and most forceful plea not to remove the work from circulation. If that is true, Nadal failed to achieve his purpose.[19] The Latin edition of Ribadeneira's biography was published in 1572 and a Castilian translation in 1583. The *Acta* no longer circulated among Jesuits, and Ribadeneira's biography remained the official source for Ignatius's life until the Bollandists Jean and Ignace Pien researched matters more thoroughly in the eighteenth century. In reaching their decision, Borja and his advisors had actually planned well. Ribadeneira's life, reflecting the times in which it was written, sought to present an Ignatius who was firmly in the countering camp of early modern Catholicism. It portrayed as antitheses the orthodox Ignatius and the heretical Luther. It claimed that Ignatius's heart was chilled by reading the *Enchiridion* of Erasmus at Barcelona in 1524, a dubious claim given that Erasmus's work had not been translated into Castilian and Ignatius barely knew any Latin. Ribadeneira's own preparatory notes indicate that he knew the version in the *Acta*, which placed the Erasmus episode at Alcalá, but Ribadeneira shifted it to Barcelona to portray an Ignatius opposed to Erasmus from the very start of his education for ministries. That manipulation of the evidence contrasts with the objective posture that Ribadeneira assumed throughout the first four books of his biography.

In 1588, five years after publishing the Castilian translation of the Ignatius biography, Ribadeneira exhorted the soldiers and mariners about to sail against English Protestants to see their enterprise as anything but difficult because they were fighting for God's cause and God would lead them to victory.[20] Borja and his associates were right to think that the circulation of the *Acta* might well undermine the view of a militant Ignatius concerned to counter dangerous theologians like Luther and Erasmus. Among the conscious decisions that Ignatius made when supplying his narrative, he chose not to stress a need to counter the progress of heresy in Christendom. On the basis of his Paris years of study alone, he had numerous occasions to address the issue. Ignatius chose instead to emphasize the opposite: that he himself had been unfairly persecuted by overzealous inquisitors and churchmen, given the novelty of what he was proposing: a revival of the apostolic life of the first disciples. First, though, Ignatius wished to warn his fellow Jesuits of the temptation to vainglory that such a lifestyle perforce engendered.

2   The *Acta* as Mirror of Vainglory

By opening his account with the siege of Pamplona, Ignatius wastes no time in portraying for his fellow Jesuits how flawed his character was. He admits his obsession with vanities and his exceeding desire to win glory (*con un grande y vano deseo de ganar honra*), especially by fighting wars. Against the better judgment of all his fellow knights, he urges ongoing resistance to the French assault on the citadel. By indulging his vainglory, Ignatius puts the garrison and the entire city and himself at great risk. A vainglorious person discerns poorly; all of the other soldiers see clearly. By implication, Christians have to work hard to discern well. Wounded seriously in that foolish defense, Ignatius falls, both literally and morally. Unlike its dramatization in fictional lore, the siege in Ignatius's account has none of the traditional heroics of a classic battle.[1] As O'Rourke Boyle argues, Ignatius does not wish us to admire his actions there. Similarly, though authors may claim that the French brought Ignatius home, as an homage to his courage, the text does not make clear who carried the wounded soldier back to Azpeitia. The siege of Pamplona, in Ignatius's memory, should not be lionized as a heroic defense of the city. William Meissner better captures the Ignatian message: at Pamplona, a cannonball shattered not only Ignatius's leg but likewise his "narcissistic pomposity," a characteristic that often masks underlying insecurities.[2] Though Ignatius had valid insights into the complexities of the human psyche, his concerns in the narrative are preeminently spiritual. Vainglory had long engaged the interest of Christian spiritual writers from the eastern and western Mediterranean.

Vainglory: Scriptural, Patristic, and Medieval Background

The Scriptures

The Hebrew scriptures treat vanity in both a narrow and broad sense. A frequently cited passage in Jeremiah (9:22–24) bears a warning about the dangers of vainglory in a narrow sense and directs that warning especially to the wealthy, the well educated, and the politically powerful. They should not boast about their status, especially in light of the great equalizer that mortality comprises. "Thus says the Lord: 'Human corpses shall fall like dung upon the open field, like sheaves behind the reaper, and no one shall gather them.'" The text supplied later generations with the image of death as a grim reaper. Vanity in the broader sense suggests that human life is futile and inconsequential. The prophet Isaiah (40:6–7) underlined that ephemeral character of human existence; so changeable is the human heart that it takes only a breath of the Lord to blow over it and it withers like grass. The scribe Qoheleth wove the theme of the vanity of human life through much of his reflection. He characterized the human situation as desolate and God's activity as enigmatic. Qoheleth urged his fellow Hebrews to avoid a faith that simplistically viewed God only as magically doing good and saving. God had created a history in which his people could encounter the divinity, but they must divest themselves of the presumptuousness that they understand God's activity. True reverence and fear of the Lord implied acknowledging that many questions generated by lived experience in that history had no answer or could not be answered. In that sense, "all is vanity," for the inconsequential and the futile distinguish human existence.[3]

In the New Testament, Paul chose to focus on vanity when communicating with the turbulent new community at Corinth, riddled by faction, inclined to boast, and proudly nonconformist. A childish pride in being different had led one member of the community to take his stepmother as a concubine. Early on, Christian thinkers tied arrogance to sexual licentiousness. Paul urged the community to assess honestly what they possess of their own that should engender pride and offered a response in keeping with the admonitions of Qoheleth: "nothing." Quoting Jeremiah's reflections, Paul urged the fractious community to unite in boasting of the Lord for the Lord's activity in human history. It is God who acts with steadfast love, justice, and righteousness on the earth. The Gospel of Matthew dissuaded believers from performing traditional acts of Jewish piety merely to gain the applause of spectators. The reward for vainglory, in such instances, went no further than such transient applause. The New Testament writers mirrored emphases of the broader Greco-Roman culture in which they were educated. The Roman philosopher Seneca, for example, moralized that "Whoever wants to publicize his virtue labors not for virtue but for vainglory."[4] The Gospel attributed to John, probably the latest to reach its final form, consistently emphasizes that Jesus does not seek his own glory. "If I glorify myself, my glory is nothing" (John 8:54). In the end, the quest for personal glory comprised a form of idolatry; Jesus seeks the glory of the one who sent him. Believers express love for God not by boasting of their accomplishments as a way to aggrandize themselves but by welcoming the one whom God has sent.

Eastern Spiritual Writers

From the fourth to the thirteenth centuries, monks in the eastern part of the Mediterranean world developed a spirituality that depicted the subtle dangers of vainglory. Classical moralists and satirists had used common sense to ridicule the boorishness of vanity. Greek monks, by contrast, used their experience of monastic life and their reading of the scriptures to develop their own critique of that vice, generally called *kenodoxia*. Numbered by Evagrius of Pontus (ca. 345–399) among the principal faults of human nature, later less properly labeled as "deadly sins," vainglory was closely associated with pride and attacked the committed ascetic at the most advanced stage of the spiritual life. Logically, anyone filled with pride in self will seek the recognition of others.[5] John Chrysostom (ca. 347–407) preached on the dangers of vainglory in the contexts of Pauline exegesis and parental education.[6] Decrying the tendencies of a "theater culture" obsessed with ostentatious clothing, physical fitness, and conspicuous consumption, Chrysostom emphasized that enslavement to vainglory inhibited sound discernment of what was beneficial to others and oneself. By way of contrast, the bishop of Constantinople adduced the apostles in Acts, who did not allow sacrifices to themselves (14:13–17), did not attribute healing to their own powers (3:12–16), found their motivation not in vainglory but charity, and treated all that they received as common resources for redistribution, especially to the community's needy.

John Climacus (ca. 579/599–ca. 659/679) suggested the intimate relationship between vainglory and pride by comparing them to wheat and bread.[7] Vainglory comprised the raw material from which pride took substance. Because vainglory made one self-righteous, it proved supremely divisive in any Christian community. Climacus tied his theories on spiritual growth to his notions of bodily energies. Whereas in the fallen, those energies move downward toward the sexual organs, in the blessed, moisture moves upward toward the supreme gift of tears. A self-obsessed heart of stone gradually becomes compassionate.

In addition to pride, therefore, vainglory was also associated with lust and with envy and avarice as well. Applying the words of 1 John 2:16 to the temptations of Jesus in the Gospels, spiritual writers generally agreed that all disordered passions had a triple source: lust of the flesh (gluttony), lust of the eyes (avarice), and pride of life (vainglory).[8] In analyzing vainglory, eastern spiritual writers identified four related characteristics. First, vainglory fosters false estimates, especially in overvaluing oneself. Evagrius underlined that vainglory attacks the rational power of the soul, distorting one's proper evaluation of self and fostering a grandiose sense of capacity. Vainglory is therefore discordant by nature, leading one to despise others in order to promote oneself. Second, vainglory fosters hypocrisy, projecting a trust in God contrary to the reality of one's way of living. Matthew's sixth chapter repeatedly derided the hypocrisy of piety performed only to be seen. Vainglorious persons become so reliant on themselves that they no longer acknowledge the gifts they have received. Ironically, that is especially true of the most prized gift of the spiritual life, authentic self-knowledge (*gnosis*). Third, vainglory creates delusions. Visions that seem to benefit a monk's faith may actually end up victimizing him, and spiritual achievements far beyond a monk's capacities seem within easy reach. The worst illusion that vainglory breeds is that of circumscribing the power of God. Fourth, vainglory constitutes false knowledge. To know oneself is to know one's vanity. Given the fundamental character of vainglory's assault on the ascetic, it is a permanent temptation of the spiritual life. Vainglory manifests itself in a variety of ways, often appearing under the guise of good, and vainglory attacks monks of every level of experience, relentlessly tempting a monk from his first to his last days. It is especially insidious that as one makes progress in the spiritual life, that demon attacks more forcefully.

Because eastern spiritual writers perceived vainglory to be so dangerous, they sought effective remedies for the vice. In keeping with their reading of Matthew 12:43–45, they adduced vainglory as the last vice an ascetic vanquishes. Evagrius noted that the demon of vainglory takes the offensive after the others are defeated. In fact, the more that one successfully overcomes other faults, the more one is tempted to glory in that success. The battle is lifelong, for, if one temporarily expels the demon but puts nothing good in its place, the demon returns accompanied by more wicked compatriots. As exorcism constitutes a supernatural cure, so natural virtues of humility, contrition, and tears lead the penitent to disdain obsession with self for love of God. The temptation may occur in any context: whether a monk fasts or eats normally, whether an ascetic dresses shabbily or dresses well. Among symptoms that indicate the vice, the writers of the eastern Mediterranean included resentment that a monk feels for the progress made by fellow monks and a lack of compunction within the monk himself. The elder brother of the prodigal son, so bitter at his father for his magnanimous welcome, constitutes a prime scriptural paradigm (Luke 15:11–32).[9]

Among remedies that heal the vice, the monastic writers took their cue once again from the sixth chapter of Matthew's Gospel, where Jesus cautioned his disciples against engaging in devout practices merely to impress others. Believers can make charity more authentic by hiding good deeds. Humiliation can also be an antidote, provided that the ascetic accepts it in a spirit of true humility. The writers noted a fine line between humility and a nonconformism that draws attention to itself. Excessive renunciation often comprised a subtle effort for personal glory. Among activities that preclude the vice, the writers encouraged committed believers to evaluate themselves honestly and regularly. They logically construed their monastic vows as an antidote: chastity for lust of the flesh, poverty for lust of the eyes, and obedience for vainglory. Ultimately, love for the glory of God frees the monk from thirst for his own glory.

Eastern spiritual writers emphasized that vainglory was a vice especially characteristic of monastic life. Typically, a monk might exalt himself for rigorous observance of the rule or might desire to make his holiness seen by abandoning the silence of monastic life away from the world and embracing the ministries of priestly life in the world. What seems good, a desire to be holy by serving others, was not so. The writers also felt that a premature desire to teach others betrayed overconfidence in oneself. Only monks tested over time and equipped with experience should give spiritual direction. Even veteran monks must beware. The temptation to vainglory was universal, and no moment of the spiritual life witnessed a truce in this crucial battle. And vainglory was terribly subtle. A monk might easily confuse a sense of vain joy with the authentic consolation of God's Spirit. Finally, vainglory turned the spiritual world upside down. It led monks to prefer their own glory to God's glory, to follow their own will and ignore God's will.

Western Spiritual Writers

In general, spiritual writers of the western Mediterranean largely endorsed the thought of their eastern counterparts and added little that was original.[10] Among shared convictions, western writers also emphasized the constant presence of the temptation. They viewed clericalism as a formidable manifestation of vainglory. Because the demon of vainglory can use any pretext to launch an attack—possessions, status, intellectual abilities, apostolic accomplishments—it comprised the most insidious of all temptations. Vainglory invited believers to reject their status as creatures. Conceited persons love themselves so much that they no longer look to God for assistance. Although the writers felt that there was no cure for the vice, to counterbalance the fault, they endorsed acting in secret, focusing on weaknesses rather than strengths, purifying interior motivations, and avoiding nonconformism. As Augustine noted, however, one could be vainglorious by struggling not to be so (*Confessions* 10.38).

In keeping with his pastoral orientation and trust in religiously informed common sense, Jean Gerson (1363–1429) analyzed the seriousness of vainglory as a sin.[11] He first noted that vainglory did not constitute a sin if one tries to win praise by glorifying God or edifying one's neighbor. Nonetheless, with Matthew, Gerson felt that sharing blessings in private safeguarded the authenticity of generosity. In itself, Gerson rated vainglory a venial sin, which could become mortal depending on the purpose for which one seeks praise or the means one uses to attain it. Ideally, all Christians, when performing good works, will renounce a desire for acclaim. Vowed religious had to be especially attentive to the ways that vainglory can lead to hypocrisy.

John Cassian as Mediator

Equipped by experience in monasteries throughout the Mediterranean, John Cassian (ca. 365–ca. 435) became the principal intermediary to the western Mediterranean of eastern thought on vainglory and the other principal faults. In the late fourth and early fifth centuries, Cassian shared with newly founded monastic communities in Gaul the wisdom of monks whom he had met in the Egyptian desert. He shifted their focus from a fascination with Egyptian wonder-workers to the more essential transformation of the inner self. Two of his works, the *Conferences with Egyptian Elders* and *On the Training for Monks*, promote at various stages of monastic experience the education of western ascetics and the path of discretion as the way to attain asceticism's challenging ideals.[12] Cassian used the Greek term *kenodoxia* and translated it as *vana* or *inanis gloria*. Once again, he impressed upon ascetics an understanding that vainglory should be feared for its subtle nature. There was no escaping the temptation, not even by fleeing to the desert. Using the metaphor of an onion, Cassian depicted a process of peeling off one layer only to find another, in the flesh or in the spirit, in attractive array or in squalid rags. Vainglory does not diminish over time and attacks us at our virtuous best. The vice had two principal manifestations: exteriorly when a monk is driven by the desire to be seen and interiorly when he is driven by the desire for praise. Presumptuousness leads a monk to welcome the devil masquerading as the "angel of light" (2 Cor. 11:14). Cassian described the case of an arrogant monk who cast himself into a well, trusting the demon's promise that no harm would befall him. He died a few days later.[13]

Cassian follows the eastern Mediterranean tradition in supplying remedies for the vice. He endorses the traditional remedies of avoiding nonconformity, especially any attempt to work miracles, and he again urges monks to work for the glory of God, not for their own glory. Nonetheless, Cassian does develop the possibilities for remedy by emphasizing education and discernment. Younger monks should seek instruction from their older peers. His writings late in life testify to his own belief in that strategy. Moreover, Cassian recommends that monks learn to discern the difference between authentic charity and flamboyant vanity. For Cassian, vainglory seemed like a debased or rusted coin, the corruption of something originally valuable. Boasting strips the spiritual life of its substance, and vanity diminishes its luster.

As a general norm, Cassian recommends that monks use discretion and avoid the extremes of fanaticism or laziness. Fast, but do not fast excessively. Pray, but do not neglect your duties in the monastery. Trust God, but avoid insolence. If you should be blessed to perform a miracle, remember that it is admirable only if done for charity, not show. Thank

God for the miracle, and hide your involvement in it. Cassian followed Evagrius in positing one way in which vainglory can actually prove beneficial. By somewhat tortuous logic, he argues that vainglory can help monks overcome lust. He intuits a dynamic process that begins when vainglory makes a monk fantasize about ministry as a priest. For one to be called to priesthood, the person must have a sound reputation for virtue. To earn that reputation, one must control lustful thoughts and never indulge them. So vainglory aids celibacy.[14] For biblical inspiration, Cassian turned to the cases of two virtuous kings of Israel, Uzziah and Hezekiah, whose righteous reigns were ultimately undermined by presumptuousness. Uzziah dared to enter the Temple to make an offering and was struck down with leprosy. Hezekiah boastfully showed Babylonian ambassadors his full storehouses, and the treasures were later carried off to Babylon. In apostolic times, Paul exhorted the Galatians (5:26) not to "become conceited, competing against one another, envying one another." Cassian urged devout Christians to seek an interior truth opposed to exterior vanity.

Ignatian Vainglory

Pamplona to Loyola: Healing, the Saints, Rudimentary Discernment

After the foolhardy defense of the fortress at Pamplona, Ignatius returns home in a way that suggests the paralytic in the Gospel. He is carried on a litter because he has been crippled (cf. Luke 5:17–26). He sets about his recovery with the same bravado that he displayed at the siege. He endures his pain without crying out or shedding tears. His martyrdom is self-imposed (*se determinó martirizarse*). His vanity leads to the "butchery" (*esta carneceria*) that his doctors practice. The wording portends the trials of his apostolic life, when he will face the butchery practiced by the Inquisition. As summer arrives, Ignatius develops such a severe fever that his doctors fear for his life. Ignatius uses the term "health" (*salud*) in a holistic sense that embraces physical and spiritual healing. When things begin to improve for him, he claims that "our Lord" gives him health, grants him healing (*nuestro Señor le fué dando salud*). For a vainglorious person, that is a difficult affirmation and a gift of God. The true miracle is occurring within. Once Ignatius repents and confesses his sins, he begins to get better. Ignatius is slowly learning which action is more difficult: to stand up and walk or receive the Lord's forgiveness. The moment of his healing is also symbolic. He almost dies on the feast of John the Baptist (June 24), and he begins to heal on the feast of Peter and Paul (June 29). Ignatius improves under the patronage of the apostles of Acts, not the hermit of the wilderness. Early in Acts (3:1–16), "in the name of Jesus Christ of Nazareth," Peter effects a miracle by curing a man lame from birth and then gives credit to the Lord.

O'Rourke Boyle and O'Malley agree that the cult of the saints among the early Jesuits had elements of conventional Catholic piety. The first Jesuits at times blurred the thin line that separates divine healing from pious superstition. As Ignatius matured, however, he tended to say little about the cult of the saints. The fact that Peter and Paul are buried in Rome is likewise significant for Ignatius's memory. O'Malley notes that the first Jesuits had an "emphatic respect" for the papacy.[15] Well they might at a moment when the orthodoxy of the *Spiritual Exercises* and the validity of the Institute were under attack. The relationship between the papacy and the Jesuits, when functioning well, was mutually supportive. Papal approbation of the *Exercises* and the Institute supplied their best defense. Peter assisted Ignatius.

During his long recuperation, Ignatius asks for books to read. It is the first of several instances in the *Acta* in which books and written texts play a crucial role.[16] Ignatius enjoys recreational reading, especially the works of chivalric literature. His reflections on what he reads reveal how far he still has to go in the process of healing. His focus remains on exterior deeds: what he can do to impress a lady of standing or surpass Francis and Dominic. His focus, as O'Rourke Boyle observes, remains on himself, especially now that he is physically lame and ethically immature. His physical diminishment engenders in him a fear of social humiliation. A lame soldier is an oxymoron. One need only recall the scene from *Monty Python and the Holy Grail* when King Arthur taunts the knight who attempts to guard a bridge after his arms and legs have been cut off: "What are you going to do, bleed on me?"[17] Ignatius's moral impairment blinds his judgment; he ponders doing the impossible (*estaba con esto tan evanecido que no miraba quán imposible era poderlo alcançar*). When he transfers his bravado from a chivalric to an ascetic context, his zeal for the spectacular is no less pronounced. As O'Rourke Boyle observes, Ignatius traded his knightly rigors for saintly rigors, culminating in a planned "attack" (*ida*) on Jerusalem itself.[18] The Spanish word *ida* can also mean recklessness.

Though still mired in vainglory and motivated by a desire to be seen doing the difficult, Ignatius is healing. There are two indications for him that this was the case already in the castle at Loyola. He discovers there the authentic issue of the spiritual life, "what possesses one's heart" (*tanto poseído su coraçon*). He recognizes that the Lord comes to his aid within, and his eyes are opened to the varying internal movements of the soul. In Luke's programmatic fourth chapter, Jesus proclaims that he came to give sight to the blind. Ignatius begins to experience the power of the promise in Luke's great commission, the good news of forgiveness for repentance (*Y cobrada no poca lumbre de aquesta lección, começó a pensar más de veras en su vida pasada, y en quánta necesidad tenía de hacer penitencia della*). Through a vision of the Word made flesh, the Madonna and Child, Ignatius overcomes his fleshly desire. Chastity for Ignatius was an early gift from God. Vainglory for him is a far more difficult problem. The attention to inner signs marked progress for Ignatius, but his ability to read those signs confirms that he still has a long way to go. He uses an overly simplistic, purely emotional criterion at this stage in his journey: if it "feels good," it comes from God. To mature spiritually, Ignatius has to integrate the faculties of intellect and will.

The early signs of a life dedicated to helping souls also indicate that Ignatius is on the path to healing at the family castle. He converses there about "matters of God." Such conversation will be a lifelong hunger for Ignatius. In conversations lacking substance, he generally remains silent. Ignatius begins to put together his own book, though he still cares too much about the externals of calligraphy and colors. The notebook, however, has an apostolic design. It is not for Ignatius alone. He desires to be healed in order that he can set out on the way to Jerusalem (*deseando ya ser sano del todo para se poner en camino*). It was on the road to Jerusalem, in Luke's Gospel, that the Lord prepared his disciples for ministry. Ignatius wishes to bring profit and progress to souls (*con lo qual hacía provecho a sus ánimas*). He experiences greatest consolation when he imagines "serving our Lord" (*para servir a nuestro Señor*).

At this juncture, though, the characteristics of Ignatius's life of service are still vague. Having heard of the rigors of Carthusian spirituality, he investigates the possibility of joining that order once he returns from Jerusalem. Medieval pilgrimages often ended with the pilgrim choosing a monastic vocation. Ignatius's major concern, however, is vainglorious:

Was Carthusian asceticism severe enough to gratify his self-loathing? For its rigorous penitence, connections to the nobility, and lifestyle of autonomy in a community setting, Carthusian religious life attracted early followers of Ignatius in Paris, like the bachelor Castro. In fact, while there, Ignatius and his companions may have attended Sunday Mass at the Chartreuse, and Ignatius did seek advice from a Carthusian about an appropriate director among various theologians on the Paris faculty.[19] In the matter of community lifestyle, Ignatius did become a Carthusian of sorts, founding an order of independent individuals who gather intermittently for prayer and meals. At the castle of Loyola, however, Ignatius remains committed to setting out along the way. Though his brother tempts Ignatius by reminding him that all he sees in the castle could one day be his, Ignatius departs. Ironically, Ignatius's brother pleads with him "not to lose himself" (*que no se eche a perder*). Jesus taught his disciples on the road to Jerusalem that they had to lose themselves to gain the kingdom.

Loyola to Montserrat: Backsliding, Chastity, Nonviolence

The first stage of Ignatius's journey and gradual conversion features parallel vigils at the Marian shrines of Aránzazu and Montserrat.[20] There is much backsliding into vainglory in those vigils. Oddly enough, Ignatius remembers that he set out, with his brother and servants, on a mule. The mule is a hybrid between a horse and an ass. It was not a mode of travel typical of pilgrims. Most pilgrims walked; only the wealthiest traveled by horse or carriage. Nor was the mule a flattering mode of travel. Typically, mules were used for plowing fields and insulting knights. The detail of the mule seems intended to reveal a larger issue for Ignatius; he identifies himself too closely with the Lord. In the Synoptic accounts of the triumphal entry into Jerusalem, Jesus rode on the colt of an ass, in keeping with a prophecy of Zechariah. In part to help Jesuits not make the same mistake, and reflective of his lifelong concern for poverty, Ignatius issued instructions in 1541 that the Jesuit missionaries to Ireland should not have a mule or a horse, and in 1553 he forbade provincials in Spain and Portugal from owning their own mule.[21]

The first of Ignatius's two vigils took place at the shrine of Our Lady of Aránzazu in the Basque territory. Unlike the second, at Montserrat, that vigil figures less prominently in later treatments of Ignatius, though the first companions felt, as Gonçalves da Câmara noted, that he made his vow of celibacy at Aránzazu. There seems a paradox in the greater fame accorded Ignatius's showier vigil at Montserrat. The shrine of Aránzazu was one of several established in Western Europe from the ninth to the thirteenth centuries, where shepherds or cow herders miraculously discovered images or statues of the Virgin Mary, often with the help of their animals. Aránzazu is located high in the mountains, in harsh terrain at the boundary between nature and civilization, and the shrine is popular among the shepherds of that region. Shepherds in Luke were the first to hear the news of the Incarnation, to gather in worship of the Word made flesh, and to share the good news announced to them (2:8–20). Marian shrines were, and still are, a place where believers seek interior healing and cripples a physical cure.[22] Ignatius found himself at a primitive moment in his religious transformation. Ultimately, his ministry will occur in a more learned, urban, and cosmopolitan context. Ignatius will settle at a shrine more fitting than Aránzazu and Montserrat, the chapel of Our Lady of the Way in downtown Rome.

Upon leaving the shrine at Aránzazu, Ignatius deviates from his path to collect a debt from the Duke of Nájera. He makes that brief visit to court as part of a ruse he used to fool his brother. Ignatius distributes to beggars some of the funds that he recovers from the duke. The beggars foreshadow the life Ignatius will soon embrace. He donates the rest to repair a statue of Mary. By embellishing the statue, Ignatius hopes to embellish his own fame locally. His vainglory also leads him to travel in reckless fashion, on the mule, but without his brother and the servants who first attended him. He goes on alone, inviting trouble from local bandits in the hills and mountains of the Basque region. Instead, he meets "a Moor" (*un moro*) along the "royal road" (*el camino real*). Ignatius uses the encounter to depict the ways in which societal values continue to motivate him and cloud his interior discretion. The characterization "Moor" was surely demeaning and may not even be accurate. After the *reconquista* of the caliphate of Granada in 1492, the Christian rulers of Spain's kingdoms soon abandoned their initial policy of limited tolerance for Muslims. By 1526, a panel of theologians, convoked at the wish of Charles I, advised the king that even the compulsory baptisms of Muslims during the recent revolt of artisan militias (*germanías*) in cities of Aragon were valid. Charles then gave all Muslims living in his united kingdom the choice of accepting baptism or leaving the reign. Given the growing pressure on Muslims in the various Spanish kingdoms to convert, the "Moor" whom Ignatius met may have been a baptized New Christian. As Ignatius makes apparent in what follows, he is actually the Christian in name only. Whatever the Moor's religion, Ignatius chooses that insidious term to indicate his prejudicial contempt for a fellow traveler.

Ignatius confesses that, at the moment he encounters the Moor, he is still pondering the great deeds he might do to attract attention to himself. He imagines penances that will exceed those of any previous saint. Obsessed with great external deeds (*obras grandes exteriores*), Ignatius ignores the interior life and the critical virtues of humility, charity, and patience. Committed Christians are to see humility and charity and patience as the generous gifts of a loving God. They are all antidotes for vainglory.[23] That helps to explain the heavy emphasis on humility in the second week of the *Spiritual Exercises*, including the meditations on the Kingdoms, the Two Standards, the Three Types of Persons, and the Three Kinds of Humility itself. Ignatian spirituality does not privilege the three traditional vows of religious life but offers a universal remedy for that principal fault. And Ignatius insists on the point about humility because his own conversion from vainglory took so long.

Ignatius and the Moor begin to discuss matters of theology, particularly the question of the perpetual virginity of Mary. The discussion indicates that the two had a language in common—the Moor did not use Arabic— and perhaps they shared a basic knowledge of Christian catechism. The topic of discussion mirrors the broader social and theological issues of the encounter: honor in Spanish chivalric culture and purity of blood in Spanish religious culture. After receiving royal sanction for their claim of universal nobility (*hidalguía universal*), the Basques of Ignatius's day exploited purity of blood as a means to reinforce their privileged status.[24] At that point in his life, Ignatius was a zealot. He has a hyperchivalric reaction to the Moor's suggestion that Mary lost her physical virginity when Jesus was born. As the Moor moves ahead and Ignatius reflects on what he has heard, Ignatius decides that the Moor has offended Mary's female honor. Ignatius has to avenge her (*era obligado volver por su honra*).[25] But Ignatius has made sufficient progress in the spiritual life that he questions his first instincts and the broader imperatives of *hidalgo* culture.

Ignatius presents himself as an odd Hercules at the moral crossroads.[26] Faced with choosing the path of virtue and not inclined to decide on his own, he leaves the decision to God through the agency of the mule. He drops the reins, the mule takes a path that leads away from the Moor, and with an eye toward the Kingdom meditation, Ignatius says that he ends up following the "royal road." Ignatius is learning to follow a God of non-violence, a God who does not require that individuals who hold a controversial position in a theological debate must pay for any error with their lives. Early in Luke's account of the journey to Jerusalem, Jesus did not call down fire on a Samaritan village as his disciples had proposed, instead continuing on his way. By letting the mule decide, Ignatius abandons a strict hidalgo code of honor. He teaches Jesuits the danger of a stance that was insulting to one's partner in spiritual conversation, righteously aggressive, and quite arrogant in presuming to exercise the power of life or death. In all spiritual conversation, Ignatius advises Jesuits to "speak little and reluctantly, listen long and willingly." Following the method of the evil spirit but for entirely good purposes, a Jesuit was to go in "by the other's door to come out by his own."[27] Their model should be the gentle and loving Christ of another Lukan pericope, the Christ who meets the disciples walking on the road to Emmaus. Successful spiritual conversation would make hearts burn within.

Jesuits should also see the encounter with the Moor as a mirror of improper ministry to marginal groups. Faith is a gift: one cannot compel another to believe by threatening to take the person's life. Among the marginal groups to whom the first Jesuits ministered, they had mixed results in achieving Ignatius's ideals. Jesuits trained women to work as spiritual directors, and Jesuits availed themselves of the sage counsel that women offered. They also treated women as "the weaker sex," as Ignatius seemed to do late in the *Acta*, when he advised Jesuits to work only with women of high standing in order to protect the reputation of the nascent Society.[28] In working with indigenous peoples, Jesuits betrayed a spectrum of attitudes ranging from paternalism to collaboration. In creative fashion, they explored new doorways to enter the world of the other: language, music, and even technology. And they at times showed a healthy discretion that Ignatius lacked at this point in his spiritual development. Jesuits treated as a practical matter the much publicized reality that indigenous peoples often went about naked. Jesuit missionaries felt that those peoples were too poor to afford clothes, and the missionaries were too poor to clothe them.

Ignatius himself learned a lesson from his encounter with the Moor. Later in life, he recommended keeping the good qualities of Muslims foremost in mind and established a house in Rome for members of other religions interested in converting to the Christian faith. The house provided room and board to give the candidate an opportunity to reflect on that choice and make the transition to Christian society more easily. By isolating the candidate from his past life, however, the house did exercise a measure of social control. In their evangelizing and educational activities in Spain, some Jesuits returned to a strategy of accommodation first proposed by the Hieronymite bishop Hernando de Talavera (ca. 1430–1507) after Granada's reconquest.[29]

The successful end of the centuries-long *reconquista* by the Catholic monarchs of Castile and Aragon bred a new spirit of militancy on the Iberian peninsula. Ignatius's father had fought in the siege of Granada and marched into the conquered city under the standard of the cross.[30] In 1492, Jews who would not convert to Christianity were expelled from both kingdoms. In 1502, the monarchs issued an edict ordering all Muslims in Granada to convert or leave. Between 1502 and 1516, formal religious conformity was achieved in Castile and Navarre. By 1526, Charles I insisted that all Muslims living in lands of the Crown of Aragon convert as well. There were many mixed settlements of Catholics and Muslims (*Mudéjares*) in Aragon, those Muslim communities were among Spain's most literate, and their resistance to conversion made them especially vulnerable to persecution.[31] The spirit of militancy led at times to an attitude of suspicion toward all converts from Judaism or Islam, distinguished as "New Christians." New Christians had to assimilate completely to the beliefs and practices of Old Christians or face investigation by the Inquisition. As Protestants made inroads in other European kingdoms, as the Turks pressured Christendom and as the raiding of the Barbary pirates intensified along Iberian shores, suspicion of New Christians increased.

Ignatius himself did not exclude New Christians from membership in the Jesuits, and Jesuit schools accepted New Christians among their students. While serving as superior-general of the Society of Jesus, Ignatius adapted his norms to the circumstances, but he always upheld a general principle of nonexclusion. Though the Society would accept any candidate with the appropriate qualities for ministry, Ignatius judged that it might be better in some cases to accept a New Christian in Italy rather than in Spain, given the militant atmosphere that prevailed in Spain. Those Jesuits who claimed that Ignatius had intended to exclude New Christians (Gonçalves da Câmara among them) were mistaken, and the Fifth General Congregation abrogated the express policy of Ignatius by capitulating to pressure and adopting that stricture. Influential early Jesuits, including Pedro de Ribadeneira, Antonio Possevino, Luis de Santander, Diego de Guzmán, García Girón de Alarcón, and Juan de Mariana, opposed the abrogation of Ignatius's policy.[32]

On the road from Aránzazu to Montserrat, Ignatius for the first time calls himself "the pilgrim" (*el peregrino*). Prior to reaching Montserrat, Ignatius equips himself as a vainglorious pilgrim. In addition to the staff and gourd traditional among pilgrims, he designs a special garment of sackcloth to set himself apart exteriorly from the normal pilgrim in a tunic and red cross. He designs his vigil at Montserrat as the performance of a remarkable ascetic. It is to last all night and be spent both kneeling and standing, an endurance contest inspired by the heroics of Amadis of Gaul.[33] However, there are elements of the positive to balance that picture of vainglory. At Montserrat the Lord inspires Ignatius to leave his weapons behind. He will no longer have the means to kill antagonists in a theological debate. Prior to the vigil, Ignatius makes a general confession of his sins. And he learns an important lesson as he leaves Montserrat to continue his journey to Jerusalem. He slips out at dawn to avoid attention, and he anonymously gives his old clothes to a beggar. Lest he be honored for his dramatic vigil at the shrine, he does not take "the direct path to Barcelona" (*el camino derecho de Barcelona*).

Montserrat to Manresa: Authentic Discernment, Confession, and Consolation

Ignatius now learns that avoiding glory can be a subtle path to seeking glory. His fear that people would learn of his vigil and pay him deference (*que le conociesen y le honrasen*) realizes itself in a way he does not foresee. On the crooked path to Manresa, Ignatius is accosted by a stranger who asks him whether he has given his clothes to a beggar. The question touches Ignatius deeply. He realizes that, by his anonymous gift, he has put the beggar's life in jeopardy. The beggar's having his clothes could easily look like theft.[34] Ignatius therefore sheds genuine tears of compassion for the beggar. His discernment has become more sophisticated than the "feel good" approach he used at Loyola. An effort to avoid respect can be a way to attract attention. Ignatius adds comments on these complexities to his notebook.[35] When Ignatius admits that he is not following the direct path, he likewise indicates his awareness of the subtleties of the interior life. Early in the Renaissance, in a letter that describes climbing Mount Ventoux, Petrarch produced a popular metaphorical account of the varying paths to a virtuous life. Petrarch claimed that his brother, a Carthusian, had taken a direct path to the summit, whereas he himself followed a crooked path. On that summit, Petrarch found a passage in the *Confessions* of Augustine that recalled him from the distractions of the exterior world and pointed him toward the complexities of the interior life.[36]

Ignatius takes three days to prepare the notes for his general confession at Montserrat, perhaps hinting at his scrupulous temperament.[37] Contemporary aids to the making of such a confession likely fed his scrupulosity. Guides to confessing in an orderly manner were written soon after Lateran IV's decree in 1215 mandating annual confession. After the introduction of printing, books and broadsheets for confessors and penitents alike were published in Spain and elsewhere. A succinct type of publication known as *confessio generalis*, though only a few pages long, had extensive lists of questions derived primarily by filtering the seven "deadly sins" through the Ten Commandments and then appending sins derived from other catechetical categories (articles of faith, sacraments, works of mercy). A confessor could read each question to the penitent, who need only respond, when appropriate, in a paraphrase of Vulgate Psalm 50: "I acknowledge my fault."[38] By contrast, a general confession for Jesuits ideally became an important way to begin anew, to repent in Lukan terms. Jesuits emphasized not an external obligation to confess but an interior desire for renewal. Confessors should emphasize not hell's punishments but Paul's hope: where sin abounds, grace superabounds (Rom. 5:20).[39] Ignatius characteristically closed his personal letters with the wish that Christ help all with his abundant grace. Jesuits were not to be harsh when administering the sacrament and had to protect against all "pharisaic self-righteousness." The sacrament of confession, like other ministries of the late medieval church, gravitated between emphasis on consoling service and juridical duty. The juridical framework of the sacrament required a thorough and accurate listing of sins.

Ignatius at Montserrat is still caught up in that juridical world.[40] As Ignatius put together the first week of the *Spiritual Exercises* and his own lessons in catechism, he mirrored the progression of topics expressed in literature like the *confessio generalis*. Around 1476, the Franciscan Giacomo della Marca published a work entitled *Regola de confessione* that structured the examination of conscience around the seven capital sins, violations of the Ten Commandments, and sins involving the five senses, the twelve articles of faith, the seven sacraments, the seven corporal and spiritual works of mercy, the three theological virtues, and the seven gifts of the Holy Spirit. As founder of the Jesuits, Ignatius still struggled at times to free himself from that juridical world. Early in his tenure as superior-general, he recommended that doctors in Rome not treat a seriously ill patient who refused to confess to a priest.

Nonetheless, Ignatius accentuated the consoling service of the sacrament. Jesuits should send a penitent from the confessional in consolation. Nadal urged Jesuit confessors to bolster the truly penitent in converting to a new life, and Polanco urged Jesuit confessors always to favor the more compassionate way of dealing with the penitent. Ignatius himself suggested that believers, in examining their consciences regularly, begin by recalling the reasons for which they felt grateful to God at that moment in their lives. The development of casuistry reveals a creative tension for Jesuits in their confessional ministry. In the dialectic between the tradition's focus on law and sin and the founder's focus on consolation and healing, Jesuits confessors saw an opportunity to console by examining the many possible sins case by case and accommodating the general norms to specific circumstances.[41] The first Jesuits were popular as confessors for their emphasis on consolation, their willingness to accommodate, and their reticence to charge for their services.

Manresa to the Cardoner: The Creature, a Norm of Discretion, Narcissus, God's Immediate Action

Confession and absolution play a crucial role in the insights that Ignatius receives during his months at Manresa. His behavior there parallels his behavior at Pamplona. As he attempts to scale great heights, he falls into the depths of the spiritual malady of scrupulosity, which cripples him even more severely.[42] Vainglory motivates his climbing, an effort to hurry along the straight path. Instead the Lord slows him down. His begging at Manresa becomes an opportunity to call attention to himself for renouncing his wealth and inheritance. He focuses obsessively on externals. He lets his hair and nails grow, he eats no meat and drinks wine only on Sunday, he leaves his head uncovered in a gesture of self-imposed dishonor that leads to illness, and he wears a single garment of sackcloth, which ensures that he will be "smelled as well as seen."[43] Ignatius reserves his greatest demonstrations for the realm of piety. He attends daily Mass, kneels to pray for seven hours, and makes confession after confession. As Ignatius steps up his piety, he discerns the movements within his soul.

For the first time, Ignatius describes seeing a creature in the form of a serpent that is attractive and has shiny adornments that seem to him to be eyes. The vision of the creature proves paradoxical. At first, it brings great happiness, but over time it provokes anxiety. Seeing the serpent makes Ignatius feel good but contributes nothing to his understanding of the interior life (*ningún conocimiento de cosas interiores espirituales*). The beautiful beast endowed with something resembling eyes fittingly makes a superficial, purely visual impact. Ignatius's spiritual life follows a similar rhythm. At first he finds great appeal in the life of a virtuoso ascetic, but over time he is troubled by the thought of spending seventy years in rigorous asceticism. The combination of vainglory and depression leads Ignatius to his most severe temptation. His scruples precipitate a crisis.

Ignatius's first remedy for the scruples is self-reliant. Writing all his sins down, however, does not remove them. His next remedy is self-designed. He hopes to find a confessor who will order him not to go over his past sins but stops short of suggesting this solution to his confessors. One day, on his own, a confessor does give Ignatius similar advice: confess only those sins that are clear. To Ignatius, however, they were all clear. At this point in the narrative, Ignatius engages in what may be purposeful irony. He expresses to the Lord his willingness to follow even "a puppy" who offers sound spiritual advice. It could be a subtle jab at his Dominican hosts, who, though the renowned "hounds of the Lord" (*Domini canes*), fail to offer an effective remedy to the scrupulous ascetic in their midst. Because no one can help him, Ignatius settles on the most extreme remedy of all, "casting himself," in the words of the existing text, "from a large hole" (*para echarse de un agujero grande*).

In her analysis of the text, O'Rourke Boyle proposes an emendation.[44] The Spanish term *agujero* does mean "a hole," but the action of "throwing oneself *from a hole*" makes little sense. One throws oneself into a hole. O'Rourke Boyle thinks that Ignatius used *agujero* for the more precise term *aguja*, which means a needle or a steeple and could therefore be understood in this context as a pinnacle. The same word, *agujero*, appears later in the narrative to describe a needle that Ignatius used to damage his shoes. In other sixteenth-century texts, *agujero* is used for *aguja*. *Agujero* can also mean a well, and Cassian once told the story of a monk who threw himself into a well. Nonetheless, "pinnacle" still accords better with the wording and context of Ignatius. One can cast oneself down from a pinnacle. Spatially, pride lifts up or exalts.[45] Moreover, there are other pinnacles that may help to explain Ignatius's meaning. Prior to reaching Manresa and while there, Ignatius describes himself as attempting to reach the pinnacle of military or chivalric or ascetic success. His vainglory drives him to scale heights from which he might be seen. O'Rourke Boyle adduces the parallels of Adam grasping at equality with God, of ascetic stylites outdoing each other in scaling the heights of sanctity, and of Gonçalves da Câmara focusing on Ignatius's facial expression after climbing up into the Red Tower at Rome. The most significant parallel is to be found in the third temptation of Jesus in Luke's Gospel. There, the devil conducts Jesus to the pinnacle of the Temple and invites Jesus to throw himself down so that angels may catch him as he falls. Jesus refuses to force God's hand by such a vainglorious action. Luke moved the temptation to the final, climactic position among the three.

Ignatius's obsession with himself leads him to the point of suicide, as he contemplates jumping from a dangerous height. He steps back from the precipice, only to attempt one last self-reliant remedy. Inspired by the account of a saint (perhaps Andrew) who did not eat until God answered his request, Ignatius declares a holy hunger strike, to continue until he reaches the point of death or is cured. However, he calls it off when his confessor bids him to do so. By allowing himself to be led, Ignatius finally begins to find a remedy for his scruples. Healing comes when Ignatius is convinced in his heart that a merciful Lord has freed him (*teniendo por cierto que nuestro Señor le habia querido librar por su misericordia).* Ignatius uses two metaphors to describe the depths of that liberation, one psychological and one educational. He feels as if he has been awakened from a dream, and he feels that the Lord is teaching him lessons interiorly when he experiences and tests a diversity of spirits.

Those lessons yield a peaceful sense for much of the rest of Ignatius's life that he is just in the eyes of the Lord. His near-death experiences thereafter troubled him not from a sense of personal loathing and unforgivable sinning but from a sense of interior healing and spiritual overconfidence. Ignatius decides that the Lord is now teaching him to moderate his extravagant asceticism. He begins to eat meat and confirms the appropriateness of that decision with his confessor. Though he finds himself consoled in prayer all night long, he reckons that those consolations were not from God because he needs to sleep. He uses norms of discretion and moderation for his external appearance, cutting back the hair and nails that he allowed to grow freely. He seeks a mean between carelessness and vanity and, in so doing, continues to move toward the apostolic life to which the Lord is guiding him. In specifying the externals and the pieties of Jesuit life, Ignatius used similar norms of discretion and moderation. Renaissance artists on occasion vividly portrayed the eremitic saints of the penitential wilderness, John the Baptist and Mary Magdalene, rail thin and their heads and bodies covered by long, unkempt hair. They were not to be the heroes, however, who inspired the spirituality of Ignatius and the Jesuits. As Ignatius sensed when beginning a new life at Manresa, he could not be an unkempt hermit because God was calling him "to be busy helping souls" (*se ocupaba en ayudar algunas almas*).

Because externals ultimately counted for little, as superior-general, Ignatius prescribed norms of discretion and adaptation. Jesuits for good reason did not have a distinctive habit. They wore what was appropriate and what was in keeping with local usage and their vow of poverty. In the new settings in which Jesuits evangelized, they adapted their dress to the customs of the people whom they served. Matteo Ricci's dressing and living as a Confucian scholar in China epitomizes a broader tendency.[46] Ricci accomplished far more, however, by his affability and scholarship than by his manner of dress. In matters of food and drink, Ignatius recommended once again that Jesuits follow local custom and consult a doctor when in doubt about the suitability of certain ascetic choices. Fasting remained a sensitive issue for Ignatius, given the ways in which he suffered from stomach problems that he brought on himself. In contrast to the extreme fasting of penitential hermits, who were often inspired by the rigors of John the Baptist in the desert, the Jesuits followed the milder example of the Incarnate Lord, who came among his fellow Israelites eating and drinking (cf. Luke 7:33–34).[47] The dynamic of Ignatius's own years of conversion often proved exemplary for the first Jesuits. Before surrendering to God, neophytes in the spiritual life often gloried in their acts of penitence. After surrendering to God, Jesuits looked on their bodies as gifts of a gracious Lord.

In matters of piety, Ignatius emphasized the need for daily prayer but forbade an excessive amount. He urged Jesuits to pray in order to deepen their affection and devotion. Tears were always his trusted sign of interior affection.[48] Like Ignatius, the first Jesuits were controversial for their willingness and, indeed, desire to receive Communion frequently. Although late medieval theologians like Jean Gerson and Paolo Maffei as well as devotional works like *The Imitation of Christ* advocated frequent Communion, the practice remained disputed. Opponents claimed that frequent reception demeaned the holiness of the sacrament and glossed over the unworthiness of those receiving. The Jesuits countered that frequent Communion had been the practice of the ancient church and had proven beneficial for their own spiritual development. Their advocacy reflected the optimistic perspectives of theologians like Maffei, enlivened by trust in God's infinite mercy and love.[49] Jesuit reception of Communion took place outside of Mass, generally on a weekly basis. Most of the first Jesuits, however, felt that Nicolás Bobadilla's daily reception of the sacrament was extreme. Finally, Ignatius tended to downplay the importance of ordination, almost never mentioning the subject in his writings. The qualification for undertaking the help of souls was membership in the Society. Priesthood comported a danger of honor and privilege. Several early Jesuits accepted ordination only when ordered to do so.

Willing to trust the Lord's promise of forgiveness, Ignatius next learns important lessons when God teaches him like a pupil in grammar school. Ignatius candidly admits the childish character of his spiritual life at Manresa. His talent is still quite unpolished (*por su rudeza y grueso ingenio*). The quality of God's lessons contrasts with the lack of satisfying spiritual advice that Ignatius seeks but rarely finds from spiritual directors.

Divine pedagogy yields important fruits for the interior life. At least four of the five visions that Ignatius experiences at Manresa are communicated through the sense of sight. Understanding for Ignatius was consistently a matter of "seeing clearly." Even the famous vision of "the keys" might have a visual matrix, if O'Rourke Boyle's analysis of that vision is accurate.[50]

The first vision of Ignatius at Manresa takes place on the steps of the monastery, another metaphorical setting for gradual progress. Ignatius finds his understanding enlightened by a vision of keys (*teclas*), referring to the keys of a musical instrument. If the text is transmitted correctly, Ignatius uses an aural metaphor to communicate his understanding of the Trinity as a harmonious composition made up of distinct musical notes. The vision meets Ignatius's primary criterion for authentic interior consolation. He weeps and sobs and no longer relies on himself. Given that Ignatius's enlightenment would be primarily theoretical and intellectual, O'Rourke Boyle questions why that would lead him to such an emotional reaction. She suggests that the explanation lies in the fact that Gonçalves da Câmara transposed Ignatius's door keys (*llaves*) to musical keys (*teclas*).[51] Here the faithful scribe fell victim to his own vainglory. He missed Ignatius's conversion from seeking personal glory and the ways in which grace healed Ignatius and integrated him into the most noble community of all, the Trinity. The "keys" to which Ignatius referred, in O'Rourke Boyle's analysis, are the keys of absolution in confession. They appeared in the artwork of the time as the distinguishing mark of Peter, who carried keys symbolizing a commission to bind and loose sins. Ignatius had begun to heal at Loyola on the vigil of Peter's feast. Ignatius's scruples ceased when he trusted the words that his confessor pronounced: he was absolved "in the name of the Father, and of the Son, and of the Holy Spirit." Kenneth Clark characterized the Catholic ritual of confession and absolution as typifying the genius of Catholicism to humanize, harmonize, and civilize the deepest impulses of ordinary human beings.[52] At its consoling best, it is a simple ritual that offers one gifted with faith a concrete actualization of the divine promise of forgiveness.

For marshaling contextual support, O'Rourke Boyle's argument deserves serious consideration. Conversely, hearing "llaves" from Ignatius and later dictating "teclas" to a secretary would constitute significant editorializing or error by Gonçalves da Câmara. In general, Ignatius seems little concerned to convey the content of his visions at Manresa because they were so personal and thus irrelevant to Jesuits. Ignatius claims that it was difficult to recall his vision of the creation of light. Ignatius appreciates the real presence of Christ in the Eucharist because it helps him experience the most significant of all of God's lessons, that God transforms believers from within (*y vió el fructo que hacía en las almas tratándolas*). For Ignatius, experiencing the Word's becoming flesh in vision meant almost the opposite: seeing a vague white body without distinct limbs.[53] In analyzing the final vision of Ignatius along the Cardoner River, O'Rourke Boyle highlights the setting as a clue to meaning, and she relates that vision to Ignatius's earlier sighting of a serpent-like creature endowed with shiny adornments that looked like eyes.

Ignatius initially sees the odd creature at a hospital dedicated to Saint Lucy and probably endowed by one of the crusading military orders. Saint Lucy is the patroness of the eyes. The creature appears at midday, and O'Rourke Boyle sees resonances of the famed "noonday devil," who deceived by offering false illumination and encouraging self-fixation. In her estimation, the flying serpent described by Ignatius was actually a peacock. Medieval bestiaries characterized the peacock as a hybrid of bird and serpent.[54] The peacock's head was deemed especially crafty. A peacock therefore fits Ignatius's description. The creature was beautiful, colorful, and had something that resembled eyes—the bright ocelli of the male peacock's tail. In medieval iconography, the peacock at times symbolized resurrection, immortality, and incorruptibility, but that was due above all to the toughness of its flesh after slaughter. Martial had once joked that "any hard-hearted woman who hands a peacock over to a cruel cook should not be surprised that he ruffles his jeweled wings at her."

Nevertheless, the peacock primarily symbolized the vice of vainglory, which might endanger one's salvation. From the time of Aristotle, the peacock was labeled a jealous and conceited animal. In his ancient encyclopedia of the natural world, Pliny described the peacock as pretentious and malevolent, always ready to spread its lustrous tail when praised (*Naturalis Historia* 10.22.43–45). Leonardo da Vinci (1456–1519) observed that the peacock had a greater propensity to vainglory than any other creature, "always contemplating the beauty of its tail," and it made others look its way by spreading out that tail and shrieking loudly. For O'Rourke Boyle, the peacock did symbolize the immortality that Ignatius sought, but it was an immortality to be won by self-reliance and personal glory. Male peacocks strutted as they displayed their exotic feathers, but they wept at the sight of their own ugly feet (or, in Ignatius's case, his ugly legs). Ignatius was learning the insidious character of vainglory as a vice. Efforts to avoid the vice often led one into a vicious cycle of ever greater vice. Even in his sackcloth at the Montserrat vigil, Ignatius had behaved like a peacock.[55]

God works with Ignatius along the bank of the river as a gentle schoolmaster, granting Ignatius the gift of his great enlightenment. That vision begins, as Ignatius acknowledges, with him staring into the natural mirror of the water in order to admire his own face (*se sentó un poco con la cara hacia el río*). A reference to Narcissus seems intended. One modern Jesuit psychiatrist diagnosed Ignatius as afflicted by clinical narcissism.[56] Such a personality suffers from grandiose conceptions of self. Allegorically, Narcissus shows that one can be tricked by vanity. Vainglory ultimately produces a fatal immobility. Deceived by the beauty of the image he observes in the natural mirror of the water, Narcissus never moves from that spot. Though tempted like Narcissus, Ignatius follows a different path. He takes refuge at the foot of the cross he encounters along the way and expresses his gratitude to a merciful Savior. The cross is redemptive. It heals Ignatius's obsession with self and transforms this obsession into a love dedicated to the service of others.[57] In Lukan terms, the cross before which Ignatius felt that transformation represents the entire range of activities—entry, confrontation, trial, crucifixion, death, resurrection, ascension—that Jesus had to accomplish in Jerusalem. For Ignatius, the self-effacing service that Jesus embraced when he became flesh and fulfilled his salvific mission means that believers find healing for their inflated sense of importance or uniqueness by imaginatively participating in the Lord's life of self-effacing service.

From this point on, all seems new to Ignatius. He feels that he better understands matters of the Spirit, of faith, and even of letters. He does not narrate particular details of his visions for his fellow Jesuits because he would rather they focus on his integral liberation. He expresses his gratitude to God for the things that God has done for him. And he can now discern the evil character of the serpent-like creature. It represents human glory exulting in self-love. He drives off the peacock with his pilgrim's staff. The immobility of Narcissus yields to the journey of a disciple with Jesus to Jerusalem. In her study of the *Acta*, O'Rourke Boyle describes an illustration in an early printed edition of the *Spiritual Exercises*. In the text for the first week, a man is shown crawling on his hands and knees. He is blindfolded, naked, and fettered. His backside supports baskets in which various animals and a devil cluster. On his buttocks, immediately behind the devil, a peacock poses with its tail displayed for admiration.[58] The first week of the *Exercises* ends at the foot of the cross not with a sense of guilt for sin but with a sense of gratitude for forgiveness—which is emblematic of Ignatius's spiritual journey to this point.

O'Malley characterizes the *Spiritual Exercises* as the most fundamental of Jesuit teachings and the fruit of the religious experience of Ignatius himself. He calls attention to the Fifteenth Annotation that Ignatius supplied for those who guide one in the making of the retreat. That explanatory note affirms that the Creator deals directly with the creature and vice versa. "This immediate action of God on the individual is the fundamental premise of the *Exercises*."[59] Ignatius sought inspiration from the Spirit of Christ at every step along the way. He posits a direct experience of the Spirit that is emotional as well as intellectual. The culminating contemplation in his *Exercises* sees God as active in all of life's experiences. That insight of Ignatius affected the ways that the first Jesuits conducted their lives and the ministries they exercised. Those ministries initially had a strong note of the charismatic evangelizing that typified the ministries of the apostles generally in the New Testament and systematically in Luke's Acts. For Jesuits, consolation was a gift accessible to all and granted abundantly by a generous God. While the first Jesuits generally tried to expand the arena of grace at work, their zealous opponents often tried to delimit that arena. The *Exercises* are, in a sense, the Jesuit adaptation of Jesus's great commission to the disciples in Luke (24:47): "repentance and forgiveness of sins is to be proclaimed in his name to all nations, beginning from Jerusalem."

Despite frustration with his spiritual advisors at Manresa, Ignatius does receive one bit of spiritual advice that helps him a great deal. A woman at Manresa expresses to him the hope that, one day, "my Jesus would appear to you." Ignatius remembers that odd wish throughout his life and probably felt that God answered the woman's prayer at La Storta. At this point in his spiritual development, the woman's words, "my Jesus," befuddle Ignatius. He has come to identify his own pilgrimage so closely with the Lord that he focuses only on "his Jesus." That visionary's prayer typifies the helpful ministry that Ignatius receives from women on several occasions at Manresa and Barcelona. They are his best spiritual companions (*entraba más en las cosas espirituales*). When women come to visit him at Manresa, he shows off for them. "If you find me at the point of death, then shout, 'Sinner! Recall how you have offended God.' "[60] When he is sick during the winter of 1522, women care for him and insist that he wear shoes and cover his head. Once Ignatius reaches Barcelona, he receives more sage advice from a woman there, who tells him that one can make little spiritual progress in Rome (*queriendo decir que se aprovechaban en Roma poco de cosas de espíritu*). For Ignatius, fresh from the great spiritual progress that God granted him at the Cardoner, that is a troubling warning, but it will be borne out by his experience in the city.

Barcelona to Venice: Pilgrimage, Begging, Benefices

The ultimate sign that Ignatius is converting is his desire to resume the journey to Jerusalem (*Ibase allegando el tiempo que él tenía pensado para partirse para Hierusalem*).[61] But he also remembers having a ways to go. Though others suggest to him that a companion would help him, because he did not know Latin or Italian, Ignatius decides to go alone. Only later in life will he fully appreciate the value of companions. Companions at this point were undesirable precisely because they would help him. "If he took a companion, he would expect help from him when he was hungry; if he fell down, he would expect him to help him get up."[62] The best companion on the road to Jerusalem, of course, is the Lord himself. But when Jesus sent out his disciples, he sent them with companions, not alone. As confirmation that Ignatius is still following a crooked path, he resumes his scrupulous behavior over the matter of obtaining ship's biscuit for the voyage. That debate with himself will be continued at the *Acta*'s conclusion, when Ignatius discerns whether Jesuit churches should have a fixed income (benefice). His confessor in Barcelona advises him to beg for what is necessary and take that with him. He takes the hardtack but leaves behind several coins he deems unnecessary. He still struggles to avoid vainglory. When asked his destination, he dissembles and says "Rome" rather than "Jerusalem," precisely for fear of that vice (*por temor de la vanagloria*).

After the lengthy interlude in Manresa, the pace of Ignatius's journey quickens as he takes ship in Barcelona. He lives the life of a pilgrim in a literal sense.[63] Those months on land and sea show that Jesuits must journey for ministry. Nadal early underlined the sense of that paradigm, when he reminded Jesuits that "we are not monks. . . . The world is our house."[64] It was a salutary reminder, given the novelty of the Jesuit way of proceeding. Many early Jesuits thought that they were monks. Ignatius wanted his companions to live the life of the early disciples, on a journey to evangelize. Like Jesus and the disciples on their journey to Jerusalem, Jesuit disciples would have nowhere to lay their heads (Luke 9:58). Jesuit ministry was carried on in the cities of Europe and the new territories to which Europeans were traveling, and Jesuit novices were to experience the hardships of that dynamic ministry by making a pilgrimage. The novitiate pilgrimage was not a devotional exercise but an existential one.[65] Likewise, the fourth vow makes Jesuits available for worldwide ministry. Its significance is apostolic.

In the narrative, Ignatius described himself as "the pilgrim" because he wanted to diminish emphasis on himself and focus on God. In fact, in the first part of the *Acta*, almost all of the human actors are described by epithets: the French, the Moor, the captain. The narrative of Ignatius has elements of an archetypal spiritual journey. Like Adam, he begins the journey in a garden and hopes to return there one day. Like Jesus, he moves resolutely to Jerusalem. Along the way, he will lapse into vice and lose his focus. He is on a crooked path to his goal, not a straight one. As the Gospel urges, he tries to take nothing for his journey. The portion of his trip from Barcelona to Rome serves as an apprenticeship for his future activities. His ministerial skills continue to evolve. Though he sets sail from Barcelona with favorable winds, they become so strong that all on board are seasick. Ominous notes mark the entire journey. On land, the threat of plague is ubiquitous. At sea, the Turks have seized Rhodes. In Venice, Ignatius is so ill that he asks a doctor whether he can risk traveling. The doctor tells him that it is fine to do so if he wants to be buried in Cyprus. On board ship, Ignatius's zealotry in chastising the crew almost leads them to maroon him.

Ignatius does have some success in helping others. He protects a woman and her daughter from an attempted rape by soldiers, using shouting, not violence, to scare away the soldiers. Shouting is a form of speech, and the aid to the women constitutes a decidedly unusual but nonetheless effective ministry of the Word.[66] Ignatius enters Rome on Palm Sunday and leaves after Easter; his encounter with the Ascension still awaits him in Jerusalem. He abides by the pilgrim's obligation to live from what one could beg, repeatedly wondering whether he should trust God entirely or raise some funds for the trip. The dilemma reflects a debate in the Gospels about the appropriate use of material possessions. Ignatius obtains several ducats by begging on the road from Rome to Venice but gives most of them to other beggars. He arrives to take ship in Venice, furnished only with a confidence that God will protect him. He so impresses the doge that he is given a place on a vessel transporting Venetian officials to Cyprus.

Ignatius remembers himself as a good beggar, and the narrative comprises something of a beggar's feast. Here is a summary of O'Rourke Boyle's thorough listing of relevant episodes from the *Acta*:[67] After Ignatius first left Loyola, he collected ducats from the duke of Nájera, he daily begged for alms in Manresa, and he embarked gratis on a ship from Barcelona, eventually discerning that he could take along ship's biscuit but had to leave behind five or six unneeded *blancas*. He traveled with fellow beggars to Rome, where he accepted for his Holy Land voyage six or seven ducats as the only internationally accepted coinage. That later struck him as untrusting, and he disbursed the ducats to the poor. A wealthy Spanish acquaintance in Venice gained an audience for Ignatius with the doge, who in turn arranged Ignatius's transport to Cyprus and from there to Jerusalem. On the return trip, Ignatius's companions begged a spot for him on a poor vessel; the pilot of a rich ship sarcastically suggested that Ignatius fly back like Saint James. Ignatius went on to note that, on the voyage home from Jerusalem, the wealthy vessel that refused him passage sank, while the poor vessel made it safely to Italy.

When he returned to Venice, a rich acquaintance gave him fifteen or sixteen *giulii*. As Ignatius traveled across northern Italy, a succession of beggars who had learned of his generosity quickly depleted that store. He obtained free passage to Spain, and he gained supporters who paid for his lodging and studies in Barcelona. In Alcalá his begging earned him insults from local clergymen, but a good Samaritan arranged for his lodging at a hospital and gave him alms. In order that Ignatius could continue to study at Salamanca, the archbishop of Valladolid granted him a place in his college and funds for any further expenses. Once Ignatius settled in Paris, he found a merchant who gave him twenty-five *escudos* as a bill of exchange, but a fellow student squandered those resources and could not repay them. Ignatius again found housing in a hospital and then traveled annually to the wealthy commercial areas of Flanders and England to beg alms sufficient for the costs of the next year of university studies. Those who made the *Spiritual Exercises* in Paris immediately began to beg for their sustenance. Ignatius hesitated to surrender the *escudo* necessary for his graduation there, since poor students cannot afford that virtually compulsory donation to the faculty.[68] When he returned home to Azpeitia, he stayed in a hospital and begged for alms. On the trip back to Venice, he found the citizens of Bologna singularly unwilling to assist him in his need. In Rome, his companions obtained a bill of exchange to cover the costs of their projected pilgrimage to the Holy Land. While awaiting ship in the Veneto, Ignatius and a few companions lived in an abandoned hovel that they repaired. The other companions lived in hospitals. They all sought alms twice a day but barely survived on what they received.

No wonder, then, that the one item of business from the Jesuit *Constitutions* that Ignatius was willing to discuss with Gonçalves da Câmara was the matter of benefices. The broader society of Ignatius's time debated the perennial question of whether poverty is a religious value. Positively, poverty calls for radical trust in the Lord. However, because physical poverty can often prove dehumanizing, the Gospel of Matthew emphasized blessings for those poor in spirit. In the economy of commercial capitalism that Ignatius used to his advantage, the poor were seen less as the face of Christ than as the epitome of laziness. Those who are physically able should work for a living, not beg.[69] Ignatius betrayed a subtle understanding of the commercial economy as he matured. He could remember all of the various types of coins he obtained by begging, and he exploited technological means like a bill of exchange that made capital liquid and contributed to the growth of Europe's economy. He followed the trail of the successful bourgeoisie to Flanders and England.[70]

In the end, though, he legislated against fixed income for Jesuit ministries. His spiritual reasoning is spelled out in the Two Standards meditation of the *Exercises*. Ignatius posited a continuum in Satan's proposal from coveting wealth to seeking vainglory and to pride in that recognition. Similarly, in Christ's proposal, Ignatius sees a continuum from poverty to insults for possessing nothing and to humility for being redeemed in Christ.[71] If vainglory was the principal Jesuit vice, then it would be inviting trouble to allow Jesuit communities to become wealthy. Accepting charity opened a Jesuit to divine charity and to gratitude for divine generosity. Jesuits were to be poor with Christ; accepting recompense for ministry would corrupt ministry. And the lack of fixed income had a prophetic note as well, inviting the burgeoning world of commercial capitalism to consider whether profit represented the best criterion for human success and inviting the cardinals of the church to consider whether church office should be treated as private property.[72] It is one of the reasons that Ignatius had Jesuits vow not to accept an ordained ministry in the church's hierarchy above the priesthood.

The stumbling block in all of this for Ignatius and the first Jesuits proved to be their schools. From the start, those institutions had financial difficulties that threatened their survival. Ignatius therefore made an early decision to endow the schools and use the revenues generated by their endowment for ministry. In fact, those educational institutions were financially viable due to the generosity of their Jesuit faculties. The reality of operating institutions for schooling soon outstripped the ideal of conducting charismatic ministries of the Word of God. Even begging to support the professed houses of the Society was soon discouraged. Demands for manpower were great as Ignatius accepted more and more invitations to establish Jesuit schools. The historical reality seems to be that begging was more viable in a feudal world than in a bourgeois world. In Renaissance Venice, boatmen were fined for ferrying the poor from the mainland over to the islands of Rialto.[73]

Venice to Jerusalem: Ascending the Mount, Stepping out of the Lord's Footprints

Ignatius leaves Venice, changes ship in Cyprus, and finally reaches the Holy Land. The Lord continues to appear to him frequently during the trip and to give him consolation. Yet his mode of engaging in pilgrimage and his description of the journey set him apart from his contemporaries, especially those who traveled with him. Ignatius did not engage in the traditional ritual to begin the pilgrimage, during which the pilgrim confessed his sins, prostrated himself before the altar, accepted his staff, and then put on his distinctive garment with a cross on the shoulder. He arranged the departure on his own. In recounting his first catching sight of the Holy Land, Ignatius does not recall experiencing the customary emotional reaction, nor does he mention singing the traditional *Te Deum* or *Salve Regina*. Throughout the description of his journey, he makes no reference to relics or indulgences. Nor does he emphasize the fact that the pilgrim is a stranger in this world. Rather, upon his return to Italy, he will conclude the opposite and seek to discover what he must do in this world. He focuses almost exclusively on the interior effects of the journey, not on the external rituals and actions. That chosen emphasis conveys to the reader the need to interiorize the Gospel message.[74]

The only portion of his pilgrimage narrated in any detail is a dual ascent of the Mount of Olives, at journey's conclusion. That narrative further underscores his focus on the interior. Following the exhortation of early spiritual writers like Paulinus of Nola (ca. 354–431), who urged visitors to Jerusalem to "adore the imprint of the divine feet in the very dust trodden by the Lord," pilgrims often collected dust from those footprints to take home as souvenirs.[75] Ignatius began his ascent focused on a naive and literal view, but he recovered the interior meaning as he descended.

Upon disembarking and approaching Jerusalem, Ignatius and his fellow pilgrims are greeted by friars carrying a cross. His first sight of the city, from the so-called Mount of Joy, fittingly gives Ignatius great consolation. But his stay in Jerusalem will provoke a new crisis, another crossroads in his spiritual journey. Ignatius decides to act on his consolation and remain in Jerusalem for the rest of his life, visiting the holy places and helping souls. In requesting permission to stay, Ignatius reveals only his pious desire, not the apostolic one. He already senses that helping souls is controversial. The Franciscan superior denies his request and orders him to return to Italy with the other pilgrims. That leads to Ignatius's crisis and a visit to the Mount of Olives, from which Luke says that Jesus ascended into heaven. The Ascension is described only in Luke's writings and is the culminating event in Jesus's ministry in Jerusalem.

Ignatius's visit to the Mount is driven by vainglory. He resents the fact that the Franciscans have rejected his plan. Although Ignatius has letters of recommendation, the Franciscans, rather ironically, are swayed more by considerations of money. They do not want to have to ransom him or any other zealous pilgrim from the Muslim rulers of the region. Ignatius makes his visit to the Mount with typical bravado. He goes secretly, eschews a Muslim guide, and bribes his way past the guards. The literalism of his youthful piety reveals itself once he climbs the hill. He is curious to know in which direction the feet of Jesus were pointing when he ascended.

One could determine the direction because Jesus had miraculously left footprints in the stone on the hilltop. Curiosity, like vainglory, is a sin of sight. The former tries to see what it should not see, and the latter tries to ensure that one be seen.[76] However, Ignatius forgets to check the footprints carefully. Thus, after a quick trip to Bethpage, he decides to return to the Mount and must bribe his way in again. All of that curious searching produces no consolation for him. The Spirit visits Ignatius only when he descends from the Mount and a Syrian Christian apprehends him. The grace that the Spirit confers in that moment proves abundant. Because Ignatius steps out of the Lord's footprints and descends from the Lord's Mount of Glory, he acknowledges the lordship of Jesus in his heart and can begin a life in service to the Lord.

Ignatius uses geography to remember his experience of God's activity in his life. As in Luke's writings, Jerusalem functions as the hinge linking Ignatius's conversion from seeking vainglory to his seeking God's glory by assisting souls in companionship. When the pilgrim Ignatius ascends the Mount of Olives, he is obsessed with the externals of his own bravado and the direction of the Lord's feet. He has to cease clutching at an equality with God in order to serve the Lord. True conversion has to be interior and profound. Jerome and Erasmus both sought to emphasize the spiritual meaning of authentic pilgrimage to Jerusalem.[77] Jerome stated, "Not to have been in Jerusalem, but in Jerusalem to have lived well is praiseworthy." Erasmus argued, "What good is it to do [something] exteriorly if interiorly one's thoughts are quite the opposite? . . . There is no great merit in treading where Christ trod with human footsteps, but it is a great thing to follow in the steps of Christ in the affections of the mind." Within Ignatius, as he warned fellow Jesuits, there was still much vainglory when he made a pilgrimage to Jerusalem. For Ignatius to serve the Lord, the Spirit had to heal his conceit. Ignatius's focus shifts from the good news of the conversion that the Lord has worked in him to the acts of the apostles he gathers as companions. Their way is the way of the Lord's disciples, a way that leads them to evangelize their entire world and involves them in trials and persecution.

Jerusalem to Barcelona: Lifetime Struggle with Vainglory

As the spiritual writers of eastern and western Christianity agreed, one never vanquished vainglory. Ignatius continues to recount his struggle with the vice. While traveling across northern Italy to take ship for Spain,

Ignatius falls back into bad habits. Contrary to the advice of Spanish soldiers, who recommend that he take secondary roads in order to avoid the fighting between French and Spanish armies, Ignatius rashly sets out on the direct route (*su camino derecho*). Three times he is taken into custody along the way, twice by the Spanish and once by the French. When interrogated by a Spanish captain, Ignatius responds in a familiar form of address that he uses with all persons, no matter what their social rank. He models that practice on the manner in which Christ and the apostles addressed each other. Both armies eventually release Ignatius from custody. The Spanish commander considers him a harmless lunatic, and the French commander embraces him as a fellow Basque. Ignatius takes ship from Genoa, sails through the privateering fleet of Andrea Doria, and reaches Barcelona. There he struggles once again with his hypocritical instincts to practice his piety before others, pricking a hole in his shoes with a needle (*agujero*) to offset the fact that his stomach feels better. The soles quickly wear out, leaving only the tops of the shoes.

Along the way to Paris and during his stay there, Ignatius continues to seek attention. When Ignatius finds that his stomach problems are diminishing, he increases his fasting and abstinence. When Ignatius hears that his former roommate, who had stolen his money, is seriously ill in Rouen, Ignatius walks barefoot and without food or drink to visit him. When Ignatius fears that he may have contracted the plague after touching one of its victims, he thrusts the hand that was then causing him pain into his mouth. The episode leads to another moment of mild humor in the narrative. Word of Ignatius's action soon reaches the university. When Ignatius returns to his room at the College de Sainte-Barbe, all the other students immediately empty the premises and run away in fear for their lives. Ignatius is banished for a few days but eventually allowed to come back. Finally, when Ignatius finds himself distracted during his studies, he goes to his master and promises never to miss a lecture. Jesuit students, take note.

Ignatius again depicts the ways that his bravado leads him into difficulty when describing his travels from his family home to Italy, in order to rejoin his companions then gathering in Venice. While journeying from Genoa to Bologna, as he is walking along a path along a river, Ignatius realizes that he has lost his way (*smarì la via*). The lofty path he follows narrows so much that eventually he has to crawl on his hands and knees. He actually reaches a point where he can go neither forward nor back (*non poteva più nè andare inanzi nè tornar' indietro*). If he moves, he fears that he will fall into the river. Brashly trusting his ability to master the lofty and narrow path, Ignatius ultimately finds himself immobilized. He characterizes that moment as the greatest struggle of his life, a struggle for humility over vainglory. In fact, just outside Bologna, he does fall off a bridge. Covered with mud, he enters the city, and the residents mock him.[78] In Pauline terms (2. Cor. 12:7), vainglory proved to be Ignatius's thorn in the flesh, and he felt that it would plague his fellow Jesuits as well.

Conclusion

At first glance, there could hardly be a stranger association than John Cassian and Ignatius Loyola. A recent translator of the former characterized Cassian's monastic spirituality as the polar opposite of Loyola's apostolic spirituality.[79] There is much to that position. In the latest English selection of Ignatius's letters, the only citation of Cassian occurs in Ignatius's most monastic letter, the poorly understood diatribe on the obedience of apostolic religious that he sent to the Jesuits in Portugal in 1553.[80] As the supreme monastic temptation, vainglory perforce seems irrelevant to apostolic religious life. Still, vainglory and narcissism provide a big tent, uniting under their spread the literary genius of Ovid, the spiritual genius of the monastic writers, the flamboyant genius of hidalgo culture, and the psychological genius of Sigmund Freud.

Dominique Bertrand has argued that the Ignatian emphasis on the role of intelligence in discerning interior thoughts and movements shares elements in common with the Desert Fathers.[81] Few works were as widely read and copied as Cassian's. Cassian mediated to western monks not only the teaching of the Egyptian fathers on vainglory but also their establishment of a network of charitable institutions to aid the poor. Cassian lauded monks who had become poor by choice for trying to assist those who were poor by no choice of their own. Those institutions reached western Europe in the form of "diaconates" (*diakoniai*).[82] Ignatius would find that charitable impulse sympathetic. And the eastern spiritual writers had underlined that monks were led by the vice of vainglory to abandon their ascetic existence and seek greater recognition in "apostolic works." By conceiving an apostolic religious order, Ignatius perforce exposed his companions to a principal fault of human nature.

In expressing their concerns about vainglory, the two spiritual writers employed the same biblical language and image of a "royal road." Ignatius described taking the "royal road" after his confrontation with the Moor. On at least two occasions, Cassian emphasized that a discerning discretion best engenders balance in a disciple of the Lord and leads that disciple along "a royal path."[83] Both men appreciated the peculiar spiritual challenge of vainglory. Cassian generally saw a causal progression from one principal fault to the next: greed inflames fornication, which work together to bestir avarice. But Cassian removed pride and vainglory from his chain of faults. As one progressed in virtue and overcame vice, the two most dangerous impulses then came into play, leading monks to flaunt their fasting undertaken to quell gluttony. Pride and vainglory were often a by-product of success in the spiritual life and implied a much greater fall. That is why discernment played such a crucial role in Cassian's spirituality. As Michel Foucault observed, "[Discerning] has nothing to do with a code of permitted or forbidden actions, but it is a whole technique for analysing and diagnosing thought, its origins, its qualities, its dangers, its potential for temptation and all the dark forces that can lurk behind the mask it may assume."[84] John Cassian and Ignatius both acknowledged vainglory as a principal fault of human nature and gave serious reflection to its avoidance. Ultimately, Ignatius had to confront his longing for notoriety through outward accomplishments, overcome a temptation to scrupulous accounting of every possible sin, and embrace the gift of conversion of heart.

Whether from Cassian or elsewhere, Ignatius had ample opportunity to wrestle with prior reflection on the spiritual dangers of vainglory. Gregory the Great (ca. 540–604) defined vainglory as "seeking the power of an empty name," saw a close tie between pride and hypocrisy, and argued that hypocrites discern poorly because they lack discretion and sin consciously because they act with malice.[85] Gregory learned much about vainglory when he left his household monastery to get involved once again in the affairs of Rome. In the *Summa theologica* (I–II, Q. 84; II–II, Q. 132), Thomas Aquinas (1224–75) argued that pride is the root sin and vainglory the first sin, agreed with Gregory the Great that vainglory should be numbered among the principal vices, and concluded that vainglory constitutes a mortal sin if it leads one to act against charity. In the *Little Flowers* (chapter 7), Francis of Assisi (1182–1226) was said to have taken along two loaves of bread for his Lenten fast on an island in Lago di

Trasimeno and to have consumed half of one loaf in order to overcome his vainglory and establish that he was not another Jesus. Late in life, for the same reason, he tried to hide his stigmata. The life of Francis in the *Legenda aurea*, which Ignatius read while recuperating, emphasized that Francis wasted the first twenty years of his life in vain activities (*vane vivendo consumpsit*), later preferred to be censured rather than praised, and eventually attracted noble and nonnoble followers who had spurned their previous pursuit of worldly vanities (*spreta seculari pompa*).[86] Jean Gerson addressed the theme of vainglory and even attributed the roots of the Great Western Schism to that vice. Likewise, Gerson carefully considered subjects like consolation, frequent Communion, and adaptability of spiritual direction that concerned Ignatius as well.[87]

Artists of the period depicted pride or vainglory or self-love as a beautiful woman gazing at herself in a mirror, at times accompanied by a peacock at her feet. A large fresco of "Iniquitous Civic Government" in the Palazzo Pubblico of Siena that Ambrogio Lorenzetti completed in the middle of the fourteenth century shows *Vanagloria* wearing a coat edged in gems and admiring herself in a mirror. Juxtaposed to her is the female figure of *Spes* (Hope), who looks not to herself but to the Lord Jesus. On the capital of a column from the same century in the courtyard of the Doge's Palace in Venice, *Vanitas* is clothed in a robe embroidered with roses and gazes into a mirror.[88]

Though Ignatius did not embrace a doctrinaire monastic view of the world as utterly corrupt,[89] he did share common emphases with monastic predecessors like Cassian. Discernment for Ignatius was critical; in fact, the struggle against vainglory taught Ignatius the subtleties of sound methods of discerning. When tempting the devout to vainglory, the evil spirit characteristically appeared under the guise of goodness. Visions that seem to benefit belief actually victimize the believer. One easily confuses the vain joy of approval with the consolation of the Spirit. In an effort to defeat vainglory, a committed believer often resorts to excessive countermeasures that can be just as conceited.

Before the Jesuits existed, Ignatius had become so convinced of those spiritual realities that, in a letter of 1536, he taught them to Sister Teresa Rejadell.[90] In keeping with previous teaching on vainglory, that same letter upheld a criterion of discretion whenever one examines one's conscience.[91] If our spiritual enemy supplies us with consolation, we should focus on our sinfulness. When our conscience becomes lax and self-satisfied, we no longer see sinfulness as sinful. If, conversely, our spiritual enemy attacks us through discouragement or depression, we should focus on our blessings. When our conscience becomes scrupulous and self-obsessed, we see sinfulness where there is no sin. The solution, however, was not to cease examining one's conscience but to shift one's emphasis in the opposite direction from conceit or self-obsession.

The examination of conscience, therefore, became a trusted remedy for Jesuit vainglory. Ignatius had good reason to insist that Jesuits practice that form of prayer twice daily and never omit it. Moreover, Ignatius structured the examination of conscience to allow the prudence and discretion he considered essential. It began with a review of the day's blessings up to that moment in time and only afterward opened up the possibility of sinful acts. Skilled practitioners vary the emphasis to counter the subtle attacks of the evil spirit.[92] Proper discernment and competent spiritual direction supplied a second Jesuit remedy for vainglory. A continual search for progress (*provecho, aprovechar*), inherent in an apostolic life of pilgrimage and a vocation realized "on the road," supplied a third antidote for the self-satisfied stasis that vainglory breeds.[93] Cultivating within the virtues of patience and charity and humility militated against the vice. Finally, Jesuit poverty played a crucial role in Ignatius's vision. As a pilgrim, in keeping with medieval tradition, he had brought no money except what he might distribute to the needy along the way. As a Jesuit, he envisioned a community like those idealized in Acts, where members held all in common and had no fixed incomes.

With his monastic predecessors, Ignatius emphasized a focus on God's glory, not one's own. Ironically, in a way that might foster vainglory, Jesuit spirituality after Ignatius has emphasized the "greater" in his cherished phrase "for the greater glory of God." Ignatius would emphasize "of God." In his own concise phrasing, he wanted to turn their eyes toward God, not toward themselves.[94] Perhaps Ignatius has so little to say about chastity because he felt that Jesuits faced a more difficult struggle against vanity. Once Ignatius determined to serve the Lord through chastity at the shrine of Aránzazu, he found himself in the spiritual dynamic described by Evagrius and Cassian, whereby his vainglory actually made the practice of chastity somewhat easier. After Ignatius committed himself to chastity, he realized that any indulging in sexual activities would erode the good reputation that he so prized.

In addition to relevant material in the scriptures and patristic and medieval spiritual writings, other cultural influences may have affected Ignatius's convictions about vainglory. His fantasy to win the hand of a lady at court reflected the cultural matrix of courtly love literature. In a world filled with roving knights, Ignatius needed to win attention at court and distinguish himself, so that he could marry into the highest level of the Spanish nobility. For years, that goal stoked the fire of his vanity.[95] His description of the confrontation with the Moor echoes the aristocratic ethos of his Spanish world, where life was conceived primarily as a contest in which one defended personal and blood claims to superiority. Honor was the fundamental motivating passion for generations of Spaniards, particularly the aristocracy, and honorable deeds needed to be seen. In Ignatius's lifetime, by statute, Spain ostracized impure lineage.[96]

The choice of what to do after the Moor had insulted the Virgin echoes the Hercules legend, which was given classic expression by the sophist Prodicus, handed on by Cicero, and discussed by medieval moralists. When Hercules stood at the crossroads between virtue and vice, he did not choose to rely on his own strength, nor did he embrace the desire for honor and glory typical of the heroic age of Greek antiquity. Rather, using his mental powers to discern, Hercules chose the path of virtue. Ignatius, with the aid of a mule, did likewise.[97] Ignatius's temptation to kill himself by jumping from a high place would put him in the minority of known medieval suicides. According to statistics from medieval French sources, jumping from a window ranked fourth behind hanging, drowning, or cutting one's wrists with a knife as a mode of suicide. In a concerted effort to prevent suicide, the medieval church used theories of the interrelationship among specific vices to identify persons who might be prone to kill themselves. Though the church's analysis suggested that one came more frequently to despair out of laziness (*accidia*), pride likewise could lead one to become angry or depressed and then to fall into despair. Behind all suicides lay an integral wretchedness that touched the physical, material, and moral dimensions of the desperate individual's life.[98]

Ignatius left telling indications of his self-obsession and bravado in the *Acta* when he suggested an affinity between himself and Narcissus at the Cardoner River and the unnamed river near Bologna. In Ovid's richly contrived narrative (*Metamorphoses* 3.339–510), Narcissus's own image deceives him: he does not realize that his image is only a reflection, nor does he realize it is his own reflection. Immobilized like a statue in his lifeless surroundings, Narcissus indulges a self-love that proves fatally unobtainable.[99] He had only a sense of his own beauty and could not see himself as anything else, certainly not ugly or, in Christian terms, sinful. He plays a solitary game, without companions. The plot needs only a lover for its protagonist, and that lover need only find the reflective waters of a tranquil spring. The beloved can offer nothing to the lover but death, and the lover, ironically, cannot bring his beloved to life. Narcissus precipitated his fate by staring at his own reflection and trying to embrace himself. The richness of his self-infatuation ends up impoverishing Narcissus. Tears destroy the desired image, which proves to be bereft of substance. The disappearance of that image from the water's surface, however, foreshadows the protagonist's own demise. Night envelopes his eyes, which remain transfixed by the image of his beloved, himself.

Freud's psychological analysis of the myth shares points in common with the acuity of Ignatius's self-knowledge and the wisdom of the spiritual writers' treatment of vainglory.[100] In his treatment, Freud emphasized three themes: self-consciousness and self-examination, human anxiety before death, and unsatisfactory relationships with the other. All infants, at a very early stage in their development, pass through a narcissistic phase, during which they realize that they do not control their world and depend on the affection of their parents. A secondary phase of narcissism, however, is generally pathological, triggered by turning back on oneself when the parents, especially the mother, do not prove empathetic. By adulthood, a narcissistic personality disorder is manifested by boasting and self-aggrandizement out of all proportion to one's actual accomplishments. Sufferers from the disorder revel in fantasies of power and success, demand excessive admiration, and manipulate others to achieve their goals.[101]

Therapy may assist one in breaking out of the bewitching power of ego in order to reach out to the other, but a narcissistic personality finds it difficult to form a bond with the therapist. Healing moves one from narcissism and megalomania to love and attachment to figures outside of one's own ego. As one matures, the focus shifts from oneself alone to one's companions. Like the spiritual writers, Freud felt that egotism could, on occasion, invest the subject with a means to defend against the pathology. Yet the circle of narcissism is truly vicious. Narcissism affords a measure of protection precisely by teaching one never to risk loving another. Until narcissistic individuals develop the capacity to love another, they continue to concentrate their attention on themselves. Like the spiritual writers once again, Freud posited that, for an individual and a society, narcissism is superseded but never altogether dismissed. A mature psyche retains vestiges of self-absorption and will at times seek its own pleasure. The struggle against vainglory never ends.

3   The *Acta* as Mirror of Apostolic Religious Life

Ignatius returns to Italy on his poor ship and then has to determine a new direction for his life. "What should he do?" (*Quid agendum*). He decides to study "in order to be able to help souls" (*y al fin se inclinaba más a estudiar algún tiempo para poder ayudar a las ánimas*).[1] It is a decision of significant consequences, parallel to his willingness in 1548 to accept the invitation of the town council of Messina to staff a school there, and he offers just as little explanation for the decision. Ignatius believes that learning constitutes an essential mode of preparation for a life of apostolic service. The intimate connection between the two supplies the basis for his later choice to make teaching an apostolic service. The goal of helping souls will influence the way that Ignatius studies and the subjects he chooses to learn. Ignatius prefers disciplines that will assist one engaged in ministries. As Nadal observed, when commenting on how hard Ignatius studied, "without letters, his ministry to help his neighbors would neither be effective, nor would it be as free from danger and peaceful."[2] At Manresa, Ignatius experiences God working as a teacher to transform him from within. He also begins to appreciate that studies supply exterior credentials. His plans to study receive the approval of his unnamed confessor and his generous friend, Isabel Roser.

Before starting school, Ignatius explores the possibility of joining forces with a holy friar (*un fraile*) whom he had previously met in Manresa.[3] His motives for exploring that option reveal his priorities at the time: to learn (*aprender*), entrust himself more freely to the Spirit (*poderse dar más cómodamente al espíritu*), and benefit souls (*aun aprovechar a las ánimas*). When Ignatius discovers that the friar has died, he goes to school. His focus remains on assisting others and preparing himself well for such ministries. When Ignatius has visions while studying, he concludes that those visions are temptations. He does not experience such distractions when praying or attending Mass, so they could not be of aid to his spiritual progress (*quán poco provecho*).

Pilgrimage, Charism, Education, and Apostolate

Anthropological Facets of Christian Pilgrimage

Victor and Edith Turner have supplied a historical anthropology of pilgrimage that helps explain why Ignatius's pilgrimage prepared him for the radical choice of what he ought to do. In its origins and for much of its history, Christian pilgrimage comprised a charismatic activity, in which one was literally moved by the Spirit. The journey initiated the pilgrim into a new and deeper level of existential belief. Pilgrims experienced the depths of authentic consolation, a healing within for sin that also held out the hope for healing physical ailment. The Turners suggest that pilgrimage was an "extroverted mysticism," whereas mysticism was an "introverted pilgrimage."[4] Prior to his decision to study, Ignatius had experienced both. Christian pilgrimage was also a communitarian experience. Once an individual decided to go, that person necessarily came into contact with like-minded individuals. It was an activity among companions. Pilgrims traveled in organized groups and participated in communal activities at way stations and the sanctuary itself. They moved from the mundane center of their everyday lives to a sacred periphery, and that very movement nurtured feelings of Catholic populism and anticlericalism as well. Finally, Christian pilgrimage was transforming, building in a slow progress of stops along the way to the climactic encounter with the sacred energies of the holiest shrine, where one was washed free of sin. As a consequence, the journey back home generally occurred swiftly and without incident.

Christian Pilgrimage in Ancient and Medieval Times

The ancient practice of pilgrimage among Christians had Jerusalem as its goal. To journey to Jerusalem meant that a believer literally embraced the call to follow the Lord. Though pilgrims to the Holy Land generally stopped at the shrines of the Annunciation at Nazareth and the Dormition on Mount Zion, they ultimately wanted to reach Calvary and the Church of the Resurrection. Their journey in imitation of Christ became a way to the source of salvation. The pilgrimage to Jerusalem consoled and often engendered intense emotion on the part of participants. Pilgrims traveled a long distance in faith, immersed themselves in the suggestive geography of the Holy Land, and reveled in a topography that reinvigorated their sense of Christianity's good news. At times, as discussed in the previous chapter, their emotional experiences had a naive literalism, expressed in such actions as gathering dust from the footprints of the Lord. Imagination likewise was crucial to their emotional participation, for the Roman general Titus had so effectively sacked Jerusalem that the vast majority of the structures from the time of Jesus no longer existed.

The medieval period brought two important changes to the practice of pilgrimage. First, once Islam had spread through the eastern and southern regions of the Mediterranean, shrines appeared in the Christian West that allowed pilgrims to mimic a journey to Jerusalem without crossing into Muslim territory. If Europe could not go to the Holy Land, then the holy places would come to Europe. In exemplary fashion, Mary's house at Nazareth was carried westward by angels until it found a new placement in Loreto. Marian shrines are interesting for the fact that they were well entrenched in the West before the flow of pilgrims eastward was restricted. The basilica of Santa Maria Maggiore in Rome, built on the spot where it purportedly snowed in August, is one such example. Loyola's Spain was blessed with several compensatory shrines, prominent among which were the sanctuary at Zaragoza, where Mary appeared to the apostle James and left a pillar with a small statue of herself, and Santiago de Campostela, where James himself had come to be buried after he fled from Muslim political authority. The two shrines indicate the evolution of James's role in Spanish Catholic spirituality, from evangelizer to crusader.

In addition to establishing a network of shrines that offset the difficulties of travel to the Holy Land itself, the medieval era also witnessed an effort by the Church's hierarchy to control the charismatic impulses of the experience. The church, through its penitentials, began to make pilgrimage an integral part of the sacrament of penance and prescribe pilgrimage as the only way to make satisfaction for specified sins that one had confessed. Bishops proved themselves deft in gradually integrating pilgrimage into the structures of authority. The freedom and, at times, anarchy that pilgrimage fostered made such "holy nomadism" threatening to church authority. From a hegemonic perspective, crusading was the ultimate cooptation of the practice. Nonetheless, the hierarchy could never strip pilgrimage of all of its charismatic qualities. The first pilgrims set off after receiving extraordinary manifestations, and their journey proved beneficial not only for the individual but the community, no matter what their personal status in society. Belief in that extraordinarily graced experience led others to set out along the way.

When placed against this background, the pilgrimage of Ignatius has elements of a return to ancient practice, sharing in the broader impulses of renaissance that characterized his cultural world. Though it is difficult to pin down his motivations for the pilgrimage—likely a mixture of penitence, vainglory, and inspiration—it is clear that Jerusalem was his goal. He stopped at only two way stations, the Marian shrines of Aránzazu and Montserrat, which both had for him personally strong resonances of the Incarnation as a new beginning and a source of universal salvation.[5] After taking ship in Barcelona, Ignatius focused exclusively upon the supraregional and universal character of Jerusalem. In addition to the goal of his pilgrimage, Jerusalem functioned for Ignatius as the place where Christ enlisted followers to help build his kingdom. The Kingdom and Two Standards meditations are set there.[6] Ignatius turned away from Santiago and crusading. Moreover, he did not treat Rome as a locus for pilgrim activities. Though he mentioned Our Lady of the Snows in the preface, when describing his first stay in Rome, he did not mention a visit to Santa Maria Maggiore or the other stational churches.

Pilgrimage as Education along the Way

The journey to Jerusalem continued Ignatius's education for ministry. He deepened his appreciation for movement rather than stasis, he tried to take nothing for the journey, he made contact with like-minded persons, and he began to appreciate the benefits of companionship. God had to teach Ignatius like a child because Ignatius still possessed elements of a pilgrim's childish literalism. He had to retreat from his rash efforts to see the Lord's footprints and put himself in the place of Lord. The Ascension provided a crucial marker in time and space: the pilgrimage fleet traditionally embarked from Venice on that feast day, and Ignatius stepped out of the Lord's footprints on that Mount. The journey continued for Ignatius well after he had left Jerusalem. Unlike other pilgrims, he did not rush home and renounce the world by entering a monastery. He did retain his pilgrim's garb, a long gray tunic; he did attempt to walk barefoot, as the most devoted pilgrims did; and he did migrate from university to university, as pilgrim students did. He struggled with residual literalism, refusing to celebrate his Mass of Thanksgiving after ordination anywhere else but Jerusalem and, when that proved impossible, choosing Santa Maria Maggiore because the relic of the manger was conserved there. There were also signs of his maturing faith, as he embraced the human Christ who practiced unrestricted solidarity. He exploited the power of the pilgrimage experience in elements of his *Spiritual Exercises*, in which Christ enlists followers for a kingdom already present and educates followers along the way, and Christ's Spirit awakens interior freedom and a love capable of finding God in all things, not merely in the geography of the Holy Land.

In the final analysis, discernment of what was to be done was a lifetime's work for Ignatius and his companions. The results of that discernment, moreover, were controversial. The choice for an itinerant lifestyle, in companionship, without money, through education, all in order to help souls, created the same sorts of tension with the hierarchy that pilgrimage created. An apostolic lifestyle was charismatic; it was worrisome; it was novel. In the spring of 1555, Ignatius rejoiced to learn that Marcello Cervini had been elected pope. What brought benefit to the community of the church, the election of a pope of Cervini's tolerant qualities, augured well for the nascent Society of Jesus. Unfortunately, Cervini died only a few weeks later. When the notably less tolerant Gian Pietro Carafa was elected to succeed Cervini, Ignatius feared the consequences for the church and the Jesuits. That election took place on the feast of the Ascension. A few months later, Ignatius completed his narration, highlighting the importance of education for service, the various ministries that he and his companions exercised, and the opposition of some church authorities to the directions embraced by that group of companions.

Ignatian Apostolic Service and Trials

Barcelona to Alcalá: Catechism, Humanism, Education, and First Trials

It takes years of memorization for Ignatius to learn "letters," which meant Latin grammar. While he studies, he tries to assist souls by giving alms to the poor, directing persons in the *Exercises*, and engaging them in spiritual conversation. There are two new dimensions to the services that Ignatius offers at Barcelona. He teaches catechism and attracts companions.[7]

Catholics had valued the importance of teaching Christian doctrine even before Luther brought catechism to center stage. Catholics had developed their catechetical methods in the broader context of their concern for fostering the art of living and dying well. That was especially true in the emphasis on examining one's conscience in order to make a good confession. In cataloging the qualities of a good Christian life, fifteenth-century catechesis emphasized the teaching of the Ten Commandments, the Creed, and certain fundamental prayers. Pathologically, that catechesis might focus excessively on matters of guilt and sin. The instructions were expanded to include the seven sacraments, the virtues, the beatitudes, and the works of mercy. In fact, teaching the ignorant was one of the spiritual works of mercy. In the Catholic world, catechism was the special concern of lay confraternities. Religious catechesis followed the methods specified by the Greek word itself: questions and answers that facilitated memorization.

In the sixteenth century, Luther's emphasis on catechism did cause Catholic adaptation. Eventually, Jesuits at times attempted to counter the progress of the evangelical reformers. And the technology of printing broadened the audience and fixed the answers in authoritative form in books. Teaching catechism went from fostering a moral way of living and dying to providing a form of religious indoctrination. The primary focus of catechism shifted from teaching Christian doctrine to ensuring confessional orthodoxy.

O'Malley argues that catechism proved to be the fifteenth-century art most compatible with Ignatius's emphasis on conversion and authentic Christian commitment. From Ignatius's days of schooling in Barcelona through his time as superior-general in Rome, he taught catechism and eventually made it an explicit ministry of the Jesuit Institute. The Ignatian focus on fundamental morals and sacramental confession as the expression of a committed Christian life provided the focus for all Jesuit catechesis. What evolved in the years of the first Jesuits were the methods employed to communicate those lessons. The Jesuits frequently used young people to assist them, and Jesuits trained their assistants to give formal sacred lectures. Jesuit methods included a rewriting of the lessons in verse form that was often set to music. Jesuit scholastics and their assistants then took to the streets, as sacred pied pipers who invited groups of children to follow them as they sang. Subsequently, Jesuits like Peter

Canisius and Diego de Ledesma wrote influential texts, which, in places such as India and Brazil, turned the teaching of catechism into a form of literacy training. Jesuit schools once again institutionalized catechetical methods and moved the pedagogy in catechism from an emphasis on faith as lived to faith as truths. Rigorous catechists safeguarded those truths from the infection of error.

At Barcelona and again at Alcalá, when Ignatius engages in the ministry of catechism, he teaches the art of Christian living. He focuses his teaching on the creation of human beings, their fall and their conversion. Women who gave depositions before the Inquisition in Alcalá said that Ignatius discussed the Ten Commandments and mortal sin, the five human senses and the powers of the soul, all of which he hoped would lead them to practice the examination of conscience twice daily and to confess and receive Communion frequently.[8] He eventually finds that he has made great progress in Latin grammar (*había harto aprovechado*) and is ready to move on to "the arts" (*ya podía oír artes*). With his three companions, he goes to the University of Alcalá.

The university had recently been established by the influential Franciscan cardinal Francisco Jiménez de Cisneros (1436–1517), who had also supported a reform of the teaching of Christian doctrine and the forcible conversion of Muslims in Granada. Humanist currents circulated within and around the university, and Ignatius remembers his own contacts with the de Eguía brothers, one of whom ran a printing press that was publishing the works of Erasmus. Ignatius gives only a schematic description of his studies: the terminological logic of Domingo de Soto (1495–1560), the *Physics* of Albertus Magnus (ca. 1200–80), and the *Sentences* of Peter Lombard (d. 1160/64). The progression from dialectic to physics or natural philosophy is traditional, but the inclusion of a theological text for a new undergraduate seems odd. Ignatius would normally not have attended lectures on Lombard's *Sentences* in a graduate theological faculty until he had completed his arts degree. Soto and Ignatius likely met when the Dominicans kept Ignatius a prisoner at San Esteban in Salamanca. After studies at Alcalá and Paris, Soto returned to Spain to teach new currents in logic at Alcalá from 1520 to 1524. He first published a textbook on the subject in 1529, entitled *Summulae logicales*. After earning a doctorate in theology in 1525, Soto joined the Dominicans and began a lengthy career teaching philosophy and theology at San Esteban. In the course of his

career, Soto participated in the neo-Thomist movement in Spanish intellectual life that focused on issues related to theology and natural law.[9]

If Ignatius's philosophical studies were traditional, the humanist studies taking root at Alcalá were new to Spain and had premises that proved
congenial to Ignatius and his Society. The humanist movement of the
Renaissance was a characteristic phase in the rhetorical culture of
the Western intellectual tradition.[10] Humanists sought to persuade by the
eloquence of their speech and the ethics of their actions. Humanists did
persuade the first Jesuits of a number of their positions. Rhetoric, not
logic, formed the basis for the humanist educational program. Humanists conceptualized their program of education to assist in the formation
of character and aid in the building of a just state. Humanists believed
that a truth that was eloquent would move human hearts and minds
more than bare assertion would. Eloquent truth engaged the whole human person and promoted interior appropriation. Good orators accommodated their form and content to the audience at hand. They could not
persuade unless they were in touch with the minds and hearts of those
whom they addressed. That sort of accommodation proved vital to Jesuit
ministry.

Just as Ignatius remembered his friendships with those affiliated with
humanism at Alcalá as controversial, so the Jesuit adaptation of humanist
ideals proved controversial inside and outside the Society. The controversy led to the erroneous belief that Ignatius disliked Erasmus and forbade the reading of his books. Ignatius and Erasmus shared a consistent
emphasis on the importance of interior conversion for authentic Christian
living. Interior conversion comprises one of the leitmotifs of the *Acta*. Ignatius did express reservations about Erasmus at a moment when the Erasmian legacy was under attack and Paul IV was preparing to place the
works of Erasmus on the Index of Prohibited Books. Ignatius typically
wished to shield his new Society from larger church controversies at a time
when the Society generated plenty of controversy on its own.[11]

The broader historical reality, as O'Malley argues, is more important.
Renaissance humanism supplied the rationale for Jesuits schools as a
ministry.[12] Humanists and Jesuits shared a common faith in education.
Humanists taught in order to develop a student's abilities and character
as a preparation for public service. Jesuits taught in order to foster a more
authentic and committed life in service to Christ's kingdom. The first

Jesuits felt no need to elaborate their own philosophy of education; the humanists had done that well already.

Historically, Jesuits stumbled into schooling. Ignatius viewed his own schooling in an apostolic and pragmatic way. He felt that studies would make his help to souls more efficacious, and he needed the credentials that schooling supplied. Jesuits took their first steps toward a ministry of schooling when they taught at Jesuit colleges affiliated with universities. Eventually, when the town council of Messina invited the Jesuits to found their own school, Ignatius decided to accept the invitation. He could accomplish two purposes at once: the college would fund training for Jesuits themselves, and it would minister to the urban public. Though some schools began to close five years after Messina's opening, Jesuit schooling survived and quickly generated its own momentum. By 1556, the Jesuit Pedro de Ribadeneira could see in education the essential qualities of the Jesuit vocation that Ignatius emphasized in his *Acta*. As a ministry, teaching young people not only fostered a Jesuit's progress in the spiritual life but addressed the needs of his neighbors, in a Lukan sense. The proper education of young people ensured the welfare not only of all Christendom but of the entire world.

Responding to a need long highlighted by the humanists, Jesuits would seek to fill the void of teachers who were virtuous as well as lettered and who would conjoin the example of their lives with the learning they proffered. In Ignatius's view, teaching in that humanist manner had already contributed to universal progress.[13] The truths that one learned, as humanists had long argued, should have an impact on the way that one lived. The first treatise on humanist education, written around 1402–3 by Pierpaolo Vergerio, focused on "the best morals and appropriate studies for adolescence."[14] While Erasmus and his fellow humanists argued that they could reconcile humanist studies and Christian theology, Ignatius made humanist studies an essential preparation for a Jesuit's study of theology.

Adopting the humanist rationale for schooling affected the ministerial public served by the Jesuits. In their ideals, the first Jesuits emphasized that they did not wish to favor the rich over the poor. In their practice, however, they adopted a curriculum based on "letters." By founding their teaching on Latin grammar, not the vernacular languages, Jesuits emphasized literary and professional skills for the middle and upper classes and effectively eliminated the lower classes. Schools reshaped the way in which Jesuits understood themselves, moving many of them away from charismatic evangelizing into stable classrooms.[15] Given their institutional commitments, they had less freedom to roam as apostles. Jesuits were the first Catholic religious order to operate secondary schools as a ministry. Though always well educated, Jesuits now learned in order to teach. Operating schools with a humanist rationale meant that Jesuits dealt with matters of secular culture and civic responsibility. In order to meet their educational commitments, Jesuits had to know the "pagan classics." The primary impact of the Society from that moment on would be cultural. Jesuits studied and taught secular disciplines to mine their relevance for genuine conversion of heart.

At Alcalá, Ignatius's success in helping souls by giving the *Exercises* and teaching Christian doctrine generates unfavorable rumors about him. In Ignatius's memory, the apostolic trials that begin in that university town were foreshadowed by the butchery (*carnicería*) he had experienced during his convalescence at Loyola, by his being led down the Mount of Olives, by his being taken captive in northern Italy, and by his ridicule at the hands of a priest and some others in Alcalá itself. The hobbled beggar of alms, the curious wearer of sackcloth, the known friend of Erasmians, and the suspected *alumbrado* comes to the attention of church authorities in Alcalá and the Inquisition in Toledo. Ignatius's interrogator warns him bluntly that the Inquisition, in investigating suspicions about him, might well "resort to butchery" (*hacer carnicería*).

The Inquisition's primary concern and the majority of its trials focused on suspected deviation from the church's teachings on theological and moral issues. Most trials involved Catholics accused of offenses such as blasphemy, bigamy, and sodomy. Secondarily, the Inquisition in Spain dealt with apostasy, suspected cases of baptized Jews or Muslims who had reverted to their previous faith or Catholics who had embraced the Protestant cause. The Spanish Inquisition operated under the aegis of the crown and enjoyed fairly widespread support. Deeply rooted prejudices led most Spaniards to be leery of heretics in general and the descendants of converted Jews and Muslims in particular. That prejudice intensified with the militancy behind the conquest of Granada in 1492 and the increasing fear after 1517 that Protestantism might make inroads into the newly united kingdom.[16]

The case of the *alumbrados* ("enlightened ones") illustrates the religious climate of Spain in the 1520s.[17] They were one of the sixteenth-century reform movements that wished to emphasize God's direct dealings with believers and exclude mediation through the institutional church. They advocated an interior faith marked by love of God and surrender to the guidance of God's Spirit. They fostered a quietist piety marked by rejection of the sacraments and liturgy. They practiced a theology that was spiritual and mystical, in opposition to the rationalism and speculation of Scholastic theologians. By the time that Ignatius came under investigation, the Spanish Inquisition had already condemned forty-eight propositions held by the alumbrados and was seeking to crush the movement. Investigations were in progress throughout the diocese of Toledo, and adherents of the movement had been jailed.

Ignatius knew members of the movement in Alcalá and chose as his confessor Manuel de Miona (ca. 1477–1567), a Portuguese priest accused a few years later of being an alumbrado. Ignatius and his *Spiritual Exercises* had an impact on Miona, who entered the Society of Jesus in 1545. Ignatius added to suspicions by sponsoring pious gatherings at the local hospital where he resided or in the homes of those who took an interest in his spirituality. Ignatius wore a plain gray robe to those meetings and arrived barefoot. His lessons on sinfulness and repentance at times produced dramatic results: women fainted or vomited or rolled around on the floor while claiming to see devils.[18] For the first of many times, at the insistence of Catholic clergy, the Inquisition would investigate Ignatius. His memories of those investigations are the most vivid and detailed elements of the second half of the *Acta*.

Harassment and persecution by church authorities run as a thread from Alcalá to Rome.[19] There were three hearings in Alcalá. In the first, Ignatius is accused of wearing sackcloth and being an alumbrado. The archbishop's vicar, Juan Rodríguez de Figueroa, investigates and finds the charges without foundation. In terminology reflective of humanist ideals, Figueroa characterizes Ignatius's teaching and his life as blameless. Nonetheless, he orders Ignatius and his companions not to dress alike and orders Ignatius to wear shoes that Figueroa would purchase for him. As Ignatius will generally do before the inquisitors, he offers begrudging compliance to those commands. Ignatius has a frank exchange with the vicar and reminds the vicar that he too will burn if convicted of heresy.

His general opinion of the Inquisition is even more telling: he can see no benefit in such investigations (*Mas no sé, dice, qué provecho hacen estas inquisiciones*).

For similar reasons and the fact that a lady of high standing had visited Ignatius at the hospital, Rodríguez de Figueroa investigates Ignatius again a few months later. Ignatius is not summoned to give account, and the vicar takes no action. On a third occasion, a rumor that Ignatius persuaded a woman and daughter to go on a dangerous pilgrimage leads to his imprisonment for forty-two days.[20] While jailed, Ignatius displays his characteristic bravado. He refuses a lawyer and considers himself imprisoned for the love of Christ, who will free him (*Aquel por cuyo amor aquí entré me sacará*). His faith in Christ as liberator is strengthening, and his identification with the imprisoned apostles in Acts is apparent.[21] On this occasion, Ignatius describes himself as "the captive" (*el preso*), not the pilgrim.[22] Ignatius explicitly adds that a notary recorded his interrogation. He is asked whether he is a crypto-Jew and responds negatively. He also denies a rumor that he persuaded the women to go on pilgrimage.

Significantly, Ignatius is joined in jail by his companion Calixto de Sá. Ignatius increasingly perceives that the Inquisition's activity is insidious because it hampers his ability to work together with his companions for the aid of souls. Years later, in 1613, while copying the depositions from the Alcalá hearings, the notary Juan de Quintanarnaya Balverde inferred that Ignatius taught an inspiring catechism and lived an exemplary life, like the apostles, realizing the love of God and neighbor in assistance to the poor, the hospitalized, and the imprisoned.[23]

In describing the final investigation at Alcalá, Ignatius confirms his frustrations by adding his reaction to the sentence, which once again exonerates him but compels him to dress as a student and refrain from speaking about matters of faith until he has completed his studies. Ignatius remembers the inquisitor's satisfaction with his Solomonic judgment. An individual like the inquisitor focuses on externals: the way one dresses and the credentials one holds. Ignatius objects that the sentence will have dire consequences, closing the door to his helping souls make progress (*parece que le tapaban la puerta para aprovechar a las ánimas*). Closure and stasis function as favored Ignatian characterizations of wrong; they impede the progress of the Gospel along the way. He appeals the sentence to the archbishop of Toledo, Alonso de Fonseca (1475–1534), who gives Ignatius clothes and a scholarship to the college he founded at Salamanca in 1525. Ignatius moves to a new university in order to be free to help souls.

Alcalá to Salamanca: Further Trials, Apostolic Vocation in Companionship, Inquisitions, and Heresy

In Salamanca, Ignatius soon arouses the suspicions of the Dominicans at San Esteban.[24] One of the Dominicans invites Ignatius to the convent for a Sunday meal, and Ignatius attends with his companion Calixto. His experience resembles that of Jesus when sharing meals with the Pharisees during his journey to Jerusalem in Luke's Gospel. The subprior initially tries to win Ignatius's confidence by offering an accurate appraisal of his little band. He has heard the good news about the life and morals of Ignatius and his companions and "their going about preaching in an apostolic manner" (*que andaban predicando a la [a]postólica*). Then the subprior poses a series of questions designed to entrap Ignatius: *What have you studied?* (Very little.) *What do you preach?* (We do not preach but only engage in friendly conversation about God.) Ignatius knew he had no license to preach. *About what things of God do you speak?* (We praise virtues and censure vices.) *Do you speak of virtues and vices through your learning—by your own admission minimal—or through the Holy Spirit?* Ignatius at first remains silent for he senses the trap. (There is no need to discuss these matters further.) *Because there are so many errors of Erasmus in the air, don't you want to respond? Why is Calixto dressed in such an odd fashion?* The ultimate question, as usual, bears upon externals. The Dominicans hope that Ignatius will convict himself as an Erasmian, by defending positions of Erasmus, or as an alumbrado, by teaching morality only from the Spirit's inspiration.

Though Ignatius gives no cause, the Dominicans keep him under house arrest until he can be handed over to the authorities. Ironically, the longer Ignatius remains at San Esteban, the more Dominicans he wins to his side through his persuasive spiritual conversation. As part of their jailing, Ignatius and Calixto are shackled and chained to a post. They have to do everything together. Ignatius seems to date the birth of a proto-Society of Jesus to his days in Salamanca. The opening sentence of that chapter speaks of *compañia* once and *compañeros* twice, and Ignatius makes a point of a collective persecution there.[25] Two other companions later join Calixto and Ignatius in jail. They are all consoled to be imprisoned for the love of God, and they do not escape when the other prisoners do. They behave like Paul in Acts (16:19–34). This time, the confinement lasts seventy-two days, and as part of the investigation, Ignatius hands over the written notes of his *Spiritual Exercises*.

Whenever questioned, Ignatius offers impeccable responses. He purposefully launches into a lengthy catechesis on the first commandment in order to demonstrate the quality of his teaching and irritate his condescending judges. When pressed on how, without the proper academic credentials, he can distinguish mortal from venial sin in the *Exercises*, Ignatius insists that the inquisitors focus on the content of his catechesis and judge it correct or in error. The pattern is the same: the Inquisition concentrates on rumor and externals; Ignatius is concerned about quality and content. In Salamanca, Ignatius's life and teaching are again judged without error, but he is forbidden to teach on the difference between mortal and venial sin until he has earned a degree. Ignatius remembers that the judges spoke kindly to him at the end of the inquest, and he interprets their kindness as an effort to win his acceptance of the sentence. He agrees to comply with the sentence, but he makes it clear that he does not accept it. This time, he says that, in addition to closing the door, they are closing his mouth and making it impossible for him "to help his neighbors" (*pues, sin condenalle en ninguna cosa, le cerraban la boca para que no ayudase los próximos en lo que pudiese*). The customary "souls" are here glossed as the individuals who arouse the compassion of Luke's good Samaritan. In the *Constitutions* that Ignatius wrote for the Society of Jesus, he used the expression "helping neighbors" more frequently than "helping souls."[26]

The brief time that Ignatius spent in Salamanca proved a watershed in his journey with the Lord. It convinced him of the justice of his cause and the quality of his catechesis, including the difference between a mortal and venial sin. It led him to take the initiative when he learned that he was under investigation by church authorities in Paris, Venice, and Rome. It deepened his loathing for rumor. And it confirmed his discernment to lead a life like that of the early apostles, by which he and his companions would help their neighbors. Because the Inquisition made that impossible in Salamanca, he decided to transfer to the University of Paris. Once settled, he intended to bring his companions to join him.

By this point in the account, Ignatius has traced a sort of process of elimination that helped him discern his authentic vocation.[27] Before leaving Loyola, Ignatius had imagined one day joining the Carthusians. The decision not to stab the "Moor" represented a subconscious rejection of that bizarre spiritual creation of the High Middle Ages, the crusading religious order.[28] At Montserrat and Manresa, he had tested the monastic vocation of the Benedictines and the eremitic vocation in a cave. Despite deep admiration for Francis, Ignatius did not seek to join the Franciscans as a way to realize his dream of living and working in the Holy Land. After returning to Barcelona, he had explored the possibility of joining forces with a holy friar. In Salamanca, he remembered earlier considering the possibility of joining a religious order that needed reform. His desire for attention influenced that consideration. In a lax religious order, Ignatius would suffer more for his observant rigor and would be insulted for his zeal. The Dominicans whom Ignatius met in Salamanca may have reanimated that quixotic venture. Ultimately, though, while imprisoned, Ignatius discerned his true vocation: to help souls, to study first so that he could do so, to gather others of similar motivation, and to keep with him those he had already gathered. He had resolved the dichotomy between entering a religious order or going about the world. Religious could live their vows while assisting the progress of their neighbors in the world.

At the moment when the Dominicans at Salamanca were scrutinizing Ignatius carefully, they were also playing a prominent role in the formal inquisition of Erasmus at Valladolid. For years the Spanish biblical scholar Diego López Zúñiga (d. 1531) had urged an investigation of Erasmus's writings. Zúñiga first censured errors in Erasmus's editions of the Greek New Testament and the annotations that accompanied those editions and then culled from the corpus of Erasmus's publications purported blasphemies and opinions supportive of Luther. Shortly before the scheduled hearing, one of Erasmus's Spanish supporters, Alonso Fernández de Madrid (ca. 1475–1559), tried to help Erasmus by publishing a Castilian translation of the *Enchiridion*, which was actually an expanded paraphrase. The second edition of that work in 1526 came from the press of Miguel de Eguía, one of the brothers whom Ignatius mentions in his *Acta*. Rather than help Erasmus, the translation increased animosity toward him, especially among those clergy and religious who resented his stinging criticisms.

Delayed by news that soldiers of the emperor Charles V were sacking Rome, the panel eventually convened at Valladolid in the summer of 1527 with the inquisitor-general, Alonso Manrique, as its chair. Though no formal verdict was issued because the tribunal adjourned when plague broke out, votes were taken and recorded that indicated the sentiments of those involved. The Dominicans and Franciscans, in general, were fairly hostile to Erasmus, and the members of the faculty of theology from Salamanca condemned him. His supporters came primarily from the Benedictines and the biblical scholars, excluding the ever antagonistic Zúñiga. The most vitriolic critic was Diogo de Gouveia (ca. 1470–1557), principal of the Paris Collège de Sainte-Barbe from 1520 to 1548. Even without a formal judgment, the charges against Erasmus received wide publicity because Erasmus felt bound to refute them. Some of those charges resemble motives for which Ignatius was also under close scrutiny. Erasmus was vilified as an innovator, and his innovative tendencies were most apparent in his effort to reform monasticism by emphasizing interior dispositions rather than exterior practices.[29] In responding to such charges, Erasmus and Ignatius followed a similar path: defending their commitment to the Catholic Church but rejecting the intransigence of ultraorthodox zealots.

Ignatius had vivid memories of his experiences with the Inquisition in Spain because he relived those experiences in the years that he dictated his *Acta*. In 1551, the archbishop of Toledo, Juan Martínez Guijeño (called Silíceo), banned Jesuits from ministering in his diocese because he resented their privileges as religious and despised Ignatius for accepting New Christians into the order.[30] Ignatius acquired letters from Pope Julius III, who ordered the archbishop to desist. In 1553, at the urging of Dominican opponents, such as Melchor Cano, Silíceo established a commission to investigate whether the *Spiritual Exercises* were infected by teachings of the alumbrados. The commission was chaired by another Dominican, Tomás de Pedroche, and it reached the conclusion that parts of the *Exercises*, especially the Fifteenth Annotation and the second method of election, were heterodox. The furor abated for a time in 1554 but was rekindled by the election of Gian Pietro Carafa as Pope Paul IV in May of 1555. The individual relentlessly fanning the flames was the Dominican Cano, who detested Ignatius because he perceived that the founder of the Jesuits was "vain."[31] Cano also detested the Society of Jesus as a religious order. He came from the culture of Scholastic theology, which fostered in him a preference for objectivity and external authority.

Cano expressed his antipathy in deed. He goaded the Spanish Dominicans to publish a copy of the condemnation of the Society issued in Paris in 1555. He impugned the orthodoxy of the *Spiritual Exercises* and prepared a censure of the book for Paul IV. Fortunately, the censure never reached the eyes of a pope himself hostile to Ignatius, Ignatius's spirituality, and the Jesuit order. Ignatius and Nadal both attributed Cano's opposition to his religious zeal. While Nadal confessed that Cano had tested his patience and elicited his prayers, Ignatius tersely observed that Cano's knowledge did not match his zeal.[32] The threats to active ministry that Ignatius first encountered in those years in Spanish universities were still real when he dictated the *Acta*. He was grateful to God for exonerating him personally and for safeguarding his ministries.

The first Jesuits ministered to criminals and heretics. The prisons of the early modern world housed debtors and those awaiting sentence or execution.[33] Jesuit ministry to those in prison focused in general on their change of heart. On behalf of the imprisoned, the early Jesuits exercised ministries of the Word of God, such as preaching and confession, and works of mercy, such as supplying food or alms. Jesuits also attempted to address the structural problems of the day by begging for funds to pay the debts of debtors.

Jesuits likewise ministered to the heretics of their time. Once again, their emphasis tended to fall on personal transformation. They supposed that the immorality of one's life eventually taints what one teaches. Only authentic change of heart would amend the quality of living and content of teaching. As superior-general, Ignatius acknowledged a range of possible responses when dealing with the disease of heresy. In a Latin letter to Peter Canisius with suggestions for Emperor Ferdinand I, Ignatius endorsed repressive measures common in that age: remove heretics from positions of authority, burn their books, and punish them harshly, even leaving open the possibility of their execution. In that same letter, Ignatius also used a metaphor of healing to recommend gentler pastoral methods that focused on education as a ministry: send qualified preachers and pastors to the German lands, publish good catechisms, and develop better seminaries. A second letter to Canisius in Italian, finished the same day

(13 August 1554), continued the theme of education by commending the multiplying effects of solid theological education, a vast network of schools, and a range of publications.[34] From the time of Pierre Favre's first visit to Germany in 1540, Jesuits were appalled by the ignorant Catholic clergy whom they met there. In the Italian letter to Canisius, Ignatius candidly acknowledged that Protestants made their strongest arguments based upon the immoral lives and theological ignorance of Catholic clergy.

At all times, Ignatius recommended prudence in dealing with heretics. Jesuits were to avoid polemics that gave free publicity to the opponent and transformed a matter of the heart into an intellectual free-for-all. The *Exercises*, like the great commission to the apostles in Luke, emphasized repentance for the forgiveness of sin. Once that conversion had occurred, Ignatius felt that the Spirit would move the believer's heart toward an ever more authentic relationship with a merciful God. For guidance, Ignatius had memories of his own zeal in theological debate with the "Moor" and the self-righteous dogmatism of some Dominicans at San Esteban.

Ignatius saw firsthand the intransigence of proponents of theological dogmatism. After the collapse of the discussions between Catholics and Protestants at Regensburg in 1541 and after the defections of leading Catholic intellectuals in 1542, Pope Paul III revived the work of the Roman Inquisition and entrusted its leadership to Cardinal Carafa. Carafa thus became the diligent inquisitor he had long wanted to be. In a 1532 *Memoriale* on the dangers of heresy in Venice, he had pressed Pope Clement VII to recognize that kindness to heretics simply made them more obdurate and more dangerous. In Carafa's opinion, Clement till then had been too clement: he was proceeding "without zeal" (*si procede freddamente*). Until the 1540s, Carafa had served on diplomatic missions to Spain and took inspiration from the centralized organization and brutal methods that the Spanish Inquisition regularly utilized.[35]

Jesuit reactions to the revival of that Roman tribunal were mixed. According to Polanco, Ignatius himself had encouraged Pope Paul III to re-establish the Roman Inquisition. That seems consistent with later positions that Ignatius expressed, though Polanco misrepresents Ignatius as the architect of that policy and the individual primarily responsible for its enactment. There is likewise evidence that Ignatius discussed with Carafa and others the need for a Roman Inquisition, but Carafa had no need to be persuaded of the Inquisition's value. In fact, Ignatius and Carafa had differing opinions on almost all issues facing the church.[36] Some of the early Jesuits backed the Inquisition and pursued heretics. Other Jesuits, however, worked for the possible reconciliation of heretics within the fold. That became official church policy under Julius III, who issued a *motu proprio* on 29 April 1550, reminding all those working with heretics to seek their repentance and reconciliation and never forget the Lord's forgiveness and his exhortation to forgive others seventy times seven times.[37]

As pope, Carafa adopted a series of radical measures to ensure religious conformity. O'Malley characterized Carafa's Index of Prohibited Books (1559) as "one of the most fanatical documents of even that fanatical pontificate."[38] Already in 1532, Carafa was arguing that the pope should stamp out the reading of heretical books, especially those written by scholars who had become arrogant through their secular learning. As a trial run for the Index, church zealots had campaigned to ban a book of devotion produced by a group of active reformers known in Italy as the *spirituali*. The book's title, *Beneficio di Cristo*, indicated its focus on the charity and kindness of Christ. It emphasized interior inspiration, reform, and dialogue, and it reflected in significant ways the ideals of Erasmus. Though Carafa and his followers wanted to proscribe the book, Ignatius and the Jesuits abstained from comment. Ignatius participated in the meetings of the spirituali living in Rome.[39]

As Carafa prepared the Index, Jesuits generally seemed to agree with the concept. At the request of the pope, Diego Laínez examined the published works of the Florentine Dominican reform preacher Girolamo Savonarola (1452–98). Laínez produced a rather judicious opinion. He felt that specific passages in the corpus needed closer examination. When the Index was finally published, however, Laínez and the Jesuits were stunned. The listing was far more comprehensive than they had anticipated, and it included the entire body of work published by Erasmus during a long, scholarly career. In fact, J. H. Elliott has observed that the Index of 1559 was "characteristically so severe as to drive most versions of the Bible out of the market, together with many famous editions of the classics and the early Fathers."[40]

In the years of Paul IV's pontificate (1555–59), Jesuits were dragged into two high-profile investigations conducted by the Roman Inquisition. The first involved Giovanni Morone, the bishop of Modena, whom the pope himself accused of tolerating heresy. Paul's accusation formed a part of his broader effort to crush the Italian spirituali. As Ignatius was accused of being a crypto-*alumbrado* at Alcalá and Salamanca, so Morone and the spirituali were accused of being crypto-Lutherans. Morone had been a friend and supporter to the Jesuits from their founding. However, while preaching in Modena in 1543, the Jesuit theologian Alfonso Salmerón had clashed with Morone and lost his preaching mandate. Years later, Morone remembered that he had objected to Salmerón's mentioning names from the pulpit, but Salmerón remembered a dispute over the crucial theological issue of justification. Prior to his arrest, Morone had apologized to Salmerón. When investigating Morone, the inquisitors twice called Salmerón to testify, and Salmerón's testimony helped to keep Morone imprisoned. After Paul IV died, Morone was immediately released. Though Morone resented Salmerón's testimony and his imprisonment, he showed his magnanimity by remaining a friend to the Society and servant to the church. Morone guided the final of Trent's three sessions to a successful conclusion.[41] Medieval spiritual writers at times adduced magnanimity as the virtue opposed to vainglory. Jesuits were embarrassed by the Morone affair and their involvement in it.

If the Morone affair was an embarrassment to the first Jesuits, the Carranza affair was a disgrace. Shortly after the Dominican Bartolomé Carranza de Miranda (1503–76) had become archbishop of Toledo and primate of Spain in 1557, the Spanish Inquisition opened an investigation of charges that his published catechism contained heretical teachings. Among Carranza's principal accusers was his fellow Dominican Melchor Cano, who had also attacked the *Spiritual Exercises*. Moreover, the unscrupulous inquisitor-general, Fernando de Valdés (1483–1568), despised Carranza for handling doctrinal problems privately and unleashed the full force of his judicial court to demonstrate the proper way to extirpate such problems. The Spanish Inquisition condemned the catechism shortly after its publication in 1558, and Paul IV upheld that judgment. Once again, Paul seemed to sense a way to attack the spirituali in Italy. One of the recognized leaders of the spirituali, Cardinal Reginald Pole of England, had supported Carranza and his book.

Carranza also asked the Jesuits for support, but Diego Laínez, immediate successor to Ignatius as Jesuit superior-general, demurred. The Spanish Inquisition had issued its own Index in 1559, which banned not only

Carranza's catechism but pirated writings of Francisco de Borja. Laínez had personal reservations about Carranza's book and feared that any open support of Carranza would make the Jesuits themselves a target of Paul IV and the Spanish Inquisition. Among the Jesuits, only Francisco de Toledo (1532–96) openly came to Carranza's defense. Though a respected theologian and a judicious scholar, Francisco's opinion was easily dismissed as that of a New Christian tainted by Jewish blood. While Carranza was imprisoned in Rome, the Jesuits sponsored a dinner for him at the Roman College. He was allowed to attend and then returned to his cell, where he spent the better part of seventeen years. Only after Gregory XIII issued an ambiguous verdict was Carranza finally released, and he died soon thereafter. The Carranza case illustrates for Jesuits that concern for the institutional survival of the organization can become a higher priority than moral clarity. Carranza was a victim of the "pedagogy of fear," and his treatment was a "patent injustice."[42] So was Ignatius's treatment on every occasion that he was imprisoned by the Inquisition.

Salamanca to Paris: Theology and Aquinas, Recruitment, Yet Further Trials

At this point in the narrative, Ignatius sets out for Paris alone and on foot, despite warnings about the dangers of that journey at a moment when the kingdoms of Spain and France are once again at war.[43] Ignatius says little about his program of studies in Paris.[44] He did not warm to the speculative and apologetic character of Scholastic philosophy and theology. He refreshed his knowledge of Latin grammar; earned a bachelor's degree, a licentiate, and a master's degree in philosophy; and completed enough theology to allow him to help souls without harassment and, if he chose, be ordained a priest.

The methods of Paris influenced elements of Jesuit education. Jesuits learned and taught in clear stages, moving from the grammar and rhetorical training of the colleges to the philosophy and theology of the university, especially the Jesuit university in Rome.[45] Jesuits employed the methods of repetition and disputation learned at Paris as a way in which to apply the data communicated in lectures. Nonetheless, Jesuit education also betrayed elements that were innovative, even from the perspective of Paris. Jesuits accepted no fees, developed a spiritual program for their schools that emphasized interior appropriation of moral values as humanist educators had, offered courses in cases of conscience, and integrated into their program festive elements like theater, a contrast to the rigors of life at the Collège de Montaigu in Paris where Ignatius first lived and, for a variety of reasons, soon left behind.[46]

External and internal factors, dating to the Paris years, led the first Jesuits to choose Thomas Aquinas as their preferred theologian. In Paris, Ignatius and his early Jesuit companions attended lectures by Dominicans on the *Summa*. When the Jesuits settled in Rome, they found themselves in a city where the Papal Court had publicly celebrated Thomas's feast for over a hundred years.[47] Internal factors also influenced that decision. By the sixteenth century, Aquinas's teachings had acquired sound credentials for orthodoxy, something Aquinas himself did not have in the thirteenth century. Aquinas had emphasized that grace built on nature. That emphasis fit Ignatian spirituality well. At the conclusion of the *Exercises*, Ignatius invites the believer to contemplate the presence of God active everywhere in creation. A generous God had abundantly poured out his grace and transformed human activity into a revelation of divine presence. Nadal emphasized that humans had a mysterious dignity as partners in the great work of reconciliation. But the first Jesuits never deified Thomas. As Salmerón expressed the matter, paraphrasing a common medieval saying, Jesuits were never more a friend to Thomas than to the truth.[48] Ultimately, the first Jesuits emphasized a style of theology that was not speculative like that of Aquinas but transforming like that of Luke. Nadal described Jesuit theology as one conducted in the Spirit, from the heart, and of practical benefit to others.[49]

Paris equally influenced the future Society as a setting for ministry and a recruiting ground for membership. Ignatius studied for seven years in a major urban center. The geography of Jesuit houses, and especially Jesuit schools, would reflect that setting. Ignatius was eventually able to study without any interruption for begging because he visited great commercial centers in northern Europe and saved his alms. Places such as Flanders and England offered Jesuit ministries financial viability. Though Ignatius had promised his Spanish companions that he would arrange for their coming to Paris to join him, he could not realize his plan. Nonetheless, Ignatius found that a large community of students in a university city was fertile ground for recruitment. In Paris, he continued to give the *Exercises*, among others to Martial Masurier (d. 1550), a professor of theology who participated in the controversial efforts for church reform that were inspired by Erasmus and centered on the diocese of Meaux.[50] The first Jesuits recruited their membership primarily from the upper middle class. In principle, there was no impediment to recruiting members from all classes of society, and the egalitarian ideals of believing communities described in the New Testament inspired Jesuit thinking on recruitment. Anyone who had emotional maturity, proven character, and intellectual talent sufficient for a university degree could become a Jesuit. However, by a priori refusing to accept candidates from the indigenous peoples, the first Jesuits contravened such egalitarian ideals. As a consequence, a good number of Jesuits died at sea as they traveled to meet the insistent demands for staffing of the missions.

In Paris, as in Spain, Ignatius's success in gathering like-minded companions dedicated to apostolic service leads to harassment and persecution. When Ignatius gives the *Exercises* to three competent tutors, they exhibit great signs of internal conversion (*Estos hicieron grandes mutaciones*). Unlike the rich young man in the Gospel, the three seem intent on realizing the radical imperatives of discipleship. They give everything they have, including their books, to the poor. They live from begging alone. They take up residence in the hospital where Ignatius had once resided. Their abandoning the college for service in a hospital leads the students whom they left behind to revolt. Thinking that Ignatius has brainwashed their tutors, the students forcibly drag them back to the college. One of the three tutors, the theologian Juan de Castro (d. 1556), later became a Carthusian.[51]

The harassment of Ignatius in Paris also has serious repercussions. Because of the great rumors (*grandes murmuraciones*) that swirl around him, Ignatius cannot study and cannot help souls. On the basis of his experience in Spain, Ignatius takes the initiative, visits the inquisitor before he has been formally summoned, and receives a verbal acquittal (and a menacing reminder from the inquisitor that "we have heard about you"). Still, Ignatius demands a full trial. When the inquisitor refuses, Ignatius brings witnesses to testify and a notary to record what they say in his defense.

Ignatius, therefore, chose to narrate his difficulties with the Inquisition in Paris and commend to his fellow Jesuits his recourse to legal protections. That narrative should be set against Ignatius's passing over in silence the vigorous role of the faculty of theology at Paris in consulting on controverted matters, conducting inquisitions, and examining books in the very years that Ignatius studied in Paris.[52] By 1528, the Paris theologians had investigated Luther's teachings, the innovative scholarship of Lefèvre d'Etaples, the preaching of reformers at Meaux, the matter of the "three Magdalenes" in the Gospels, and the writings of Erasmus. From 1528 to 1532, though working at a less vigorous pace, the faculty published a condemnation of Erasmus, voted against Henry VIII's petition for an annulment, actively pursued errors in the biblical scholarship of Cajetan, and prepared the grounds for the execution as a heretic of the aristocrat-turned-translator Louis de Berquin (d. 1529). In the period from 1533 to 1534, when issues of reform erupted in Roussel's evangelical Lenten sermons, Cop's All Saints' Day sermon, and the Placards episode, the faculty "relentlessly continued its prosecution of heretics."[53] Ignatius and his Paris companions knew personally and studied with some of the protagonists of that prosecution, theologians like Jacques Berthélemy (d. 1543) at the Collège de Sorbonne, who on twenty-one different occasions examined for heresy books by authors such as Erasmus, Josse Clichtove, Henry VIII, and Cajetan. In 1525, Berthélemy suggested that Erasmus's *Complaint of Peace* was "worthy of the flames."[54] With every opportunity to endorse that vigilant stance, Ignatius passed it over in silence and chose to narrate his own ongoing persecution by the Paris Inquisition.

Subsequently, the first Jesuits received an even more chilling reception in the conservative environment of Paris. A coalition including Bishop Eustace du Bellay (d. 1565), the Parlément of Paris, and particularly the faculty of theology at the university, adopted a formal condemnation of the Society of Jesus in December of 1554. The condemnation described the Jesuit Institute as subversive. The order went by the name of Jesus, it had privileges accorded no other religious order, especially with regard to the obligations of choir in common, and it focused on the individual's relationship with the Spirit of God. As Ignatius had done during his years of study, he turned to witnesses and gathered their written testimony to counter the charges. Ignatius acquired testimonial letters in favor of the Society from rulers and bishops and other universities. And as he had consistently done, Ignatius once again answered the content of the charges to show that they were false. Other religious orders, such as the Gesuati (a group of Hieronymites) and the Trinitarians, had taken names from the

Godhead, and the mendicants were accorded special privileges, especially with regard to preaching in any diocese. Eventually, as Calvinist Protestants made serious inroads into the kingdom of France, the Parlément of Paris granted the Jesuits conditional entry in 1562.

Paris to Azpeitia: Apostolic Religious, Poor Relief, Preaching

By the time that Ignatius leaves Paris to take the airs of his Basque homeland, he seems firm in his intent to found an apostolic religious order and clear in his mind that the founding would prove controversial. By giving the *Exercises* to his roommates, Pierre Favre and Francisco Xavier, Ignatius wins them for his project. He agrees to return home in part so that he can attend to business for them, now that all have chosen a common path. They have a concrete plan for the immediate future: go to Venice and try to take ship for Jerusalem in order to be of help to souls or, failing that, go to Rome and let the Vicar of Christ determine what they could best do for the glory of God and help of souls.[55] The pope's focus on universal needs would counteract the Jesuit focus on vainglory.

Ignatius's knack for gathering companions had finally led to a society. In Spain, prior to his trip to Jerusalem, he had befriended women whose spiritual conversation was substantial, whose ministry charitable, whose generosity palpable, and whose advice about vainglory incisive. After returning to Spain from Jerusalem, he had gathered male companions who engaged with him in charismatic ministries of the Word and suffered with him in prison. In the *Acta*, Ignatius added brief summaries of the lives of three of those companions whom he could not bring to Paris as he had originally planned. Their later lives took different directions from their exhilarating time together in Spanish university towns. In Paris, he had persuaded tutors to embrace the life of disciples and fellow students to become his lifetime associates. To accept companions had proven difficult for an individual as self-reliant as Ignatius. Now Ignatius worked to protect that companionship from the skepticism of church authorities.

Toward the end of his life, Ignatius expressed regrets that he had too easily admitted new members into the Society of Jesus.[56] Some criteria for membership in the initial years were generic: maturity, prayerfulness, courage, a modicum of learning. Others, however, were distinctive of Ignatius's spirituality, particularly the sound judgment he expected from

Jesuits. They needed to live their daily examination of conscience: to find the Lord active in their lives, test results, learn from mistakes, and adapt to times and circumstances. Inflexibility did not assist disciples on a journey. Ignatius especially seemed to regret that some of those seeking membership were doing so to flee the world in order to save their souls. They reversed the essential charism of Jesuit spirituality. Nadal likewise felt that some of the first Jesuits were inept from a psychological point of view. From the first days of the order's existence, there was one constant tension related to membership in the Society of Jesus, an unresolved dilemma of the Jesuit way of proceeding. Members were strongly encouraged to be indifferent and available for any ministry, but the Institute insisted that one's talents and interests dictate one's apostolic assignment.

Despite anxieties about a return home, Ignatius climbs on his horse and sets out from Paris. He admits, in Lukan terms, that he feels much better "along the way" (*trovandosi per la strada molto meglio*). In Azpeitia, he refuses accommodation in the family castle and takes up residence in the local hospital. That gives him the freedom to speak of the things of God openly. He teaches catechism, preaches on Sundays and feast days, assists the poor, and seeks to reform morals, especially the vices of gambling and clerical concubinage. His efforts for poor relief in his hometown reflect broader sensibilities he encountered during his time of studies in Paris. Ignatius likely shared a meal around 1529 with the humanist Juan Luis Vives (1492–1540), theoretician of poor relief for Bruges and other cities, and Ignatius learned firsthand the welfare practice of cities in Flanders and England when he begged for alms there. Ignatius was also resident in Paris when the theology faculty endorsed the relief program of the city of Ypres.[57] In all of those cases, Ignatius witnessed efforts to move poor relief beyond private charity and make it a concern of urban governments.

Thanks to his education, Ignatius now had the credentials to preach. In the later Middle Ages and the Renaissance, preaching had become the focus of much theoretical literature. At the universities, theologians wrote handbooks on the "Art of Preaching." According to university theoreticians, preachers should instruct. Preachers best accomplished their goal by choosing an appropriate verse of scripture, dividing the verse into its constituent phrases, and demonstrating the importance of each phrase by analyzing the content and citing the relevant authorities. The entire sermon became an exercise in proving a single or even multiple theses. Effective preaching was logical and appealed to the intellect of the audience. According to the Franciscans, however, preachers should move listeners to a better life. Franciscan sermons focused on the subjects of virtue and vice and succeeded as much for their appeal to the emotions as to the intellect. The friars often used their vernacular preaching to ensure that the faithful confessed once a year as required. For humanists like Erasmus, preaching would best be renewed if Christian preachers learned the classical tenets of effective public speaking. Preachers might then achieve all three duties of the orator specified by Roman theoreticians such as Cicero: they would instruct, delight, and move. Erasmus was especially interested in the preaching methods of the patristic era, when the fathers of the church exploited their philological training to articulate a verse-by-verse commentary on a scriptural passage.

When Ignatius included his moral concerns in his sermons at Azpeitia, he proved a moving preacher. The government adopted laws against concubinage, and his brother amended his ways. Preaching was another ministry of the Word listed in the Formula of the Jesuit Institute. Three qualities emerge from an examination of the sermons delivered by the first Jesuits. Their preaching was charismatic, relying on the inner inspiration of the Spirit. A range of persons from Jesuit scholastics in Europe to indigenous boys in Brazil preached under the Spirit's inspiration and Jesuit auspices. In those initial years, Jesuits rarely preached in churches. Rather, they imitated the apostles of Acts by preaching in the streets and public squares of cities. When, as a young Jesuit, Juan Alfonso de Polanco was chided by his relatives for disgracing the family by preaching on the street, Polanco claimed such preaching as proof for the authenticity of his vocation, and he threatened to preach before Florence's merchants, to whom his father and brothers marketed their wool. Jesuits preached on the normal occasions, the Sundays of Advent and Lent, but they added other Sundays during the year and weekdays during Lent. Like the apostles in Acts, the first Jesuits preached a lot.[58]

Second, Jesuit preaching, as Ignatius specified, focused on moral issues. It followed the rhythm of the *Exercises*, moving from vice and remedies for sinfulness to virtues and consolation for conversion. Jesuits preached to touch one's heart and change one's behavior. They sought not only to teach but to delight and move their audience. As God had enlightened the mind of Ignatius and changed his heart, so Jesuits preached a word taught by the Spirit in scripture and engraved by the Spirit in human hearts. The vices of clerical concubinage and usury particularly preoccupied the first Jesuits.

Finally, Jesuit preaching was modeled on classical norms. Jesuits embraced the persuasive oratory of classical rhetoric, not the academic preaching of university theoreticians. In so doing, they emphasized the three qualities that characterized any classical art: ability, training, and practice. A competent preacher first needed the requisite talent. Preaching was not a Jesuit's birthright. Next, a good preacher needed formal training. Jesuits used the classical handbooks on rhetoric to accomplish that training. That well illustrates the Thomistic principle that grace (persuasive preaching) builds on nature (pagan textbooks). Last, Jesuits worked at their preaching. During community meals, Jesuit scholastics often delivered sermons that were critiqued by recognized masters of the art.

Azpeitia to Venice: Confraternities, Hospitals, Carafa and the Theatines, Yet Further Trials

Ignatius's final departure from home mirrors in ways his departure years before for Jerusalem. Once again, his siblings are primarily concerned with matters of honor. They ask Ignatius not to embarrass the family by leaving on foot. To please his brother, Ignatius does leave on horseback, but once out of sight, he dismounts and walks to the border of his home province. When he visits the families of his companions, he refuses the donations that they offer him, taking nothing for his journey or his companions. He sails to Italy through waters frequented by Barbary corsairs. After a mocking reception in Bologna, Ignatius continues to Venice, in order to rejoin his companions. As unreceptive as Bologna and its university renowned for legal studies has proven to Ignatius, Venice and its mainland empire prove more congenial.[59]

By the time the first Jesuits came to Venice, the city had already established a sophisticated network of assistance for the poor and the sick of the city. That network had its institutional grounding in five prestigious confraternities (*Scuole Grandi*). The members of those confraternities engaged in a variety of charitable activities: giving alms to the poor, building endowments for charitable ends, supplying rowers for state galleys, supporting the various works of hospitals, and patronizing the arts. Venetian

Scuole Grandi assisted other persons in need, not simply their own members. Confraternities in Venice were a lay brotherhood, but they welcomed members from all social classes. By law, their membership was restricted to 500–600 persons, who could be priests, aristocrats, merchants, or artisans. However, only the "original citizens" of Venice, a social class just below the patricians and clergy, could hold office in a leading confraternity. The Scuole Grandi of Venice also functioned as a social pressure valve, alleviating possible tensions in a republic governed by a strictly defined oligarchy of patricians. By broadening participation in the charitable affairs of the city, the confraternities lessened resentment for the restrictive nature of the government and helped their neighbors.[60]

Though some of the first Jesuits and Ignatius himself were for a time members of confraternities, Ignatius eventually changed that practice. For Ignatius, membership in a confraternity might affect a Jesuit's willingness to move. He also felt that laymen were perfectly capable of running their confraternities, as they had proven for centuries. Jesuits did establish or reform a variety of confraternities, which were just as varied in their membership, their emphases, and their relationship to local churches. In keeping with a fundamental desire of Ignatius, Jesuit confraternities were to be, like the Society itself, places of substantive spiritual conversation. At a later moment, the Marian confraternities introduced a new phase in this Jesuit ministry. Those Marian congregations had ties to each other, and they looked to the confraternity at the Roman College to articulate norms for all.

While fostering the vitality of lay congregations that performed charitable services, the early Jesuits also engaged directly in ministries of charity, as the official charter of the order bade them do. They followed the inspiration of the disciples, whom Jesus commissioned to heal in his name and who did so from the beginning of Acts. Once Ignatius sets out along the way, he seems much at home in a late medieval hospital. Hospitals of that era differed from our own. They offered accommodation to those near death, and they also provided general welfare services to the indigent.[61] As Ignatius discovered, they were not always a good place to get well. They proved costly to the early Society in terms of fatigue and lives lost.

Jesuits likewise assisted believers in the art of dying well, a medieval devotional practice that emphasized preparing oneself to meet death and writing a will.[62] Despite his limp, Ignatius hurries to Simâo Rodrigues when he learns that Rodrigues is gravely ill. For Ignatius, the hour of death was a moment for pastoral assistance. Ignatius attempted to reform the art of dying well by extending pastoral care to the family of the person near death. Jesuit healing before death did not emphasize the dangers posed by devils hovering nearby or the indulgences made available by specific pious practices. Nor were Jesuits to solicit donations to the Society in the will of the deceased.

Finally, the first Jesuits sought to be peacemakers and decried the ill of factionalism. That may be one reason why Ignatius explicitly remembers never pairing up Jesuits by nationality. While serving as superior-general in Rome for sixteen years, Ignatius left the city only on five occasions, two of which were efforts to make peace. In 1548, he went to Tivoli to end the antagonism between that community and Castel Madama. Four years later, when Ignatius tried to reconcile Giovanna d'Aragona (1502–77) and her estranged husband, Ascanio Colonna (1495–1557), his methods were insightful, though not successful. He urged the couple to set no conditions for reconciliation, and he suggested that one of them would have to swallow their pride and make a first gesture toward reunion.[63] Eventually, Jesuits who worked in places like Naples were inspired by earlier mendicant preaching against civic violence to develop a formal ritual of reconciliation between warring urban factions. At the village of Casola, near Naples, Francesco de Geronimo (1642–1716) extended that ritual to bring together an inept pastor and his alienated parishioners. Jesuit opposition to aristocratic values of honor was articulated in the claim that God honors only those who forgive their enemies.[64]

Renaissance Venice was a cosmopolitan crossroads, and tolerance was a key factor in the city's economic success. As a capital city, a commercial emporium, and a publishing center, Venice nurtured a variety of international contacts. The open atmosphere of Venice influenced the reconciling spirituality of Cardinal Gasparo Contarini (1483–1542), who dedicated his life to reforming the Catholic Church, especially the Papal Court in Rome, and to fostering dialogue as a way to heal the religious divisions of his day. Early in life, on the basis of an experience of consolation in confession, Contarini determined to respond to God's vast love not by following his friends to a Camaldolese hermitage but by charitably serving his fellow citizens in Venice. Late in life, Contarini led the Catholic delegation at the Colloquy with Protestants at Regensburg in 1541.[65]

Exposure to life in Venice, by contrast, affected the vigilant spirituality of Cardinal Gian Pietro Carafa, who dedicated himself to repressing heresy and reforming the clergy by imposing strict rules of cloister. After living in Venice for a time, Carafa decried the absence of the patriarch, the reading of dangerous books, the apostasy of unfaithful religious, the heresy of Conventual Franciscans, and the failure of most patricians to fulfill their Easter duty.[66] Ignatius was a friend of Contarini, who proved instrumental in gaining influential support for the Society of Jesus. Ignatius was an antagonist of Carafa, who showed his distrust for Ignatius and his Society on more than one occasion. While living in Venice, Ignatius stayed with Andrea Lippomano, prior of the community at the Chiesa della Santissima Trinità, which stood near the southern end of the Grand Canal (Dorsoduro). Lippomano let Ignatius use his library and offered him a place of quiet reflection. Close to the church, at the monastery of San Gregorio, lived a new congregation of reformed priests, cofounded by Carafa and known as the Theatines.[67]

By previous agreement in Paris, Venice was to be a crossroads for Ignatius and for his companions. From Venice, they would go either to Jerusalem or to Rome. While living in Venice, Ignatius offers to give the *Spiritual Exercises* to a young man named Diego Hoces, but Hoces for a time refuses Ignatius's offer. Hoces later admits to Ignatius that he had feared Ignatius's "evil doctrine," a characterization he had learned from someone else. Besides Ignatius, Hoces had also visited Carafa regularly and knew the lifestyle of the Theatines. At that time, rumors circulated in Venice that, due to heterodox teachings, Ignatius was burned in effigy in Spain and Paris. According to Nadal, Carafa fomented the rumors. In Venice Ignatius again solicits a formal trial and is fully exonerated by the inquisitor. However, Ignatius still chooses not to accompany his companions to Rome, when they go to seek a papal blessing for their intended pilgrimage. He gives as an explanation his fear of Cardinal Carafa and Dr. Pedro Ortiz, a Paris professor troubled by Ignatius's influence on Spanish students there.

Nadal probably learned from Ignatius himself that Carafa was encouraging the persecution in Venice, and Ignatius drafted a letter to Carafa to air his differences with the cardinal. The letter, apparently, was never sent.[68] In it, Ignatius criticized the cardinal for his extravagant lifestyle and his Theatines for their monastic lifestyle. Ignatius felt it contradictory that Theatines did little charitable work, locked themselves inside their cloister, and then expected charity in return. It was no surprise that they had a difficult time finding support. As a result, while they chanted the Liturgy of the Hours together, prayed twice daily, and fasted rigorously, they were increasingly miserable.

The experience of life in Venice and the writing of that letter helped Ignatius define his own ideals of apostolic spirituality in contrast to the cloistered ideals of Theatine spirituality. Ignatius focused his spiritual goals on interior transformation and fostered among his companions a flexibility for ministry. Carafa focused his spiritual ideals on external conformity to the rule and fostered among his Theatines a rigor in observing the norms of cloistered life. Some years later, when Carafa invited Ignatius and the Jesuits to consolidate with the Theatines, Ignatius politely refused his invitation.

Venice to Rome: House for Prostitutes, Formal Trial, the Papacy

In 1537, with travel to Jerusalem interdicted by the conflict between Christians and Turks on the Mediterranean, Ignatius and his companions set off on the road to Rome. As Rome marks the ultimate goal of Paul in Acts because Rome ruled a world community and made universal ministry possible, so Rome will mark the ultimate goal of the Jesuit journey.[69] Ignatius notes that, in contrast to his years in Paris, his years in the Veneto produced consoling visions. But it is, above all, in his journeys that Ignatius has the substantial visitations that he accentuated (*per tutti quelli viaggi hebbe grandi visitationi sopranaturali*). Ignatius's journey to Rome illustrates why he feels that way. Not far from the city, at a place known as La Storta, Ignatius has "a very special visitation from God" (*in questo viaggio fu molto specialmente visitato da Iddio*). In typical fashion for the *Acta*, he does not specify the content of the vision. Located roughly nine miles from the center of Rome, La Storta had the last inn (*mansio*) for changing dispatch horses on the way into Rome or the first when leaving Rome. It likely derives its name from a curve or a series of curves in that section of the Via Cassia. Ignatius may have found the name significant for one like himself who had followed a crooked path to his goal. The special character of the vision may indicate that Ignatius saw it as the fulfillment of the visionary woman's prayer for him at Manresa: her Jesus now appeared to him. He understands his self-obsession and accepts the Lord's healing. The first sights Ignatius has of Rome may also hint at the content of the vision. He points out that the windows of the city are closed to him and realizes that he will meet opposition there. Ignatius and his companions are traveling on a road similar to that of the disciples in Luke, a road along which Jesus first traveled.

In Rome, the little group works to assist souls, and they soon find themselves persecuted once again for doing so. Many residents of the city, however, were open and receptive to Jesuit ministries (*opere pie*). In addition to giving the *Exercises*, teaching catechism to children, and preaching on the streets, the first Jesuits ministered to Rome's prostitutes and orphans and lectured at its university. Sacred lecturing had become popular in Italy during the Renaissance. Late in the fifteenth century, the Dominican Girolamo Savonarola filled the cathedral of Florence with persons anxious to hear his provocative lectures on scripture. For the Jesuits, such lecturing became a form of systematic adult education in the faith. Jesuits offered the lectures in the evenings to facilitate attendance by working people and used as their focus texts from scripture, especially Paul's letter to the Romans.

In their work with prostitutes, the Jesuits established the innovative House of Saint Martha (*Casa Santa Marta*).[70] Prostitution had acquired a new status in Renaissance Italy because some courtesans were well educated and well read. Prostitution also threatened the public health as the ranks of prostitutes swelled and new diseases such as syphilis reached Europe. By 1600, the number of prostitutes in Rome was around 2 percent of the population, a percentage that was, as Carlo Cipolla wryly observed, high for a holy city.[71]

Though enthusiasts had long urged prostitutes to reform and prostitutes were at times open to conversion, those women confronted serious social and economic obstacles. Once converted to a new way of life, prostitutes lost their source of income. They could seek a husband but would have difficulty providing a dowry. They could also become servants, or they could enter one of the monasteries for reformed women of the street (*conversae*). What made the Jesuit ministry to prostitutes in Rome innovative was their effort at the House of Saint Martha to prepare converted prostitutes adequately for their future. While preaching repentance and conversion, Jesuits attempted to address the economic and social roots of the problem. They originally gave those women skills for life. Eventually, however, the House of Saint Martha became yet another monastery for reformed prostitutes.

There was a direct link between Jesuit ministry to Rome's prostitutes and Jesuit assistance to Rome's orphans. Among the primary groups of orphans to whom Jesuits ministered were the daughters of Rome's prostitutes. Jesuits focused on those girls in an effort to break the malicious cycle generated when a daughter inherited her mother's trade. In their work with orphans, Jesuits were inspired by the shelters that Girolamo Miani (1486–1537), a Venetian nobleman who had experienced a religious conversion as a prisoner of war, created for the street children of various north Italian cities. Miani's homes for orphans provided them with life's physical necessities and with training in literacy and a viable trade.

The windows of Rome were closed to Ignatius and his companions by those who resented the novelty of itinerant apostles intent on professing religious vows in an order sanctioned by the Catholic Church. Ignatius's opponents quickly began to harass the companions and speak ill of them (*dar fastidio et dir male*). Ignatius remembers that the governor of the city of Rome banished a Miguel Landívar for making defamatory statements about Ignatius. Shortly thereafter, two other calumniators (Mudarra and Barreda) claim that Ignatius and his companions were actually fugitives from the Inquisition's justice.[72] When summoned before the Inquisition, however, the two retract their claim and admit that the "morals and teachings" of the Jesuits are without error. Ignatius's memory reflects his consistent emphasis on quality of life as the source of good teaching. The report of the Inquisition chiastically echoes his emphases. Ignatius and his companions "have attempted and will daily attempt to help believers through their learning, their morals, and the example of their good lives." The papal legate orders all involved in the case to keep silent, but Ignatius insists on a full-blown inquiry and public sentence. With papal support, a formal inquest is held, and Ignatius is judged innocent. Among the depositions gathered were several from the church officials who had conducted previous investigations of Ignatius in Spain, France, and Venice. Most were in Rome at the time of the inquest.[73]

Ignatius receives further confirmation that the Spirit is inspiring Jesuit ministries in Rome. He gives the *Exercises* to several residents, including Cardinal Contarini. Ignatius also gives the *Exercises* in Rome to Dr. Pedro

Ortiz, his former adversary in Paris. In order to see his retreatants, Ignatius has to walk a good distance across the city. The *Exercises* are literally and figuratively a ministry "on the way." Ignatius eventually settles at the little church of Our Lady of the Way in downtown Rome. And Ignatius receives consolation from a vision he has of the first Jesuit to enter heaven, the young Hoces. He shed tears as he sees that heavenly imprimatur for the Jesuit way of proceeding.

By any measure, Jesuits were peculiar priests. Ignatius's final dilemma in his *Acta* reflects that fact: Should Jesuits accept ministries with benefices attached to them? While traveling, Ignatius debated whether to accept assistance or trust God alone. Though the latter might seem the obvious choice, for Ignatius it could be vainglory masquerading as virtue. Ignatius came to discern that Jesuits should not accept ministries with benefices attached to them. That was the choice that led him to tears of consolation. Among Ignatius's possible motivations, there was his admiration for Francis of Assisi, his sense that the vow of poverty was contrary to a beneficed life, his belief that parish ministry was the province of diocesan clergy, and his intuition that benefices would impede Jesuit mobility to minister on the way. Unlike the beneficed clergy, who would especially assist a fixed congregation in fulfilling its Easter duty to confess and receive Communion, Jesuits would freely attract their own congregation by their ability to persuade to repentance and conversion of heart.

Ignatius's decision intimated several important characteristics of the peculiar nature of his new religious order. Jesuits were not to be pastors of churches but would work outside that primary Catholic institution. Jesuits had circumscribed involvement with sacramental ministries. Moreover, Ignatius and the first Jesuits did not focus their energies on church reform. In light of the Avignonese residence of the popes in the fourteenth century, the Great Western Schism bridging from the fourteenth to the fifteenth century, and Luther's evangelical reform movement in the sixteenth century, church reform had become an obsession in the Western world. Whereas church reformers focused upon programs to improve the juridical structures of the organization, particularly the papal curia in Rome, the Jesuits focused on interior conversion, particularly a better relationship with God. Before the founding of Jesuit schools, the ministries in which Jesuits initially engaged were generally charismatic. Jesuits primarily sought to facilitate the immediate experience of the

Spirit working in the believer's heart, as their own experience of the *Spiritual Exercises* had taught them to do.

Ignatius and the early Jesuits were even peripheral to the program of church reform adopted at the Council of Trent (1545–63). In many ways, the experience of the Jesuits at the Council, like the experience of Ignatius with the Inquisition, helped them to gain a better sense of their peculiar ministerial identity. Because Jesuits focused on God's abundant grace and a change of heart, they found matters of church reform marginal to their primary concerns. Trent's reform stressed the role of bishops who should be pastoral and disciplinary leaders in their dioceses and should not, therefore, reside elsewhere. Trent legislated for parish pastors and curates and insisted on conformity in matters of external discipline. The way that Jesuits lived meant that Trent's legislation had little effect on them. By rule, Jesuits enjoyed exemption, which granted them pastoral privileges outside the control of the local bishop. Jesuits were not obliged to recite the Liturgy of the Hours in common, a privilege essential to their itinerant ministries. Jesuits vowed not to accept appointment as bishops. Jesuits enjoyed a special relationship to the pope as the believing community's universal pastor.

As Ignatius sensed when he reached Rome, the Society's Institute did cause resentment. Jesuits were peculiar, and their manner of living seemed dangerous. Ultimately, the resentment threatened not individual members of the order but the existence of the order itself. So, in Rome, Ignatius insists on a trial by the Inquisition and receives a just verdict of innocence. He intuits a future need for such formal exoneration. Though actively concerned about church persecution, Ignatius, by contrast, barely mentions the Protestant Reformation in the *Acta*.

Ignatius finishes his narration by tweaking the zealous inquisitors who had dogged him throughout his life. Yes, he had committed many sins after dedicating himself to the service of the Lord, but none was mortal. That generic confession also indicates how far he has traveled along the road of healing for his vainglory. He had sinned, but he did not exaggerate by describing each one in detail. God had blessed Ignatius interiorly with consolation. His tears were the exterior signs of the interior transformation that allowed Ignatius to see clearly. As he had urged Gonçalves da Câmara to do, he concludes on a note of gratitude to a generous God. The beauty of God's creation is not destroyed by the sinfulness of God's sublime creature. The proof lies in God's unconditional love as demonstrated in the journey of Jesus to Jerusalem and his being crucified, raised up, and glorified for his fidelity to the mission entrusted to him by the Father. For Ignatius, obedience to the will of God yields another antidote for vainglory. In October of 1555, Ignatius calmly ends his narration amidst the storm swirling around himself and the Society.[74] The historical circumstances of that moment illustrate the complex relationship of the Jesuits to the papacy.

From the beginning, many Jesuits lived in Rome, in order to administer the order and to staff various institutions for the education of the clergy, themselves included. Several factors complicated the relationship between the Jesuits and the pope. Though the first Jesuits were confirmed supporters of the universal ministry of the papacy, Ignatius advised them not to exaggerate when publicly defending papal authority. Ignatius himself recognized that Jesuits needed the authority of the papacy to protect the Society. That is why Ignatius used the influence of Paul III to ensure a formal trial for himself in Rome, against the wishes of Paul's local administrators. After the definitive breakdown of discussions between Catholics and Protestants at Trent in 1550, defending Catholicism implied defending the pope. However, the relationship between Jesuits and the pope was affected by Jesuit thinking about the church. For ancient models, they had the churches of the Acts of the Apostles, charismatic urban communities that pooled their resources to alleviate need among believers. Their favorite image for the church was the vineyard of the Lord, where apostles are sent to minister. Their emphasis was not uniquely hierarchical. Helping souls implied reciprocity, not social control. Ignatius had substantial conversations with the marginal, especially women, and had frustrating conversations with inquisitors and clerics.

Professed Jesuits therefore make their fourth vow to God, not the pope, as an expression of their desire to evangelize universally and their willingness to journey to do so.[75] That is why the *Acta*, like the Acts of the Apostles, end in Rome, not with some grandiose announcement of the founding of the Jesuits but with the promising beginnings of ministry in the center of the church's world.

With a pope such as Paul IV, all of the complexities of the Jesuit relationship to the papacy became apparent. In the *Acta*, Ignatius only hinted at the stormy dealings he had with Carafa. In Venice around 1537, Ignatius had criticized the extravagant lifestyle of the cardinal and the monastic asceticism of his Theatines. In Rome in 1538, Carafa had encouraged Doimo Nascio to attend lectures by the companions and see whether their teaching was orthodox. In Rome in 1545, Ignatius had refused Carafa's invitation to merge the Society of Jesus and the Theatines. And in Rome beginning late in 1553, Ignatius had resisted Carafa's efforts to have him order Ottaviano Cesari, a Jesuit novice, to return home to his well con-nected parents in Naples. Their differing nationalities and the realities of international politics also affected their relationship.[76] By the time that Carafa was elected pope in 1555, Spaniards had occupied Carafa's home-land of Naples for approximately fifty years. As a cardinal, Carafa had suffered humiliation at the hands of Spanish soldiers who participated in the sack of Rome from 1527 to 1528. Carafa suspected and disliked all things Spanish, including Ignatius. Their relationship was also affected by the differing ways that their spiritual lives had evolved. The zealous and vainglorious Ignatius matured spiritually into the more flexible and prudent Ignatius. Carafa's zeal, in contrast, became over time more vocif-erous and adamantine. The Roman Inquisition was Carafa's favored insti-tution, and various Inquisitions were the bane of Ignatius's life.

Once Carafa became pope in May of 1555, the personal relationship affected the Society of Jesus as well. Paul IV insulted Ignatius by refusing to receive Ignatius after his election. He received Nicolás Bobadilla in formal audience before Ignatius. Bobadilla held no office in the Jesuits, but he shared Paul's enthusiasm for the Inquisition and the repression of the Jews.[77] By the end of 1555, Paul IV and Ignatius had so deepened their mutual suspicions that both took action. Ignatius had gathered testimo-nial letters on behalf of the Society of Jesus in the event that the pope moved to suppress it. For his part, Carafa sent the papal police to search the Jesuit headquarters for weapons. None were found.[78] Throughout his pontificate, Paul IV put pressure on the Jesuits to recite the Liturgy of the Hours in common. Ignatius tried to mollify the pope by holding vespers at Jesuit churches, but he never wavered in his efforts to protect the Jesuit focus on itinerant ministries. In 1558, after the death of Ignatius, Carafa ordered the Jesuits into choir. Laínez stalled before enacting the order, hoping that Paul's ill health might soon lead to his death. When Paul IV did die in August of 1559, Laínez interpreted the order as binding only while Paul was alive. After the death of Ignatius in 1556, Carafa blocked the gathering of the Jesuits' first General Congregation. Though he eventually relented and allowed the Congregation to meet, he insisted on a three-year term for the superior-general, so that no future Jesuit might exercise "the tyranny" that Ignatius had exercised.

In the *Acta*, Ignatius recalls that his own reaction to unjust decisions was to fulfill the letter of the mandate but not accept its spirit. He is respectful of church authority, never obsequious. In the controversies with Paul IV, Ignatius and Laínez demonstrated that the fourth vow did not extend to papal commands to change specific elements of the Jesuit Institute. The Institute had already received papal approbation in writing. Ignatius prepared his resistance carefully in advance of those decisions, and Nadal urged that Jesuits resist them by every means at their disposal. To abrogate the privilege dispensing Jesuits from common recitation of the Hours threatened the integrity of the Jesuit way of "proceeding." Those who recited the Liturgy of the Hours together in choir every day of the year were perforce not generally free to minister on the way.

Over the course of his spiritual education, Ignatius had learned to fear zealotry. Toward life's end, as Ignatius narrated his *Acta*, he felt grateful to have matured beyond a zealous posturing motivated by vainglory. The instincts of vainglory fostered a zeal that had led Ignatius to consider killing a "Moor" and almost led Ignatius to try killing himself. Ignatius therefore bequeathed to his companions an apostolic ideal of ministry, conducted by pliant disciples along the way of the Lord.

There was one area of ministry in which the first Jesuits and Pope Paul IV worked in more complementary ways. They shared common assumptions in their ministry to the Jews of the city of Rome.[79] After the fall of Granada in 1492 and the expulsion of the Jews from the Iberian kingdoms in the 1490s, the question of the Jews provoked increasing hostility in Italy. The popes of Ignatius's day adopted measures to address the Jewish question in Rome and the Papal State. Paul III tried to convert the Jews of Rome to Catholicism, and Paul IV persecuted them for not converting. Once the Jesuits were founded, Ignatius did support Paul III's efforts to proselytize the Roman Jews. In his massive biographical dictionary, Pierre Bayle (1647–1706) publicized Ribadeneira's claim that Ignatius played a role in the drafting of Paul III's 1542 constitution on evangelizing Jews, *Cupientes Judaeos*. Whether influenced by Ignatius or not, the document gave Jews an added incentive to convert by allowing Jewish catechumens and converts to keep their personal property.[80] Jesuits in Rome preached sermons to Jews who were forcibly herded to the place of preaching. In 1554, in the city of Ancona, Nicolás Bobadilla presided at a burning of the Talmud. And Jesuits established a house in Rome for prospective converts, particularly Jews. Pope Julius III compelled all of Rome's synagogues to contribute to the maintenance of that institution. Jesuit support for papal proselytizing fostered an environment conducive to Paul IV's persecution. Near the Tiber River, Paul created a walled ghetto inside which the Jews of the city were all forced to reside. No subsequent pope ever overturned that law. Jesuit involvement in the mistreatment of Rome's Jews illustrates the challenging character of the flexible ideals that Ignatius proposed for himself and Jesuits. In the case of the Jews of Rome and the Papal State, the Jesuits failed in large part to live up to their ideals.

Controversial Apostolic Companions

After returning from Jerusalem, Ignatius traces two parallel trajectories that guide his memories of events until reaching Rome. The first focuses on the gathering of companions to conduct apostolic ministries. The second focuses on the controversy that such an apostolic group engenders. Both trajectories involve education, and both trajectories mirror the experience of the apostles in the Acts attributed to Luke. By the time that Ignatius and his companions reached Rome, their vision of their goals in banding together had clarified considerably. In their original draft of the Formula of the Institute, they concisely expressed their vision. They wished to be religious who would not recite the Liturgy of the Hours in common in order not to be "drawn away from charitable works, to which we have dedicated ourselves completely." That formulation ultimately proved too succinct for inclusion in the bull approving the Society of Jesus.[81] They had finalized those convictions during their activities in Venice, while still hoping to reach Jerusalem. Venice nurtured the convictions of Ignatius and his companions. As William Bouwsma observed, the Venetian Republic fostered a Christian spirituality that "emphasized the immediate spiritual insights and experience of the individual believer, and it conceived the Christian life as loving action in the world rather than contemplative withdrawal from it."[82] Italian humanists like Giannozzo Manetti

(1396–1459) in the fifteenth century had celebrated human dignity as expressed in the building of a truly humane city. Inspired by their appreciation for humanist education, the Jesuits embraced that sort of civic mission. Late in the sixteenth century, Jacopo Bassano used his paintings of the Lukan narratives of the Good Samaritan and the Rich Man and Lazarus to move his fellow Venetians not to be indifferent about inequities in the distribution of wealth among rich and poor and to show greater compassion toward those in need.[83]

While working in the Veneto, Ignatius and his companions generally chose to live in hospitals.[84] Their choice reflected a conviction that hospitality was an act of solidarity to be offered without restriction. Venice was known for a network of hospitals where one might stay for an extended period. It is little wonder that the Jesuits found themselves at home in the Veneto. Ignatius himself had lived in hospitals in Alcalá, Paris, and Azpeitia, and he had his companions do volunteer work in two Venetian hospitals. In addition to lodging the indigent, hospitals often gave hospitality to pilgrims. As the plague recurred cyclically after 1348 and the poor were assigned a key role in transmitting the disease, Renaissance cities created quarantine hospitals for workers, vagrants, beggars, prostitutes, Jews, and destitute foreigners. Ironically, that intended compassion also made marginal groups seem more dangerous and increased the likelihood, once gathered into a single place, that they would die. The arrival and spread of syphilis late in the fifteenth century accelerated the specialization of hospital services and the stigmatization of the threatening poor, particularly Amerindians, Jews, and prostitutes.

Ignatius and his early companions, however, found hospitals a place for solidarity and expression of their ministerial priorities. At times, rather than live together, they divided up into smaller groups to work in hospitals. The early Jesuits took their place in a tradition that included medieval confraternities, who sponsored hospitals around the Mediterranean, and the patriarchate of Aquileia, which adopted a pastoral guideline in the thirteenth century describing the hospital as a "place of great compassion" (*locus magnae misericordiae*).[85]

When Francis Xavier, indefatigable evangelizer in South Asia and Japan, first settled in Goa, he wrote back to Ignatius to inform him that "I have taken up residence in the hospital." When Pierre Favre arrived in Mainz, the first Jesuit sent to German lands, he wanted to establish a hospital where the needy could be gathered. In planning for the Jesuit apostolate in Japan, the regional superior and architect of a policy of accommodation, Alessandro Valignano (1539–1606), projected a series of therapeutic and foundling hospitals as part of a network of charitable foundations.[86] When the Jesuits reached Granada in the 1540s, they quickly found parallels between their own spirituality and the movement of Juan de Ávila (1499–1569), promoting interior transformation and serving the needy in schools and hospitals. Though Ignatius was favorable to the idea of absorbing Juan's group, some of his fellow Jesuits objected because Juan had Jewish blood.[87] In Rome, the Jesuits joined other orders in encouraging work in hospitals. The city soon became a model for the charity practiced through that institution. Rome's hospitals served diseased persons, abandoned children, battered women, and the city's destitute.[88] Christian spirituality affected the spirit in which care was provided in Renaissance hospitals and the willingness of the wealthy to donate to their support. Hospices had a long tradition of service and support from confraternities in various Italian cities. Houses for the conversion of prostitutes were a different matter.

Ignatius established his House of Saint Martha in Rome as part of an effort to build a humane city. The goal that he set for that ministry paralleled the goal that he set for the Society of Jesus: to prepare repentant individuals for incorporation in the world. Until that time, prostitutes who had embraced the call to repentance and conversion had only one viable option: entering a cloistered monastery. Ignatius conceived of an institution that fostered the interior freedom those women experienced during a process of conversion. In addition to a program of spiritual direction, Ignatius proposed to supply the women with the skills requisite to earn a living. Naming the house for Martha, not Mary, suggests the value of training those women to do work and endorses the active life as a path to holiness.[89] Those who had been married prior to taking to the streets had the possibility of working toward a reconciliation with their spouse. Entering a monastery was an option but not the only option. To facilitate the work of the community, Ignatius had all prospective members fill out a detailed questionnaire. Once Ignatius had in place a sufficient endowment for the work, a confraternity to run it, and Jesuits to advise it, he himself took to the streets to recruit the prostitutes.

The work quickly proved controversial in Rome, reflecting an increasingly confessional environment that threatened to extinguish a spirituality that was public and inclusive. Within a few years of its founding, members of the board that had endowed the House worked to have it shut down, spreading rumors that it served merely as a front for a bordello for Jesuits only. Early in the seventeenth century, the controversial character of the work inspired the Jesuit Alonso de Sandoval (1576–1652) to offer Ignatius's ministry as a paradigm for his own controversial use of black African interpreters in evangelizing the slaves of the New World. If Ignatius was seen with Rome's prostitutes, Sandoval saw no shame in being seen with Cartagena's blacks.[90]

The genius of that ministry in seeking to address the structural problems that led women to prostitute themselves survived the Roman onslaught. The network of houses for prostitutes operated by Jesuits was exceeded in numbers only by Jesuit high schools and Jesuit orphanages. Mary Elizabeth Perry has highlighted the creative contributions of Jesuits in Seville, especially Pedro de León. In keeping with Ignatius's impulse to foster interior freedom, Jesuits in Seville raised funds to pay dowries for reformed prostitutes. León himself worked with women in brothels and wrote a book on the subject, in which he advocated the providing of dowries and denounced those who pawned women into brothel service. It was a more compassionate approach than the civic effort to stigmatize such women by forcing them to wear yellow hoods. By having to wear a special dress and a short veil covering their faces, Roman prostitutes were burdened by public opprobrium, though viewing them still constituted a principal form of entertainment for males in the city.

There were strong social and economic incentives for economically poor women to prostitute themselves. Such women had few other ways to earn their sustenance, and by prostituting themselves, they supplied income to the network of individuals who earned their living from the industry. Were all the prostitutes simultaneously to withdraw the funds that they had deposited in banks, the banks would risk failure. It is estimated that in Rome, by the end of the sixteenth century, the persons who earned their living from the industry numbered up to ten times the total of women working the streets themselves. Perry numbers pimps, procuresses, property owners, innkeepers, room renters, and secondhand-clothing sellers among those profiting from prostitution in Seville.[91]

Ignatius never wavered in his conviction that the Spirit could work wonders in the hearts of all persons, prostitutes included. That same

Spirit brought the community of the church together in concord. Ignatius felt confident that the Spirit and the church cannot contradict each other; what the Spirit inspired in the heart of an individual would ultimately prove to be in harmony, not in conflict, with the inspiration of the Spirit in the community.[92] But Ignatius also felt that the Spirit was greater than the church. While studying in Alcalá, Ignatius knew that the Inquisition in Toledo had recently condemned positions of the alumbrados, and Ignatius had acquaintances there who were associated with the movement. He recalled nothing about the situation except that he was unfairly investigated by persons associated with the Inquisition. Ignatius knew, too, that the Dominicans in Salamanca had played a critical role in the formal investigation of the works of Erasmus. He recalled nothing about the situation except that he was, once again, unfairly investigated at the instigation of the Dominicans. He stonewalled their attempts to link him to Erasmus, but in the *Acta* he stated his friendship at Alcalá with the de Eguía family, who were engaged in publishing Erasmus's spiritual writings.

In Paris, Ignatius studied at a university whose Faculty of Theology had passed judgment on many of the controversial figures of the day, including Luther, Erasmus, and Calvin. He recalled nothing about the situation except that he twice took the initiative to dispel unfair suspicions in his own regard. In Venice, Ignatius knew Gian Pietro Carafa's efforts to repress dissidence and support a new, rigorously monastic order of priests. He dissociated himself from both activities and once again took personal initiatives to clear his good name before the pope's legate. In Rome, he went all the way to the pope in order to exonerate himself, his spirituality, and his companions. The weight of evidence in the *Acta* suggests that Ignatius, late in life, feared the desire of the Inquisition to stifle his innovative spirituality, and he alerted Jesuits to that danger.

Recent study of the newly opened archives of the Roman Inquisition helps us understand the depth of Ignatius's concern.[93] Once Carafa was elected pope in 1555, he unleashed the repressive apparatus of the Inquisition, giving that institution his full moral and practical support. Carafa personally rented a house in which the tribunal might meet, and he supplied the first locks for its jail cells. He attempted to assuage the conscience of inquisitors, twice issuing written briefs that explicitly allowed ecclesiastics to torture, mutilate, and shed blood, even if such sentences on their part resulted in death for the accused. At the insistence of the pope, who for his entire pontificate personally presided at the weekly meeting of the Congregation, rules were suspended, unconditional obedience was demanded, and violence was practiced.

While still a cardinal, Carafa had targeted dissident mendicants because he felt that they were preaching heretical doctrines. He likewise targeted religious orders who shielded their preachers from interrogation. Beginning in 1551, he forced superiors-general of religious orders to kneel before him and swear to incarcerate members of their orders judged guilty of heresy. He threatened to suspend any superior-general who did not turn over members of his order who had been cited to appear in Rome before Carafa's Inquisition. Those were procedures that Carafa had advocated as early as 1532 and now put into effect. Once pope, Carafa continued to seek new ways to flush out dissidents, even discussing but then rejecting a plan to exploit confession and violate its seal in order to identify heretics. His most traumatic actions were directed against Jews and Judaizers, especially those in Ancona. He actually tore up bulls he had signed, granting temporary reprieve to Jews and Portuguese *conversos* in that city of the Papal State. On 23 April 1556, Paul IV ordered that, from that time on, meetings of the Inquisition were to be secret.

The extent to which the Inquisition under Paul IV emphasized repression is evident in the Jewish policy. Since Jews were not baptized, they were not officially subject to the Inquisition. The actual trials of Jews by the Inquisition, it is true, represent a small percentage of its total caseload. But the use of the Inquisition against the Jews, the burning of the Talmud and other sacred Jewish books, and the efforts to convert the Jews all had the same goal of eliminating them.[94] By the 1550s, the policies were being enforced with zeal, the very quality that the inquisitors-general, Carafa in first place, called for in their 1553 order to uproot the blasphemy that study of the Talmud had supposedly caused.[95] Roman copies of the Talmud were burned publicly in Campo dei Fiori, over 1,000 copies of the Talmud were destroyed in Venice in 1553, and as many as 12,000 were confiscated in Cremona in 1559. In December 1558, the secretary to the Venetian ambassador quoted Paul as saying, on the subject of refugee Iberian Jews and Judaizing converts, often of Iberian descent and commonly derided in Italy as "pigs" (in Italian, *marrani*, from the Castilian *marranos*): "we want to see the whole lot burned."[96]

Paul's approaching death in August of 1559 unleashed a riot of celebration in the city of Rome. The crowd stormed the headquarters of the Inquisition, destroyed its records, released its prisoners, and then torched the building. When the statue of Paul on the Capitoline Hill was toppled, a yellow hat of the type that he made the Jews wear was placed on its head. The burial of the pope's remains took place after dark, and a guard was placed around his tomb dug well below ground in St. Peter's. Excluding his letters, in all of his other writings, Ignatius Loyola used the word "inquisitions" only once, in order to confess his perplexity about the good that such inquests accomplished.[97]

4 The *Acta* as Mirror of Luke

In the narrative of the *Acta*, Ignatius travels on a journey whose broad lines and final destination mirror the spiritual geography of Luke's two New Testament writings. The first of the two major portions of Ignatius's *Acta* begins in the region where Ignatius was raised, moves to Jerusalem, and ends on the Mount of Olives. The second portion begins in descent from that Mount, moves to places of education for the help of souls, witnesses the gathering of a group of fellow apostles engaged in charismatic ministries of the Word of God, discloses the opposition and persecution they experienced as disciples, and ends somewhat anticlimactically when Ignatius and his companions reach Rome. If the Gospel is to be proclaimed to the entire world, it must reach Rome. It did so both in Luke's Acts and in Ignatius's *Acta*. Following the path of those travels would help Ignatius recall the actions of God at specific points in his life and help his secretary commit to memory and then consign to notes the dictation that Ignatius gave.

As scriptural commentators have demonstrated, Luke likewise employed geography to structure his narratives, and Luke's geography has theological import.[1] It is "on the way" that Jesus educates the Lukan disciples and prepares them for ministries of the Word. Though the entire Bible often employs a journey motif, Luke betrays his originality by demonstrating a link between journey and mission. Ignatius took inspiration for a new start in his life from images of the child Jesus and his mother, Mary. Luke alone narrates the Annunciation to Mary. Ignatius realized the depths of his vainglory when he stepped out of the Lord's supposed footprints on the Mount of Olives. This was the only event from his Jerusalem pilgrimage that he chose to narrate at any length.[2] Luke alone narrates the Ascension of Jesus from the Mount. Ignatius gathered companions for charismatic ministries of charity in word and deed. Luke alone narrates the charitable acts of the apostles.

While organizing the contemplation of episodes from the life of Jesus for his *Spiritual Exercises* and engaging in a long process of formal education, Ignatius had to scrutinize all four Gospels. From his days of convalescence, he had developed a serious interest in the life of Jesus stimulated by his reading of Ludolph of Saxony's account and reflected in his desire to make a pilgrimage to Jerusalem. His formal study of theology at the University of Paris began with years of following lectures on scripture. Among theologians at Paris whom the first Jesuits had heard lecture, the Dominicans Jean Benoist (d. 1565) and Thomas Laurent (d. after 26 July 1560) in 1534 edited a work by Guillaume Pepin (ca. 1465–1533) on the exegesis of Exodus, and Robert Wauchope (d. 1551) later published a book on the Mass based exclusively on the evidence from scripture and devoid of the era's customary polemics. Ignatius may have heard John Mair (ca. 1467–1550) lecture at the Collège de Sainte-Barbe in the years that Mair was finishing his commentary on the four Gospels; the work was published in Paris in 1529. During those years in Paris, professors known personally by the Jesuits examined the scriptural commentaries of Erasmus, Cajetan, and Sadoleto. Nicolás Bobadilla remembered his Paris professors using the commentaries of Ambrose and Denys the Carthusian when they lectured on Luke.

Beginning at the time that Ignatius served as superior-general and continuing well after his death, his early companion, Alfonso Salmerón, worked on a multivolume commentary on the New Testament, and his close associate, Jerónimo Nadal, worked on an illustrated life of Christ based on the Sunday Gospel readings. When Ignatius's personal secretary, Juan Alfonso de Polanco, studied theology in Padua, he read scriptural commentaries by Rupert of Deutz, Denys the Carthusian, and Cajetan as well the notes that Erasmus appended to his *Paraphrases* of all four Gospels. Jesuit colleges in Spain followed the practice of the University of Alcalá in inaugurating the school year on the feast of Saint Luke. Most important, the *Spiritual Exercises* refer explicitly to Luke on fifteen occasions. Unlike other spiritual writers whose books of prayer Ignatius may have consulted as he put the *Exercises* together, Ignatius ended his own series of contemplations on the life of Jesus with the Ascension, a uniquely Lukan account.[3]

Refracting Ignatius through Luke

Four themes in Luke seem particularly relevant to the emphases of Ignatius's *Acta*: the theological significance of geography and especially of the

city of Jerusalem, the dynamism of the apostolic life, the cost of discipleship, and the universalism of ministry in the Spirit of Jesus.

Geography and Theology

More than any other New Testament writer, Luke focused on geography,
and he did so for theological reasons.[4] Reflecting a broader conviction of
ancient culture, Luke felt that geographical structuring assists the re-
membrance and assimilation of a text. He used geography to furnish a
mental map for his narrative.[5] As a map, however, Luke's geography
proves less than exact at times. Luke was not conducting a guided tour of
Palestine. His geography serves the theological purposes of the Gospel
and Acts.[6]

The city of Jerusalem functions as a hinge linking Luke's two writings:
Jerusalem is the city of destiny for Jesus, and Jerusalem is the source of
witness to Jesus.[7] That witness will spread from Jerusalem to "the ends of
the earth" (Acts 1:8, 13:47). The precise location for the shift from the era
of Jesus to the era of the people of God is the Mount of Olives, from which
Jesus ascended to the right hand of the Father. Once Jesus is exalted to the
Father's right hand and seated on the throne of David, the Holy Spirit is
sent upon the disciples as the promised power that will enable their witness to Jesus. As proof of the theological importance of Jerusalem to Luke,
one can adduce the fact that he names the city thirty times in his Gospel
alone, whereas Mark names it ten times and Matthew twelve.[8] Ignatius
underlines the universality of Jesuit mission by setting the contemplations
on the Kingdom of Christ and the Two Standards of Christ and Satan in
Jerusalem and having Jesus issue a call to evangelize the "whole world"
and be willing to help "everyone." For over a year after his ordination,
Ignatius waited to celebrate his first Mass of Thanksgiving, hoping to do
so in Jerusalem. Eventually, Ignatius fell back on the chapel of the manger
at Santa Maria Maggiore in Rome, because he believed that it contained
a relic of Christ's birth and therefore his Incarnation.[9]

Throughout the Gospel and the Acts of the Apostles, Luke highlighted
the crucial theological role of Jerusalem. The Gospel may be divided
into the Infancy Narrative (1:1–2:52), Preparation for Ministry (3:1–4:13),
Ministry in Galilee (4:14–9:50), the Journey to Jerusalem (9:51–19:27),

Ministry in Jerusalem (19:28–21:38), the Passion Narrative (22:1–23:56a), and the Vindication of Jesus (23:56b–24:53). Luke's Gospel is the only one to begin and end in Jerusalem. The Gospel opens in the Temple, with the announcement to Zechariah of John the Baptist's birth. That annunciation is followed by a second to Mary, which brings with it a promise that Jesus will sit on the throne of David. As the infancy narrative unwinds, the parents of Jesus twice bring him to Jerusalem. The transition to Jesus's life of itinerant ministry occurs with his baptism by John and his temptations in the desert. Only Luke concludes with the temptation that Jesus throw himself from the pinnacle (*pterygion*) of the Temple in Jerusalem.[10] He gave the Jerusalem temptation a climactic position in the list of three. Under the appearance of good, the devil proposes the contrary, suggesting to Jesus that a prophet can force God to spare him suffering and death in Jerusalem. Jesus rejects the devil's invitation to force God to protect him; he will not from vainglory dramatically display his own importance.

The ministry of Jesus in Galilee begins and ends with programmatic scenes that Luke carefully arranged. Jesus initiated his ministry by reading a text of Isaiah about a Messiah who liberates the poor, the blind, and the prisoners.[11] That scene in the synagogue presents an altogether different Messiah from the one the devil proposed. Jesus's journey to Jerusalem becomes the physical illustration that he has overcome temptation. Rather than conform to simplistic ideas of what a messiah should be or make a spectacle of himself, Jesus expresses his sonship by fidelity to the mission entrusted to him by the Father.

At the end of his Galilean ministry, Jesus is transfigured on the mountain, in the presence of three disciples. On the mountain, Jesus discussed his "departure" (*exodos*) with Moses and Elijah. That departure includes all the significant events that transpire in Jerusalem: his entry, his ministry, his death, his burial, his resurrection, and his ascension. Christologically, Jesus must fulfill his destiny; ecclesiologically, Jesus must prepare his disciples to preach in his name. Jesus attends to both these missions along the way.[12] There is much work to do with the disciples. Just after the Transfiguration and just before he sets out along the way to Jerusalem, he rebukes them for arguing about their own importance and failing to understand his predictions of suffering. The disciples not only fail to comprehend; they engage in a lively competition for self-promotion. As divine glory is revealed on the Mount of the Transfiguration (and again on the

Mount of Olives), so vainglory is revealed on the plain. Ironically, as Jesus descends from the Transfiguration, he encounters disciples who could not exorcise a demon from a child. Jesus later contrasts the humble acceptance of a child to the egoistic pretensions of his followers.[13]

Because Luke wishes to depict a special relationship between the ministry of Jesus and the city of Jerusalem, he devotes much of his Gospel to Jesus's journey from Galilee to Jerusalem. Luke himself assembled most of the material in the travel account. The materials he stitched together for eight chapters of the journey (9:51–18:14) are independent of Mark, whereas the briefer materials in the final segment (18:15–19:27) follow Mark closely. Jesus had a theological motive for traveling: the time was drawing near for him "to be taken up" (9:51). He is therefore resolute about his goal to reach the holy city. At three points in the narrative (9:51–53, 13:22, 17:11), Luke reminds readers of that goal. That is important because, while traveling, Jesus makes little physical progress.[14] Along the way, Jesus encounters Pharisees who are often so filled with self-esteem as the guardians of the Mosaic Law that they fail to offer Jesus the appropriate services of hospitality. Whether speaking to Pharisees or disciples, Jesus berates those whose faith is contaminated by a "vainglorious view of their leadership over others."[15] In contrast, at the house of Simon the Pharisee, a genuinely repentant woman offers Jesus appropriate services and reveals her inward transformation by her tears (7:36–50).

After reaching Jerusalem, Jesus enters the city as a pilgrim (19:28–40), one "who comes in the name of the Lord" (Ps. 118:26). Luke modified the scene of the pilgrim coming to the Temple by adding to the crowd's acclamation the word "king." Ironically, the superficial acclamation that the crowd shouts at Jesus ends up mirroring the words of the angel to Mary about David's throne. The road to Jerusalem led over the Mount of Olives; to receive acclaim as "king," Jesus had to "descend" from the Mount. His true or greater glory—in geographical terms his ascent from the Mount—is achieved in a more profound way, which includes suffering. After entering Jerusalem, Jesus weeps a second time for the city, in stark contrast to the acclaim that surrounds him. As a prophet, Jesus must announce the reconciling Word of God that liberates human beings. He laments that the city, which should welcome that Word, gives the Word only superficial hearing and ultimately rejects it. Jesus prophetically purges the Temple (19:45–46).

As the Samaritan village rejected Jesus at journey's inception, so the Temple officials reject him at journey's end. At the moment of death, Jesus entrusts himself peacefully to his Father, confident of his fidelity to the Father's will.[16]

Luke recounts appearances of the risen Jesus only in the vicinity of Jerusalem. As Jerusalem is the end point for the ministry of Jesus, so it is the starting point for the ministry of the Church. God's Word spreads from Jerusalem to Rome. Because Rome rules a vast empire, by reaching Rome, the Word reaches the ends of the inhabited world (*oikumene*). Luke thereby links the Gospel geographically to Acts, which comprises a narrative of gradual and universal evangelizing (Luke 23:5, 24:47; Acts 1:8). Among New Testament authors, Luke alone describes the Ascension of the Lord. The Ascension likewise comprises a link between the Gospel and Acts: there is a brief account in the Gospel and a fuller account in Acts. The Ascension is a vital element in Luke's Christology. Jesus is exalted "in glory" to the right hand of the Father. It is the final moment in the process of his "departure" (*exodos*), which included the other transcendent elements of Jesus's life (prophetic preaching and action, death, burial, resurrection, exaltation to glory). Unlike the resurrection, which no disciple saw, the Ascension is seen, though not "seen clearly" at first.[17] The attention of the disciples is fixed on heaven, whereas the incarnation of the Lord and the gift of his Spirit have made flesh and the world the setting for revelation and ministry.

Jerusalem is just as important theologically to the message of Acts. To demonstrate the continuity of God's salvific action in history, Acts begins in Jerusalem. The book addresses a logical dilemma for the primitive Christian community: If Jesus fulfilled the whole of the scriptures, why do Jewish religious officials reject Jesus and persecute his followers? In other words, "how could non-Jews find value in a movement that had roots in Judaism but which most Jews repudiated?"[18] Luke's typically inclusive approach depicts a tie historically from Israel and Jesus to Jesus and the church, and Jerusalem is the theological locus of that continuity. For Luke, the church is not a new Israel but a transformed Israel. The disciples never cease to preach the Word of God in synagogues, and from the beginning to the end of Acts, Jews embrace a call to repentance for the forgiveness of sins. In fact, Luke does not use the term "church" (*ekklesia*). He prefers the term "people" (*laos*) precisely because he wishes to emphasize the continuity between Israel and the church as God's people. Of the

142 occurrences of the word "people" in the New Testament, eighty-four (60%) are found in Luke's writings.[19] When Stephen delivers his speech in Jerusalem (Acts 7:1–53), he does not engage in polemic about the Mosaic Law or the Jewish heritage. Rather, Stephen criticized the hypocrisy of the Temple elite and the rigidity of their legalisms. Consistent with the message of Acts, Stephen argues for a more inclusive Israel.

Peter begins the movement toward greater inclusiveness when he visits the home of the centurion, Cornelius, a Gentile already attracted to the way of Judaism.[20] Despite Peter's misgivings about entering the house and sharing a meal with "the unclean," Peter does as Jesus taught him along the way and gives priority to moral purity over ritual purity. The ascended Jesus has become the judge of the living and the dead (Acts 10:42–43). God generously bestows the power of his Spirit on all who believe. When the disciples in Jerusalem chide Peter for baptizing a Gentile, Peter replies, "Who was I that I could hinder God?" (Acts 11:17). Through the tears of his repentance, Peter has been transformed interiorly from the bravado of his earlier conduct to the humility of his present service. A medieval legend taught that Peter had shed those tears beneath a rock, and authors of Ignatius's day identified that rock with the one on the Mount of Olives where Christ left his footprints.[21] Peter's response echoes that of Rabbi Gamaliel about believers in Jesus earlier in Acts: "if this plan or this undertaking is of human origin, it will fail; if it is of God, you will not be able to overthrow them" (Acts 5:38–39).

Dynamism of Apostolic Service

Luke portrays the entire life of Jesus as a pilgrimage or "a way" (*hodos*). From existing tradition, Luke appropriated the role of John the Baptist as one who "prepares the way." Luke uses the word "way" to indicate the salvific mission of Jesus, and Luke uses geography to depict the role of John and Jesus in the Father's plan of salvation. The journey motif is ubiquitous in Luke's writings. His Gospel explicitly mentions or alludes frequently to journeying.[22] In Acts, the way becomes a characterization of the community that believes in Jesus: it is literally a "Jesus movement."[23]

For Luke, the life of faith is a pilgrimage, implying that believers need to keep moving. Luke repeatedly uses the verb *poreuesthai* and its compounds; the root verb means "to go" or "to move along." When applied to Jesus, the verb can take on subtle connotations. For example, in Luke 4:30, the verb is used to indicate that Jesus "passed through the midst" of a hostile crowd in Nazareth. Despite opposition, Jesus moves to his destiny.[24] The "way" of Jesus comprises more than his physical entry into Jerusalem or his progress to the Passion. It begins with Jesus's "entrance" (*eisodos*) after John the Baptist had begun to preach, and it continues until Jesus's "departure" (*exodos*). Theologically, Luke understands "the way" to mean fulfilling the will of God. Because the Spirit leads, there is for the believer an element of authenticity in the going. As Ignatius put it in 1524, "[f]or the love of God our Lord, aim always at going forward."[25] According to Nadal, Ignatius wanted Jesuits to travel to any part of the world. Jesuits were to be most at home along the way.

The appearance of the risen Lord to the disciples on the road to Emmaus typifies Luke's emphasis on dynamism (Luke 24:13–35).[26] The disciples "were going" (*poreuomenoi*). Jesus approached and "went with them" (*suneporeueto autois*). The narrative twice emphasizes the setting "on the road" (*en tō hodō*). During their time walking together, Jesus instructs them on the overall meaning of the scriptures, that "the Messiah should suffer these things and then enter into his glory." Once the disciples recognize Jesus, they rush back to nearby Jerusalem to tell the others "what had happened on the road." The narrative likewise demonstrates that Luke closely ties the way of Jesus to his ascension into glory (cf. Luke 9:51; Acts 1:2, 11, 22). That exaltation is an essential quality of the departure of Jesus, without which the departure would not make sense. As Jesus's final commission to the disciples in Luke suggests, disciples truly witness when they follow the Lord through a journey in stages. The content of the disciples' preaching reflects the ministry of the Lord: repent (turn away from sin) and convert (turn toward a merciful God).[27] Salvation is a gift and a process because it involves a personal relationship. Believers are graced to embrace the kerygma, accept baptism in "the name of Jesus," and receive forgiveness by the power of that name and the indwelling of the Spirit.

Disciples understand the import of Christ's pilgrimage only when Christ himself, through his Spirit, opens up the subtle meaning of the entire scripture and its fulfillment in the dynamic way of the Lord. In Acts, Luke does not focus on the character and accomplishments of the human actors. Luke focuses on the progress of the Word of God preached in the name of Jesus. God's plan of salvation and God's Spirit explain the progress made in the course of the book. The dominant actors are not the apostles; the dominant actor is the Holy Spirit.[28] The narrative of the fourth chapter of Acts directs the reader's attention to what Peter and John say and do. The narrative does not dwell on the fact that Peter and John are uneducated fishermen who have come a long way from their humble past. In other words, the narrative of Acts is focused on giving glory to God, not on any acclaim that the apostles might win for themselves. They are recognized as being with Jesus, his companions.

Cost of Discipleship

The journey to Jerusalem in the Gospel of Luke becomes the privileged moment when Jesus trains his witnesses. Luke has therefore incorporated into that account much saying material. That particular section of Luke's Gospel exemplifies why Luke speaks of a "connected narrative" in his preface to Theophilus. Luke sees his community as deeply rooted in the teaching of Jesus himself. At the outset of the journey, as Jesus heads resolutely to Jerusalem, the disciples see him rejected by Samaritans who refuse to believe that he must go there to suffer and die. Whereas Jesus accepts his prophetic vocation and the likelihood of rejection and persecution that often accompany divinely willed prophecy, James and John, like the Samaritans, fail to understand. Jesus berates them for wishing to call down fire on the Samaritan village that did not offer them hospitality (9:51–55). Jesus rejects the role of a fiery reformer in the mold of Elijah (cf. Luke 7:19) and embraces the role of a gracious liberator in the mold of Isaiah (cf. Luke 4:14–21).[29]

John Meier proposed that Jesus may well have moved away from his initial following of the eschatological preaching of his cousin John to carve out his own path of compassionate preaching in word and deed.[30] Jesus teaches his disciples that they are not to punish vengefully those who reject the word. Immediately thereafter, he teaches his disciples that they must follow him no matter what the cost to themselves. In keeping with the theme of "the way," the disciples of Jesus must move along as he does, embracing his teaching by fulfilling his Father's will. As Jesus reached his destiny despite opposition, so the disciples, despite opposition and persecution, should preach forgiveness in his name to the ends of the earth. Jesuits embrace an apostolic life in contrast to that of John the Baptist and like that of Jesus. Whereas the Baptist called people out to the wilderness, Jesus went to their towns and villages. Whereas the Baptist portrayed the end as near and fiery punishment awaiting the unrepentant, Jesus preached that the end has broken in and joyful salvation awaits the repentant. Whereas the ascetic lifestyle of the Baptist mirrored the severity of his message, Jesus ate and drank at an inclusive banquet. Ignatius felt convinced that, no matter what the costs, authentic consolation would keep the disciple moving. "When a person is going forward with this fervor and warmth and interior consolation, the heaviest burden seems light, the greatest penances or hardships seem sweet."[31]

In contrast to the other two Synoptic evangelists, Luke offers his own version of Jesus's final commission to the disciples (24:44–49).[32] Mark emphasizes the preaching of the Gospel. Matthew emphasizes baptism, making disciples of all nations, and, characteristically, teaching them to observe what the Lord has commanded. Luke emphasizes the preaching of repentance and forgiveness of sins, ministries of the Word of God to be carried on once the power of the Holy Spirit has come upon the disciples. In one of her sonnets, Ignatius's friend Vittoria Colonna (1490–1547) paraphrased the commission, capturing its positive emphasis on abundant help toward a fundamental change of heart: "Neither does the everlasting support remove its grace nor hide from us its beautiful light when our repenting corrects our faults."[33]

Acts portrays the disciples engaged in those ministries. There are twelve occasions in Acts where Luke depicts "ministries of the Word," fifteen occasions where he uses the phrases "Word of God" or "Word of the Lord," and single occasions where he uses the phrases "Word of salvation" and "Word of the Gospel."[34] Among New Testament writers, only Luke closely associates the Twelve with "the Apostles." And Luke uses the term "apostle" far more often than the other evangelists do. "Apostle" appears on thirty-three occasions in the Lukan corpus, whereas it appears only once in each of the other three Gospels. For Luke, apostles are the crucial evangelizers, whom Jesus sends to preach the Word to the ends of the earth. The opening verses of Luke's account of the journey to Jerusalem purposefully repeat the verb "send" (*apostellein*, 9:52; 10:1, 3, 16). Though the Twelve eventually disappear in Acts, apostles continue to preach into the sixteenth chapter of the book.[35] In other words, key disciples in Luke have an apostolate comprised of ministries of the Word of God.

The more elaborate scene of the Ascension in Acts underlines the need for the power of the Spirit, even for eyewitnesses of the events of salvation. The same power through which Jesus healed will enable the disciples to carry out his commission.[36] When the disciples see Jesus ascend, with all of the apocalyptic trimmings to assist their understanding, they still miss the point. The disciples stare up into the sky, entranced by the spectacle. They need the sarcastic question of the "two men" to shake them from their lethargic incomprehension: "Why do you stand looking up toward heaven?" Jesus is exalted in glory with the Father. As his witnesses, apostles need to testify that God has come among us to offer forgiveness for sin and reform individual and community lives in accord with justice. When the Spirit is poured into the hearts of the disciples on Pentecost, they are shaken from their stasis and no longer fear to evangelize. Luke's Gospel first prepared disciples for the totality of their commitment: they will need to leave all behind (Luke 5:11, 14:33), expect opposition daily (9:23), and never reverse course (9:62). In the course of Acts, benefits consistently accrue to the Jesus movement when its exponents suffer opposition and persecution.[37] The initial persecution of disciples in Acts leads to the establishment of the vibrant community at Antioch (Acts 11:19–26); the final persecution of Paul in Jerusalem leads to the establishment of the universal community at Rome. Luke believed that such opposition fostered the progress of God's Word. In other words, disciples share in the prophetic vocation of Jesus.

In the Lukan corpus, there is one issue about which Jesus left his disciples an appropriately complex teaching. That is the question of the proper use of material possessions by believers. The Gospel speaks forcefully about rich and poor and inequitable distribution of wealth, and it bequeaths to disciples a creative tension.[38] At times, Luke endorses a moderate path: his writings recommend the prudent use of material wealth to assist those in need and foster receptivity to the message that Jesus proclaims. At other times, Luke endorses a radical path: his writings advocate the surrendering of all material wealth in order to endow a common fund and ensure that no one ever be in need. In Luke's beatitudes, the materially poor are blessed, and the rich are cursed. Though all of those blessed in the beatitudes receive blessings in the course of Luke's account, only the rich, among the cursed, suffer consequences.[39]

Universal Ministry in the Spirit

Luke links his geographical perspective to universal ministry by depicting the diffusion of the Word of God in the Gospel and especially in Acts. In Acts, disciples preach the Word to the Jews resident in Jerusalem or present for Temple liturgy; to the Samaritans; to an Ethiopian worshiper; to Jews in the diaspora of Lyda, Sharon, and Joppa; and finally to the Gentiles, beginning with the conversion of the Roman centurion Cornelius. Luke's theology sees a reconstituted Israel, an Israel transformed by belief in Jesus that will become the locus of salvation. The Gentiles who embrace the Word are associated with the Jews who do so, to form together the people of God. There are five sections of travel by disciples in Acts, each of which concludes with a summary that indicates redaction by Luke. The final section of the book (19:21–28:31) narrates Paul's journey to Rome, by way of Jerusalem. That section, however, says nothing of Paul's martyrdom in the city because the emphasis is not on Paul but on the progress of the Word of God.[40] Similarly, when Ignatius has reached the point in his *Acta* where he and his companions take up residence in Rome, he sees no need to elaborate, even to the extent of omitting any discussion of the pope's approval of his new institute. Rome symbolizes the universal ministry of the church, and, by entering Rome, the future Jesuits come to participate in that mission.

In addition to crossing ethnic and religious boundaries, the Word preached in the name of Jesus crosses social and economic boundaries. Luke has special parables of mercy (the Prodigal Son) and special concern for the marginal (Samaritans, toll collectors, the poor, and women).[41] The parable of the Good Samaritan is unique to Luke. That parable juxtaposes the world of Temple privilege, represented by the priest and Levite, to the world of Temple ostracism, represented by the Samaritan. Whereas the priest and Levite are concerned not to defile themselves through contact with "the dead," the Samaritan is concerned to assist an unfortunate victim by offering effective healing. The Samaritan Law had the same proscriptions on defilement as the Jewish Law, but the Samaritan puts compassion first. Thus, the narrative also juxtaposes heartfelt solidarity to heartless dogmatism. By so depicting privileged religious officials, the parable forms a crucial part of Luke's larger effort to have Jesus seek out those of little importance in Palestinian society. And the Samaritan acts charitably while walking along the way (Luke 10:33). Till Ignatius's time, exegetes had usually allegorized the Good Samaritan as Jesus. Believers assumed the role of the traveler in need, whom Jesus came to assist. Ignatius now wanted the priests and brothers of the Society of Jesus to be good Samaritans, awarding precedence among moral imperatives to the love of neighbor and not walking by those in need.[42]

Even on the cross, Jesus gives concrete witness to divine compassion toward the least. Although one evildoer who was crucified with Jesus taunted him, as the religious authorities and Roman soldiers had already done, the other evildoer rebuked his compatriot and implicitly testified to Jesus as an innocent victim. In a gesture of unusual familiarity, the second criminal then calls Jesus by his name and pleads for the mercy that only a king can grant. In return, the evildoer is promised an abundance of grace: salvation and entry with Jesus into the presence of God, the richest paradise imaginable. Rather than saving himself and making a scene by throwing himself down from the cross, Jesus saves the other and partially fulfills the taunt of the first evildoer. As Jesus promised to liberate in his first words to fellow human beings in Luke, he does liberate in his last words to a human being before his death in Luke. Throughout Luke's Passion narrative, Jesus acts with unconditional solidarity, healing the servant's ear, expressing concern for the women of Jerusalem, and praying that the Father forgive those who crucified him, Roman and Jew alike.[43]

In Acts, Luke goes out of his way to depict that Christianity is an inclusive faith. The Word of God crosses geographic, ethnic, and social boundaries. Geographically, Luke has the Word spread from Jerusalem (1:1–8:3) to Judea and Samaria (8:1–40), to the Gentiles along the coast of the Middle East (9:32–11:18), to Jews and Gentiles in Asia Minor (12:14–16:5), and to Greeks across the Aegean (16:5–19:40). With Paul's journey to Rome, the Gospel had reached the entire world (21:1–28:31).[44] Luke communicated his message by exploiting tenets of Jewish belief and Roman imperialism. The table of nations in Genesis 10 taught Jews that God distributed all of the nations on earth. Luke may well have exploited that table in his organization of Acts. For example, the "Cushites" of the Masoretic text of the table became the "Ethiopians" of the Septuagint text. By including the story of the conversion of the Ethiopian eunuch, Luke may illustrate the successful beginning of the mission to the people descended from Noah's son, Ham.[45]

That same story would have special resonance for a Roman audience. For the Romans, Aethiopia comprised the southernmost boundary of the inhabited world (*orbis terrarum*, Greek *oikumene*). That specific conviction reflects the practical intent of Roman geography in general. The Romans wished to use geography to demonstrate that they had conquered "the world," by which they meant the three continents of Europe, Asia, and Africa. The emperor Augustus in particular orchestrated that geography to teach that Rome's rule had reached the whole inhabited earth.[46] Acts, therefore, ends in Rome: the disciples have taken the Word of God to the ends of the earth. Acts likewise maintains the Gospel's solidarity toward all those in need: the destitute (2:43–45; 4:34–35; 10:2; 24:17), the widows (6:1–6; 9:36–42), the sick (5:12–16; 9:32–35), and women (12:12–17; 16:11–40; 17:10–12; 18:24–28; 21:8–9).[47]

Conclusion

Shortly after Ignatius succumbed to a fatal illness, the Jesuits received a consolatory letter from a community of Barnabites in Milan. Those fellow religious celebrated the ways in which Ignatius and his companions had contributed to the birth of "a new Church emulating the first apostolic community, with new apostles, new martyrs."[48] Their sentiments reflected a broader hope that the power of the Spirit was saving a church that had been on the verge of collapse. The letter has insight. Ignatius did establish a group of religious whose mission imitates the first apostles because the mission is consciously charitable and consciously universal. The narrative of the *Acta* suggests that Ignatius discerned that God was calling him to found such an order in part through a process of elimination. Ignatius rejected the zealous crusading of a military order, he abandoned his plan to embrace Carthusian asceticism while appropriating elements of Carthusian community life, and he decided not to join the Franciscans or Dominicans while following them in evangelizing in poverty. Likewise, Ignatius decided not to become a radical hermit in the wilderness or a perpetual pilgrim in Jerusalem, the latter discernment aided greatly by the Franciscan guardians there.

For his innovative Society of vowed religious dedicated to apostolic service, Ignatius found inspiration in the apostles of the New Testament. Luke proved especially helpful when he orchestrated a great journey to

Jerusalem as a way to educate the disciples for ministry. Jesus had to go to Jerusalem because he freely embraced the Father's plan of salvation. Following the will of God, no matter what the cost, led ultimately to the saving events of Jerusalem and the return of Jesus in glory to the Father. Because the costs of discipleship are readily underestimated, disciples need education for ministry. The conversation on the road to Emmaus proves just how difficult the scriptures are to understand properly and how demanding the way of the Lord proves to be. When Matteo Ricci presented that Lukan passage to the Chinese early in the seventeenth century, he stressed in the caption for the scene's illustration that "[t]wo disciples, after hearing the truth, reject all vanity." That was a distinctively Ignatian interpretation of the passage. In the woodcut that accompanies Ricci's text, Christ and the disciples all carry the walking staffs of pilgrims.[49]

In addition to the geographical framework of Luke, there are a number of specific passages in that Gospel that reflect the spiritual emphases of the *Acta*. The Annunciation portends the ultimate new beginning, the urge to throw oneself from the Temple's pinnacle represents the ultimate temptation, the Samaritan's desire to respond charitably to needs encountered along the road epitomizes the authenticity of ministry, and the final commissioning of the disciples entrusts them with the good news that repentance can lead to conversion of heart and salvation. The protagonist of the Acts of the Apostles is the Spirit of Jesus, who inspires the words and actions of the disciples.[50] The protagonist of Ignatius's *Acta* and his *Spiritual Exercises* is that same Spirit, who works in the heart of every believer. It is not purely accident that Jesuits early on were called the Society of the Holy Spirit and that Ignatius wished them to minister "in the name of Jesus" (Acts 3:6, 4:8–12).[51]

There are two further passages that bring together important themes shared by the Gospel and by Ignatius's *Acta*. The first is the account of the Pharisee and the toll collector in Luke 18:9–14, which Luke draws from his particular tradition and places at the end of his own material on the journey to Jerusalem, just before the material he derives primarily from Mark. In essence, that story, which exegetes have categorized as a rhetorical exemplum, constitutes the heart of Lukan teaching on the ways that vainglory obstructs the work of God in one's heart and on the abundance of mercy that God offers to the humble.[52] Believers do not receive righteousness by boasting about piety beyond the norm; believers receive righteousness by acknowledging their sinfulness before the Lord. In posture within the Temple and in manner of prayer, the Pharisee and the toll collector are worlds apart. The Pharisee has wasted the benefits of studying God's Law intimately and chosen a path of self-reliance. The toll collector has embraced the heart of God's Law and begged for mercy. More than a little of the Pharisee remains in everyone, and as Ignatius warned, probably a good deal remains in Jesuits. The genius of the exemplum is evident in the almost instinctive reaction of believers to think to themselves, "I am so glad that I am not like that Pharisee." The *Acta* remind Jesuits that they are probably, by inclination, like the Pharisee, for they have embraced the Ignatian way of serving in the world.

The second passage in Luke regards the pardon of the sinful woman (7:36–50). Once again, Luke draws the material from his particular tradition, not from Mark or the source called Q.[53] The story teaches that repentance and the forgiveness of sin have come to one of the outcasts of Israel. Because the woman has tasted the abundance of grace, in a banquet setting, she pours out signs of love and gratitude by her washing, her anointing, and, significantly for Ignatius, her tears. Because God forgives sinfulness, the repentant woman experiences a change of heart within that impels her to practice a love that is self-giving. Repentance and conversion make the woman more open to God's mercy, and she can go in peace. Her interior generosity and external courtesies differ from the stingy hospitality and lack of decorum shown by the banquet's host. Like a vainglorious monk who feels resentment for the spiritual progress of his fellow monks, the host, despite wishing to honor Jesus at the banquet, upbraids the woman for her generosity in response to Jesus. As Jesus urges, she goes in peace and consolation.

In Ignatius's time, scholars debated whether the woman in the Lukan passage should continue to be identified with Mary Magdalene and seen as a prostitute. The theological faculty at the University of Paris intervened in that dispute and argued, incorrectly, that the three Marys of the Gospels (Mary Magdalene; Mary of Bethany, and sister of Martha; the sinful woman in Luke 7) were one and the same person. In the *Spiritual Exercises*, Ignatius followed that mistaken interpretation.[54] It is little wonder, then, that ministry to prostitutes achieved such a prominence for Ignatius and the first Jesuits. It epitomized the broader commission of Luke, and it came right from Luke.

5 Ignatius, His *Acta*, and Renaissance Culture

Among the signs that Ignatius successfully focused his *Acta* on the Spirit's action in his own heart, one can point to the fact that Ignatius has never been all that popular a saint. Despite an early resolve to outdo Francis of Assisi, Ignatius does not enjoy the popularity that Francis enjoys worldwide. In the summer of 2005, the Women's Society of St. Ignatius parish on Grand Cayman tried to purchase a statue of Ignatius for their island church. It proved an instructive lesson in pious consumerism. At that time, there were literally hundreds of statues of Francis of Assisi available on the market but only a few of Ignatius and none especially appealing.[1] Still, those who meet Ignatius through his *Acta*, and not a statue, might well feel admiration for the courage of one who so candidly shared his struggles with vainglory. Virtually every aspect of Ignatius's life, as he remembered it, was infected by that thirst for public recognition.[2] He exhibited foolhardiness throughout in war, whether defending the fortress at Pamplona or journeying through warring French and Spanish armies or voyaging through fleets of pirates and privateers. His flamboyant asceticism led him to forgo all grooming for a time, wear ridiculous outfits of sackcloth and disintegrating shoes, torment his ill stomach with imprudent fasting and abstinence, and plunge into his mouth a hand he assumed was infected with bubonic plague. He displayed similar bravado in captivity, unwilling to seek the help of counsel or escape when the opportunity presented itself. If O'Rourke Boyle's analysis of *agujero* is correct, then Ignatius, while still mired in vainglory, saw himself tempted like the Lord to throw himself from a pinnacle. Ignatius's temptation, however, reflected his self-reliance and a lack of trust in the Lord's power to heal. If Ignatius had given in, he may well have died.

Alasdair MacIntyre has observed that humility is a decidedly Christian virtue. Heroism in ancient culture consisted of winning personal glory through great achievements. Aristotle would consider humility a vice, especially for society's wealthy and powerful elite.[3] Ignatius appreciated the gift that humility represented, and he made it a primary emphasis of his spirituality. It had to be difficult for an individual as conscious of his reputation as Ignatius was to share his failings with friends who admired him.

To become humble, Ignatius had to reject his Spanish society's code of *hidalgo* honor. Ignatius did so to help others. Nonetheless, Ignatius had learned to share with discerning discretion and not with scrupulous guilt or false humility. His contentment to reveal, near life's end, that he had not committed a mortal sin implies two things. First, once Ignatius took his vow of celibacy, he kept it. Second, like Jean Gerson and other moralists, he considered vainglory a sin but, under normal circumstances, not a mortal sin. And vainglory was not a sin at all when an individual vindicated his good name against calumnies.[4]

Medieval Hagiography

In contextualizing Ignatius's narrative, it is helpful to review the broad lines of hagiography in the Middle Ages. In any epoch, accounts of the acknowledged heroes of a believing community provide a privileged source for that community's spirituality of holiness.[5] As a genre, medieval hagiography, especially prior to the thirteenth century, tells stories in which little happens, and the spirituality of this era largely deemphasized belief in the Incarnation. Much of that literature assumed that the human order does not conform to the divine. The divine plan, therefore, must impose itself, and the literary composition must manifest the divine order. When narrating a saint's life and miracles, the principal dimensions of human existence, time and space, are neglected. Rather than living in a specific era or locale, the hero of the story was portrayed as an idealized type, a living lesson in catechism. The true protagonist of events is God. Divine Providence intervenes to shape human history, and the miraculous, by definition extraordinary, becomes an ordinary, even ubiquitous feature of saints' lives.

After 1200, Western hagiography, while maintaining those traditional emphases, developed a new stream, principally as a result of the life and preaching of Francis of Assisi. Ascetic hermits and monastic Cistercians protected the traditional emphasis on divine order imposing itself and were celebrated for conducting their lives accordingly. Mendicants, however, introduced a novel element of devotion to the human Christ and saw holiness as an effort to follow and imitate that Christ. Their emphasis began to affect the tradition. Hermits joined themselves to the human Christ and his suffering at Calvary by punishing their bodies as the domain of evil. Their fasting and self-flagellation became primary expressions of their holiness. In the period from 1198 to 1280, however, other saints focused less on external mortification and more on internal transformation. They renounced sin, not themselves or their bodies, and they imitated the poor Christ in their begging. The mendicant spirituality of holiness, therefore, was innovative not in its goal, the imitation of the human Christ, but in its means, the voluntary embrace of poverty. Whereas contemporary Cistercians sought to rise above the flesh toward mystical union with God, mendicants sought to imitate Christ through begging for sustenance and giving pastoral assistance by preaching and hearing confessions. The thirteenth century witnessed an important evolution in the conceptualization of holiness, moving from an eremitic contempt for self or a monastic contempt for the world that began immediately outside the walls of the monastery to a willingness to witness to the Gospel through pastoral assistance and mendicant poverty. A century of demographic and economic growth made the towns of Europe and particularly Italy a laboratory for experimentation.

The fourteenth century ushered in a period of crisis for the mendicant ideal, motivated by developments in church and society. First, poverty had become more suspect to religious authorities. Pope John XXII, whose tempestuous reign ran from 1316 to 1334, declared that Christ and his apostles had owned and used property, and he condemned Spiritual Franciscans and Beguines for claiming otherwise.[6] For the church hierarchy, holiness in the fourteenth century rested largely on safer values, like private devotion, obedience, and orthodoxy. Second, a bourgeois ethos began to pervade Western society, challenging the assumption that all the poor were especially beloved by God. Only a worthy beggar, not a lazy one, deserved the community's compassion. In the fiscal policies of the papacy at Avignon, bourgeois values received an imprimatur. Third, the promotion of learning clashed at times with the promotion of poverty. Even an abbot as learned as Bernard of Clairvaux (1091–1153) at times saw academic learning as an impediment to holiness. Bernard especially mistrusted any undue confidence in human reasoning that might lead theologians to presume themselves capable of explaining mysteries of the faith.[7]

Tensions built, however, as the papacy promoted university learning and bishops sponsored schools to assist their pastoral goals. Those tensions are reflected in the varieties of fourteenth-century saints' cults. Thomas Becket (ca. 1118–70) long remained the prototypical saint-bishop who gave his life to defend the church's liberty against the encroachment of secular rulers, but in an effort to promote learning, the popes also canonized some scholar-bishops.[8] Such official actions, however, had little popular resonance, where the mendicants continued to enjoy greater esteem and encourage laypeople in their pursuit of holiness. The popular mendicants included the great early Franciscans, Francis himself and Anthony, and their Dominican counterpart, Dominic. In the popular imagination, Francis reigned supreme, and Francis had made no secret of his ambivalence about learning or status. The same friar might be revered as saintly by the people for his asceticism, compassion, and piety, while his own religious order looked down on him for an ignorance demonstrated in consistently poor preaching. In the end, if learning was a valid path to holiness, one's innate talent proved more palatable to many believers than the learning acquired in schools.

The period of the Great Western Schism (1378–1417) exacerbated the distrust for learning. In the popular mind, stubborn scholars intent on defending the validity of the claim of each pope had prolonged the Schism. During the Schism and immediately thereafter, the criteria for holiness included anti-intellectual fideism and quietism, and the media of sanctity became prophetic denunciations or apocalyptic revelations. Believers achieved heroic status through poverty and rigorous asceticism, given that the hierarchy had become so secularized and the clergy so lax. In an era when God's ordinary channels of communication were corrupted, God chose to communicate through an elite corps of mystics granted extraordinary gifts. As prosperity turned to depression, as plague recurred in cycles and as the Schism wore on, a psychological alarmism manifested itself in tortured souls who were ill at ease in this world and yearned for the next. Late fourteenth-century saints betrayed an intense spirituality of self-mortification, absorption in Christ's passion, and ecstatic experience.[9] Generally educated only to a basic level of literacy, they emphasized the darker side of life and urged patience on believers in the present world. They were skeptical about efforts to improve that world. In their telling, the gap between divine and human had grown immense; it was proven in Christ's crucifixion and bridged only by the gift of mystical union.

World-Affirming Spiritualities

The world-affirming style of holiness to which Ignatius discerned God calling him had less in common with those late medieval trends and more in common with trends born in Italy during the Renaissance. With the mendicants, Ignatius did share a devotion to the humanity of Christ and the importance of poverty, for him a key antidote to vainglory.[10] In a world where cardinals estimated that they needed an annual income of 6,000 ducats, ten times the income of a contemporary lawyer in Florence, and saw the cardinalate primarily as a way to establish their family's prestige and ensure its wealth, Ignatius decided that Jesuit houses needed no fixed income and Jesuits should not rise higher in the hierarchy than priesthood.[11] A perhaps unwitting by-product of Ignatius's prohibition against prelacies meant that talent was not drained away from the order. Nonetheless, Ignatius did not share Francis's ambivalence about living and ministering in the urban world of the Mediterranean. From his days recuperating at Loyola, Ignatius experienced healing in the company of the great apostles Peter and Paul, not in the company of the great hermit John the Baptist.[12] Moreover, Ignatius felt no compunction about the relationship between learning and sanctity. As he had discerned the need for a university education, he insisted that most Jesuits obtain one, which helped to make the Society of Jesus attractive to prospective candidates.

As Ignatius celebrated all of the good things that God had done for him till arriving in Rome in 1538, his commitment to education, appreciation for the Incarnation, and desire for rebirth of the apostolic age reveal a dialogue with the world of Renaissance humanism.[13] Following Luke's Gospel, Ignatius organized the first portion of his *Acta* as the narrative of a journey to Jerusalem. During that journey in Luke, a dynamic Lord instructed the apostles as evangelizers and equipped them to debate with their adversaries.[14] Ignatius's spirituality of education had much in common with the emphases that Luke presented in the Emmaus story: it was vital to teach the ignorant so that the slow of heart would be transformed by hearts that burned with love. His narration of his own pilgrimage to Jerusalem had little in common with other contemporary narratives, which were unabashedly autobiographical and filled with details about fellow pilgrims and personal experiences. The account of Felix Fabbri, finished around 1484, runs to over 1,300 pages in its English translation, whereas that of Ignatius could fit comfortably into seventy-five pages and much of what Ignatius dictated did not deal with his pilgrimage per se. In fact, anyone seeking detailed information on Ignatius's journey to Jerusalem is better advised to consult the accounts of his fellow travelers.[15] From Manresa to Paris, Ignatius consistently envisioned Christ as his teacher. As he progressed, therefore, he sought to discern what Christ was teaching him. The God of the *Acta* and the *Spiritual Exercises* cannot ultimately be inscrutable as God is for the mystical tradition.

Ignatian spirituality is premised on the conviction that God speaks to the heart of every human being and humans speak to God. The *Spiritual Exercises* thus have rhetorical premises. The entire process of that transforming spiritual experience is set in motion by Ignatius, the only persuader involved in the *Exercises* who speaks but does not engage in dialogue. By contrast, the guide speaks to the exercitant and the exercitant to the guide. Most important, the Spirit speaks in the heart of the exercitant while the exercitant prays to God.[16] From experience, Ignatius knew the danger of vainglory in prayer, of projecting one's image of God onto God and praying only for what one wants. That is why Ignatius advocated practicing twice a day a style of prayer that began from experience, searched for signs of God in the complex, not the simplistic interpretation, and functioned best when one focused on sinfulness in times of consolation and God's superabundant grace in times of desolation. In the *Acta*, Ignatius reaffirmed his lifelong confidence that God is engaged with human beings and will speak to them. So confident was he of that dialogic relationship that he supplied a set of flexible rules to assist one in finding what God wills. Dialogue, persuasion, and flexibility were all values of the humanist style of education that Ignatius made a formal part of Jesuit training. When Ignatius matured from a rhetoric to persuade only himself to a rhetoric for reforming faith in Europe and evangelizing an expanding world, as Marc Fumaroli argues, he endorsed the program of Renaissance humanists and placed rhetoric for two centuries at the center of the Jesuit enterprise.[17]

Humanist Education and Rhetoric

The humanist movement of the Renaissance represented a characteristic phase in the rhetorical culture of the Western world. Humanists taught the arts appropriate to humanity, disciplines such as rhetoric, which educated one to speak well, and ethics, which educated one to live well. Like their ancient Roman predecessors, Renaissance humanists hammered away at ethos as the principal mode of persuasion: to persuade effectively, a speaker had to live the values that the speaker publicly advocated. Especially during adolescence, students profited from schooling that focused on the formation of character. The physical changes of adolescence, puberty above all, engendered new moral challenges. The truth that mattered for humanists, then, was a truth relevant to the way that one lived. Such a truth could not be necessarily true or logically certain; if rhetorical truth were apodictic, humans would not possess authentic freedom.

Humanists saw benefits in their education not only for the individual but for the city as well. A rhetorical education took seriously the premise of Isocrates, Aristotle, Cicero, and Quintilian that human beings by nature are creatures of the polis, a civic society. A humanist education could spur citizens to reshape the polis into a more ethical community.[18] At least by the time that Ignatius left Paris and went home to Azpeitia, as he indicated in his *Acta*, he had come to share humanist convictions about shaping a more humane polis. Ignatius proposed, as part of a broader program of moral renewal, that his hometown take action to relieve the plight of the poor. Poor relief was a cherished cause of the humanist Juan Luis Vives, who in 1526 had elaborated principles for its implementation in the city of Bruges. Vives urged the city's magistrates to address the causes of poverty, particularly the need to create job opportunities for citizens capable of working but forced without work to beg. For those citizens physically or mentally incapable of working, a strengthened network of hospitals should address their needs. In all cases, the magistrates should endeavor to raise consciousness by educating citizens who were committed to eliminating the structural evil of poverty.

Beyond poor relief, Vives and Ignatius shared other concerns: persecution by inquisitors who saw heresy in what they could not understand, polarization of Spanish Catholic society over the Inquisition's zealotry, tolerance and concord as healthy Erasmian alternatives, and the appropriateness of the best Latin literature for the moral education of adolescents. Near the end of Ignatius's life, books written by Erasmus, Vives, and the ancient comic dramatist Terence came under scrutiny and were censored by church authorities.[19] Though Ignatius approved restricting access to those books, he never forbade their consultation. More important, he incorporated social reforms pressed by Vives in his own apostolic program, he required a humanist education for the Jesuits and students in Jesuit schools, and he shared with Erasmus and Vives an appreciation for the elegance of Terence's comic verse but a need for caution when teaching his plays to young boys. With all three, to paraphrase Terence, Ignatius shared a concern for everything about the human experience. Jesuit schools daily required hours of study of Latin and Greek while offering an optional hour of catechism on Saturday mornings after the regular lessons. The Roman College of the Jesuits in Rome had one of the largest collections of printed works by Erasmus, including his edition of Terence, because Jesuits used the books to teach Latin grammar and research the church fathers.[20]

Once Ignatius had chosen to complete his education in order to help souls, he likely had an easier time choosing schooling as an apostolate. Nonetheless, the decision constitutes proof of Ignatius's flexibility, discernment, and openness to change. In 1541, he had forbidden Jesuit houses from accepting non-Jesuits among the students in courses offered there, but by 1545 he had given permission to the Society to teach non-Jesuits.[21] By the 1540s, when Jesuits encountered the movement of Juan de Ávila in Granada, they felt an immediate kinship with a group that engaged in pastoral preaching, hospital service, and schooling from the elementary to advanced levels. The quality of Ignatius's discernment on schooling is confirmed in another way. Those most opposed to the idea were ascetic Jesuits like Alfonso Rodriquez (1526–1616), novice master and spiritual writer who claimed that education was not an appropriate ministry for a religious order like the Society of Jesus. That organization, in Rodriguez's mind, should be dedicated to nourishing the spiritual growth of its own members, not to teaching others.[22] Aware of the novelty of founding a religious order engaged in the world, Ignatius fought hard to defend the innovative character of the order and ensure a training that equipped its members for that engagement. Likewise, he invited all those who entered for wrong and selfish reasons of pursuing individual perfection to grow past that vainglorious motive, as he had, and help others.[23]

That same flexibility and openness are hallmarks of the rhetorical quality of Ignatius's spirituality in general. Ignatius designed the key meditations of the second week of the *Spiritual Exercises*—the Kingdom, the Two Standards, the Three Types of Humility—as appeals to ethical values that he found in the life of Jesus and that he presumed would be appealing to others. The meditations should help one make a good choice, in keeping with the inspiration of God's Spirit, but they do not force the choice. Those meditations are set within a broader series of contemplations that allow the exercitant to make his own pilgrimage to Jerusalem, all the way to the Ascension. Ignatius started from the data of the Gospels and endowed the events narrated there with a sense of concreteness and drama. Nonetheless, the contemplations that he prescribed supply only the outlines of the story and leave much room for coloring by each individual's imagination. Still, he elicits a vividness comparable to the narrative paintings of events from the life of Christ that proliferated during the Renaissance.[24] And that vividness contrasts to the opacity of Ignatius's description of his visions at the Cardoner River. That is well illustrated in the case of the Incarnation. As a mystical vision, Ignatius described the Incarnation as "seeing a vague white body without distinct limbs." As a contemplative exercise, Ignatius portrayed the Incarnation as a great act of solidarity by the Trinity with human beings in need.

Centrality of the Incarnation

It was crucial to Ignatius and to Renaissance theologians affected by humanism that believers appreciate the significance of the Incarnation. In simplest terms, there can be no *Acta* or Ignatian spirituality without the Incarnation: it is the essential and indispensable belief for both. That means, of course, that Ignatian spirituality is Christian. If the Word did not become flesh, then there would be no pilgrimage to Jerusalem.[25] During his own pilgrimage, Ignatius had to mature beyond the external superficiality of a magical piety focused on the direction in which the Lord's feet were pointing to reach the interior freedom awakened by the gift of the Lord's Spirit. He posed the question to himself that the two men in white robes posed to the apostles at the Ascension: Why am I staring up to heaven? The question jolted the disciples back to an incarnational faith where the world and the flesh constitute the principal locus of revelation and ministry. Ignatius came to appreciate the depths of the Lord's own human experience as Jesus enlisted servants for a kingdom already breaking in and educated his disciples along the way, and Ignatius came to embrace a love capable of finding God in all material things.

If there were no belief in an Incarnation, there would be no need to travel to any part of the world. Without the Incarnation, the contemplations of the *Spiritual Exercises* become ridiculous; their meaning is predicated on flesh, on seeing and feeling and touching through the powers of imagination. Because Jesus was fully human, his experience was relevant to that of all human beings. Ignatius exploited the belief in the Incarnation to have those making the *Exercises* imaginatively attend the birth of Christ, eat with Christ, and journey to Jerusalem with Christ. It follows that the five senses were crucial to Ignatius's catechism lessons. For him, the most powerful sense was sight. He shared that conviction about sight with his Renaissance world.

Renaissance culture explored the mystery of the Incarnation in the culture's ritual time, its preaching, its art, its drama, and its theology.[26] The cities of Florence and Pisa began their calendar year on the feast of the Annunciation, and the Venetians believed that their city had been founded on that feast day, 25 March, in the year 421. The way in which Renaissance preachers treated the Annunciation likely assisted viewers in interpreting the various ways that artists depicted the scene. By examining Luke's account carefully, those preachers identified five successive moments in Mary's reaction to the news that God would become flesh in her womb. She went from disturbed to reflective, to questioning, to submissive to God's will, and finally to experiencing consolation as her reward. Etiquette of the time and common sense identified physical gestures that betrayed those inner feelings. Artists who represented the Annunciation had to choose a particular moment and then show Mary making the appropriate gesture for that moment. For example, if Mary crossed her arms over her heart, she was submitting to the divine will. Having heard a sermon on the five moments, viewers could then apply the lessons they had learned. All of those factors combined to invite believers to enter more deeply into the mystery portrayed. From his bedroom in Azpeitia to the churches of Italy, Ignatius viewed representations of the Incarnation, which were hugely popular during the Renaissance. To emphasize that Jesus had truly become flesh, Renaissance artists depicted him as a naked child unashamed of his genitals.[27]

Laudesi companies in Florence annually sponsored a theatrical production of the Annunciation. In the weeks after Easter, those companies staged multiple Lukan dramas (the Annunciation, the Ascension, and Pentecost), and they presented the events on elaborate sets that united heaven and earth in joy. The best artists of the day, Brunelleschi and Masolino, contributed to the design of the sets, and the most powerful politicians of the day, the Medici, financed the production, often as members of the sponsoring company. Renaissance theology of the Incarnation tied that mystery to the pervasive theme of the era, the dignity of the human person. If God's creation of human beings in God's own image and likeness endowed all human persons with dignity, God's coming among humans in the flesh exponentially increased that dignity. Trained in the techniques of classical rhetoric, preachers of the day used classicizing panegyric to celebrate God's great, beneficial deed.

The emphasis in much Renaissance theology, therefore, did not fall on a reparational Christology, Christ's redemptive sacrifice on the cross for sin. As depicted in the events from Jesus's life frescoed on the walls of the Sistine Chapel, the crucifixion was present but consigned to the background. The emphasis in much Renaissance theology fell on an incarnational Christology, Christ restoring humanity to greater dignity than before the Fall by becoming flesh. The decision to have the Word become flesh realized the plan that Ignatius imagined the Trinity devising together: the Godhead helped humans in need.[28] In itself, the Incarnation accomplished profound transformation, restoring harmony to the universe, reconciling human beings to God, and offering humans the power to effect meaningful change in their world. An incarnational theology affirmed the value of engagement in the world and validated a measure of fulfillment for humans here and now.

Unlike monastic or anchoritic spirituality, Ignatian spirituality was not premised on the need to flee the world or reject secular culture. Nor was the spirituality of Luke's Gospel and Acts. The Lukan writings tell a world-affirming story, where Jesus is understood in terms of what he did and apostles act on a public stage to foster the creation of a reconstituted Israel, a people who testify to their commitment to justice in word and deed. So abundant is the grace showered on the community that, by sharing material resources, no member need any longer be in need. Luke testified to his affirmation of the world by casting his message of a liberation already under way in a rhetorical prose reflective of refined classical standards.[29] For medieval monasticism, by contrast, everything beyond the perimeter of the monastery constituted the "world" in a negative sense: to embrace

holiness, monks left that world and rejected its values. Monasteries became ideal cities, self-contained and insulated. Renaissance humanism
inverted that belief: in Thomas More's *Utopia*, the cities became ideal
monasteries, regulated by a daily order and humanized by sharing all resources in common.[30]

Ignatius used the spiritual geography of his travels to underline his
embrace of ministries like those of Jesus in Luke's Gospel and the apostles
in Luke's Acts. He began the journey in the pastoral wilds of Aránzazu,
moved to the monastery of Montserrat, and spent time as a hermit at
Manresa. None of those places satisfied his discernment as to what should
be done. So he next made a pilgrimage to the Jerusalem of Jesus, stepped
out of the Lord's footprints, embraced an education at various urban universities, and finished his journey in the city that symbolized universal
ministry, Rome. In Rome he also cast off the ambivalence of the friars
about living within the city's walls, establishing his headquarters in the
heart of downtown Rome at Our Lady of the Way.[31] The depth of Ignatius's commitment to urban ministries is proven in his embrace of ministry to prostitutes. That ministry moved from repentance and change of
heart to education and reincorporation in the world, whether by acquisi-
tion of life skills or by funding a dowry. Ignatius did not found a House of
Mary Magdalene; he founded a House of Martha. Ignatius did not focus
on the desexualized saint, aged, covered only by her own long hair, and
driven to do penance by living as a hermit; he focused on a transformed
individual who might contribute to the common good of the urban community. Ignatius did not use the ministry in a vainglorious way to advertise
his patronizing assistance to lost women.[32] Instead he focused on interior
transformation and social benefits for all involved. In terms of numbers, the
network of Jesuit houses for prostitutes was exceeded only by the network
of Jesuit schools and orphanages. They all establish that Ignatius was no
longer staring up to heaven.

Rebirth of Apostolic Times

Ignatius was engaged with his world, particularly the urban world, where,
in ancient conceptualization, human beings developed their natural
speaking ability in order to become constructive citizens. Of the approximately 160 uses of the term *polis* in the New Testament, fully half occur

in Luke's writings. In keeping with rhetorical pedagogy, Luke used the term to represent the place (*topos*) of ministry.[33] That engagement with cities led Ignatius to embrace a fundamental cultural imperative of his day, the desire for a rebirth of the greatness of antiquity. Ignatius especially promoted a rebirth of the greatness of the apostolic age of Christianity, as that age was portrayed in the Acts of the Apostles. Scattered through the narrative of the *Acta*, particularly its second half, are resonances of the activities of Luke's apostles and the charismatic days of Acts when the Spirit reconstitutes God's people in a universal way. In Paris, Ignatius experienced consolation when he imagined his professor as Christ and his fellow students as the various apostles. He would give an individual student the name of Peter, John, and so on, until all twelve apostles' names were used.[34] Following Acts consciously, Ignatius decided to use the familiar form of address with all persons, no matter what their social status. He could likewise find inspiration in Acts for his conviction that it was essential for Jesuits to hold all things in common; Jesuits would not, therefore, accept benefices. He embraced ministry as the defining quality of apostolic religious life, and he embraced the specific ministries that are celebrated in Acts: journeying to evangelize, preaching repentance for the forgiveness of sins, gathering frequently for a Eucharistic meal, and healing the sick. Jesuits evangelized in the streets and public squares of European cities, and they built urban communities among the indigenous peoples of the Americas to lead those peoples to a civilized faith and a charitable polity.[35]

Early friends and enemies of the Jesuits alike recognized that effort to foster a rebirth in the sixteenth century of the apostolic minister of the first century. Friends like the Barnabites in Milan and the followers of Juan de Ávila in Granada explicitly acknowledged the effort, as did enemies, such as the unnamed Dominican at San Esteban in Salamanca, the Dominican Melchor Cano, and Gian Pietro Carafa. Ignatius emphasized that he was harassed and persecuted because of the novel charism of ministering in university cities. Like the wider world of Renaissance culture, Ignatius believed that one need not withdraw from engagement in the world to become holy. Like the apostles in Acts, Ignatius and his companions tried to achieve holiness by focusing on charitable ministries. To achieve that goal, they had to abandon common recitation of the Liturgy of the Hours. For apostolic religious, more prayer does not necessarily mean a holier life. Ignatius eventually realized that sleep and study were higher priorities than prayer. Ignatius saw his mystical visions as God's gift to him personally. He saw his benefits from study as God's gift to the order. Jesuits needed to be learned and engaged with culture, and they prayed less than other religious in order to attain those goals. That was what should be done.

As Adriano Prosperi has observed, the Jesuit effort to effect a rebirth of the apostolic minister led to something new and modern.[36] The apostolic manner of evangelizing was rhetorical: in sharing a gift, apostles engaged in gentle persuasion, accommodated their message to the language and culture of their audience, and focused on integrity as the crucial mode of persuasion. In the Middle Ages, evangelizing had acquired a more philosophical and juridical tone. Focusing on conformity and social control, the church resorted to compulsion, even through violent means, and exploited the coercive power of the confessional and the Inquisitions. In the *Acta*, near the end of his life, Ignatius expressed his perplexity about the value of Inquisitions, especially in terms of progress. Ignatius grew to appreciate evangelizing in a rhetorical manner. He insisted on training Jesuits in classical rhetoric because ancient theorists had conceptualized the effective modes of persuasion, and Jesuits sought to persuade their listeners to repentance and conversion.

In Acts, the apostles on Pentecost successfully communicated to Jews gathered in Jerusalem from all parts of the world and speaking different languages. From language as a factor of division among proud humans at the Tower of Babel, language became a ground for unity in a reconstituted Israel at the Temple in Jerusalem. When preparing for his own ministry, Ignatius began with "letters" (*litterae*), by which he meant Latin grammar. Latin was already a dead language, though still an essential element in priestly training. With the humanist emphasis on letters, Latin likewise became constitutive of elite culture. Nonetheless, by insisting that the Jesuits study letters, Ignatius also made the Jesuit program of education inherently cross-cultural. Students were challenged to enter, by the door of a language no longer spoken, the foreign culture of ancient Rome. Shedding an emphasis on social control, Ignatius gained a sense of the richness of the gift of the Spirit and the human conscience. The Spirit transformed human hearts and inspired harmony among believers.

The subsequent history of Luis Gonçalves da Câmara illustrates the difficulty of the ideal of the apostolic preacher and the influence of vainglory as a leading fault of human character. For apostolic religious, narcissism is an especially dangerous psychological affliction. Narcissistic persons are so captivated by their own beauty that they cease to move along the way. Ignatius dictated his *Acta* because he recognized in Gonçalves da Câmara that same thirst for self-promotion that often drove Ignatius. After receiving Ignatius's narration firsthand and dictating it to fellow Jesuit secretaries, Gonçalves da Câmara eventually returned to Portugal, where he found his way into a ministry at court that included serving as confessor to the *infante* Sebastian (1554–78).

When Alessandro Valignano (1539–1606) brought a group of Jesuits to Portugal to prepare them for ministry in Asia, Gonçalves da Câmara worked with the provincial, Jorge Serrão (1528–90), and a third influential Jesuit, Leão Henriques (ca. 1524–89), to obstruct Valignano at every turn. In contrast to Valignano's criterion of a "gentle manner" in educating young Jesuits, Gonçalves da Câmara urged a rigorous, even violent manner. Against Valignano's desire to keep all of those Jesuits together for training, Gonçalves da Câmara tried to separate them and send some to missions in the New World. Moreover, he tried to bar from missionary activity all Iberian Jesuits with Jewish ancestry. In contrast to Valignano's effort to protect the independence of the Asian mission, Gonçalves da Câmara tried to maintain the custom of examining all mail that arrived from that part of the world. The superior-general, Everard Mercurian (1514–80), backed Valignano in all of those disputes.

Gonçalves da Câmara showed no less rigor in advocating a change in the Society's willingness to accept New Christians.[37] When Jesuits of the Portuguese Province led the way in pushing for that change, they cited as their authority Gonçalves da Câmara, who had wrongly claimed that Ignatius wished to keep Christians of Jewish descent out of the Society. Gonçalves da Câmara proved himself willing to command, well beyond his canonical status, but, as Ignatius had intuited, he proved himself less willing to obey.

In matters of purity of blood (*limpieza de sangre*), the Morisco Jesuit Ignacio de Las Casas (1550–1608) proved a more lucid guide. Critical of any policy of forced conversions in general, Las Casas decried the bad example thereby given by spiritual authorities, political rulers, and Old Christians as a body. He specifically called for the repeal of racial laws, ghettoes, and the compulsion exercised by the Inquisition through its

"Edicts of Grace." For a limited period of time, such an edict allowed Moriscos to confess privately to sins of heresy and receive absolution for them. However, during their confession, penitent Moriscos also had to denounce their accomplices, including family members and close friends. Las Casas felt that the church should jettison those coercive, sinful measures and focus on training the clergy in Arabic. Ignatius would concur, and he would find, in the tolerant advocacy of Las Casas, a confirmation for the wisdom of his policy of accepting New Christians into the order. It was one concrete step toward Luke's universal community of believers.

The universalism of ministry as portrayed in Luke's writings helped inspire the first Jesuits to undertake a bold journey. Nadal urged Jesuits of every generation to embrace the whole world as their home and to bring help to souls wherever and whenever they are in need. Ignatius candidly acknowledged the costs of discipleship because he had experienced them. By advocating a universal mission and generous service, Luke taught believers that they must travel with the Lord all the way to Jerusalem. One could expect problems from the zealous, particularly zealous religious authorities. The day that Ignatius arrived in Rome, he found the windows closed. His response, however, was not to become a zealot himself. Even the mule had enough sense to lead Ignatius away from murdering the Moor, no matter whether he was a believing Muslim (*Mudéjar*) or perhaps even a Christian convert (*Morisco*).

Charity and Solidarity

Ignatius also candidly acknowledged the spiritual risks in such a choice. To minister in the world could lead apostolic religious to practice vainglory. After all, they were ministering in a context for all to see. Vainglory was embodied in the climactic temptation in Luke's account of Jesus's encounter with the devil, and vainglory became a more dangerous temptation as one had success in ministries. Long before Ignatius, Pope Gregory I (ca. 540–604), advocate of a servant model of the church, had left his own reflections on that dilemma.[38]

Gregory had been forced to abandon the monastery in order to minister to his city of Rome. His ministries as pope had a political dimension: he sought to defend the city from attack, conduct diplomacy by corresponding with rulers, administer the properties of the church of Rome, and feed a population swollen by a huge influx of refugees. Having learned of diaconates from the writings of John Cassian, Gregory established a network of those charity centers in the city. While so engaged, Gregory offered reflections on his spiritual experience. He found power and honor beguiling and vainglory a logical consequent of pride. His honest assessment of human nature emphasized the difficulty of acting from pure motives. One often acted both to serve God and win acclaim from fellow citizens. He prayed that he speak words in order to praise God and not to solicit praise from others. Like Cassian, Gregory felt that discernment was crucial, but Gregory placed greater emphasis on interior motivation and intention.

Ignatius saw riches, honor, and fame as beguiling; supplied rules to assist in discerning properly, not simplistically; and focused on interior transformation through the power of the Spirit. Soon after Ignatius and his companions arrived in Rome, their charitable instincts came to the fore. An especially harsh winter had led to conditions of famine in the city. When Ignatius and his companions found many homeless people begging for food on the streets, they immediately set about trying to get them off the streets and fed. The earliest formulation of Jesuit ministries, not surprisingly, described them essentially as charitable works. In the end, although faithful to what Ignatius and his companions instinctively determined that they should do, charitable works proved too concise a wording for the variety of apostolic ministries they had embraced.

In the *Acta*, Ignatius revealed a lifelong struggle against his vain personality, and he realized that he had to shed his focus on self in order to help others.[39] Charitable works comprised a key element in authentic conversion because vainglory shatters solidarity. John Chrysostom argued that nothing is more opposed to charity than vainglory.[40] It pits us against our neighbor, undermines friendships, and blinds the heart to the plight of the poor. Ignatius sought to foster a different dynamic: by embracing poverty, one no longer will treat the other as a means to enrich oneself or win acclaim.

To guide Ignatius in his evolving convictions, he had the witness of lay confraternities. In the Middle Ages, those confraternities had begun as a place for the devout elite to gather and engage in private devotions. They initially reflected an aristocratic ethos and manifested no little vainglory. Subsequently, confraternities expressed their piety in public activities, often the flashy asceticism of flagellation on city streets. In their final stage of evolution, confraternities turned to activities expressive of their civic solidarity, such as assisting the poor, maintaining bridges, caring for prisoners, and burying the dead.[41] Some of the confraternities chose to have their members provide charitable services while hooded, adopting anonymity as a remedy for vainglory, the remedy that Matthew originally supplied in his Gospel and spiritual writers frequently endorsed. Ignatius not only found inspiration in the spirituality of the confraternities, but he valued the vital contribution that they might make to charitable works. He made them collaborators in Jesuit ministries and even gave them responsibilities of leadership in key ministries.

Another medieval institution inspired Ignatius in his dedication to charitable works. That was the hospital, where charity was a way of life and solidarity ideally unconditional. Confraternities often managed hospitals as a way to practice charity. Though the Mediterranean world of the fifteenth and sixteenth centuries witnessed a movement to build much larger civic hospitals, the classic hospital of the time had anywhere from ten to twenty beds, welcomed the poor, sick, and foundlings, and offered free lodging to indigent residents or pilgrims. In a world of widespread poverty, those little institutions claimed that they would not refuse anyone who requested treatment. And in a world where vagrants and other wanderers aroused increasing suspicion, those institutions opened their doors to house them.[42]

Sante Bortolami called attention to a short set of fifteenth-century rules to guide the husband and wife running the small hospital of San Leonino in Padua. The rules specified that they would attend to cooking, cleaning, gardening, emptying bedpans, lighting the charcoal fire in the central hearth, and adding an aromatic substance to it. While doing all of that, they would never turn anyone away.[43] The hospitals had become a place to practice all of the corporal works of mercy at once, successor to the diaconates of John Cassian and Gregory the Great. From 1525 to 1529, the workshop of Giovanni della Robbia placed a frieze with all seven of the corporal works of mercy on the entrance porch to the Ospedale del Ceppo in Pistoia.[44]

Ignatius had first experienced the depths of conversion in his heart while he was healing from his wounds. When studying or visiting his family, Ignatius preferred to live in a hospital. Ignatius and his companions chose to live in hospitals even when it meant that they could not live together. In the early years of the Society of Jesus, his companions tried to establish hospitals as part of their ministry in Germany, India, and Japan. In the years immediately after the death of Ignatius, many Jesuits living in Rome contributed to a renewal of the network of hospitals there. Instead of viewing marginal groups as dangerous sources of contagion best quarantined, the first Jesuits felt called to live and work among them.

Historians have recently debated the appropriateness of seeing a confessionalization of Christendom as a result of the Reformation.[45] That theory proposes that the differing Christian confessions of early modern Europe tried to clarify who belonged and who did not by defining their doctrine, controlling their rituals, propagandizing their own positions, and censoring the dangerous ones of their opponents. The theory has not been without its critics, particularly for its excessively top-down approach. Still, the confessions emerged with distinctive qualities. Although all Christians prize the three theological virtues as a common patrimony, major groupings within Christianity tend to emphasize one of the virtues as central to their spirituality. The mainline Protestant churches have emphasized faith, and the evangelical Protestant churches have emphasized hope. As H. Outram Evennett pointed out years ago, early modern Catholicism emphasized active charity.[46] Ignatius, through his *Acta* and his broader spirituality, contributed to that emphasis. Ignatius's *Constitutions*, a book of law, use the word *caridad* on fifty-six occasions, the word *amor* on fifty-eight occasions, and the two together in the fundamental affirmation of the book, summarizing all the legislation as "the interior law of charity (*charidad*) and love (*amor*) which the Holy Spirit writes and engraves upon hearts."[47]

Ignatius knew that charitable activities would severely limit a Jesuit's time for prayer, but he was likewise convinced that every moment spent in charitable activity pleased God no less than prayer.[48] In elaborating his proposed ministry to African slaves, Alonso de Sandoval made a verse-by-verse application of Paul's paean to charity in 1 Corinthians 13. In Sandoval's interpretation, the apostles in Acts had rhetorically moved people to believe by making the love that the Holy Spirit inspired in their hearts their principal language.[49]

As a way to praise God, Ignatius dedicated himself to helping souls and eventually gathered companions for that purpose. Because Ignatius's phrase is deceptively simple, one can underestimate its import. "Helping" implies a consistently positive approach to ministry as well as a consistently humble one. God saves, whereas ministers only help.[50] One tests for the Spirit's guidance by asking whether what one does and the way that one does it makes things better for others, fosters their progress (*provecho*). When a minister is, appropriately, helping someone else, that minister will likely experience authentic consolation in an Ignatian sense. Ignatius was convinced that the sacrament of confession will genuinely console if confessors do not cause fear in penitents but encourage them to embrace God's abundant mercy. "Souls" suggests that human beings are created in the image and likeness of God and have a special dignity among creatures. That dignity was enhanced by the Incarnation. In the *Acta*, Ignatius himself glossed "souls" as "neighbors," building a note of compassionate solidarity into the Jesuit apostolate. With Luke, Ignatius warned those in ministry not to let a sense of admiration for the quality of their own living of the Gospel blind them to the needs of others. Ignatius imagined that those who embraced his spirituality would travel to any part of the world. As they traveled, like Luke's Samaritan, they should stop along the way to assist those wounded and left for dead.

Notes

Preface

1. See, e.g., John W. O'Malley, "The Historiography of the Society of Jesus: Where Does It Stand Today?" in *The Jesuits: Cultures, Sciences, and the Arts, 1540–1773*, J. W. O'Malley, G. A. Bailey, S. J. Harris, and T. F. Kennedy, eds. (Toronto: University of Toronto Press, 1999), 3–29; and Simon Ditchfield, "Of Missions and Models: The Jesuit Enterprise (1540–1773) Reassessed in Recent Literature," *Catholic Historical Review* 93 (2007): 325–43. In general, see Ignacio Iparraguirre, *Orientaciones bibliográficas sobre San Ignacio de Loyola*, 2nd ed., Subsidia ad historiam Societatis Iesu, 1 (Roma: Institutum Historicum Societatis Iesu, 1965); Manuel Ruiz Jurado, *Orientaciones bibliográficas sobre San Ignacio de Loyola*, vol. 2, *1965–76*, Subsidia ad historiam Societatis Iesu, 8 (Roma: Institutum Historicum Societatis Iesu, 1977); vol. 3, *1977–89*, Subsidia ad historiam Societatis Iesu, 10 (Roma: Institutum Historicum Societatis Iesu, 1990); László Polgár, *Bibliographie sur l'histoire de la Compagnie de Jésus, 1901–1980*, 3 vols. (Roma: Institutum Historicum Societatis Iesu, 1981–90); and Paul Begheyn, "Bibliography on the History of the Jesuits: Publications in English, 1900–1993," *Studies in the Spirituality of Jesuits* 28, no. 1 (1996): 1–42. For recent scholarship on Catholicism in the period, see, e.g., Francesco C. Cesareo, "Review Essay: The Complex Nature of Catholicism in the Renaissance," *Renaissance Quarterly* 54 (2001): 1561–73; and Diarmaid MacCulloch, Mary Laven, and Eamon Duffy, "Recent Trends in the Study of Christianity in Sixteenth-Century Europe," *Renaissance Quarterly* 59 (2006): 706–20.

2. Noëlle Hausman, "'What Ought I to Do?' *The Pilgrim's Testament*, a Source for the Apostolic Religious Life," *Centrum Ignatianum Spiritualitatis* 20, nos. 1–2 (1990): 21–22, 25–29.

3. Marjorie O'Rourke Boyle, *Loyola's Acts: The Rhetoric of the Self*, The New Historicism: Studies in Cultural Poetics, 36 (Berkeley: University of California Press, 1997), 2–3, 17, 169–70.

4. See, e.g., Philip Endean, "Who Do You Say Ignatius Is? Jesuit Fundamentalism and Beyond," *Studies in the Spirituality of Jesuits* 19, no. 5 (1987): 12–36; and María-Paz Aspe, "Spanish Spirituality's Mid-Sixteenth-Century Change of Course," in *The Spanish Inquisition and the Inquisitorial Mind*, Angel Alcalá, ed.,

Atlantic Studies on Society in Change, 49 (Boulder, Colo.: Social Science Monographs, 1987), 421–29.

5. Louis Beirnaert, *Aux frontières de l'acte analytique: La Bible, saint Ignace, Freud, et Lacan* (Paris: Éditions du Seuil, 1987), 199–204.

6. Roland Barthes, *Sade, Fourier, Loyola*, Richard Miller, trans. (New York: Hill and Wang, 1976), 39–40; and Marjorie O'Rourke Boyle, "Angels Black and White: Loyola's Spiritual Discernment in Historical Perspective," *Theological Studies* 44 (1983): 241–53, 257. Ignatius wrote a clear script, and his autographs would benefit from paleographical study. There is presently only Carmen M. Affholder, "Saint Ignace dans son écriture," *Archivum historicum Societatis Iesu* 29 (1960): 381–98.

7. Julia Bolton Holloway, *The Pilgrim and the Book: A Study of Dante, Langland, and Chaucer*, American University Studies, Series IV: English Language and Literature, 42, rev. ed. (New York: Peter Lang, 1992), 27–47; and Bolton Holloway, "The Pilgrim in the Poem: Dante, Langland, and Chaucer," *Jerusalem: Essays on Pilgrimage and Literature*, AMS Studies in the Middle Ages, 24 (New York: AMS Press, 1998), 123–27. Until the mid-sixteenth century, the Catholic Church heavily influenced nascent theater in Spain. See, e.g., Melveena McKendrick, *Theatre in Spain, 1490–1700* (Cambridge: Cambridge University Press, 1989), 34–36.

8. Carla Rahn Phillips, *Six Galleons for the King of Spain: Imperial Defense in the Early Seventeenth Century* (Baltimore: Johns Hopkins University Press, 1986), 19–21, 47–48; and Pablo E. Pérez-Mallaína, *Spain's Men of the Sea: Daily Life on the Indies Fleets in the Sixteenth Century*, Carla Rahn Phillips, trans. (Baltimore: Johns Hopkins University Press, 2005), 191–97, 237–38.

1. The *Acta* as Privileged and New Source

1. For the criticisms of Melchor Cano, see, e.g., Constance Jones Mathers, "Early Spanish Qualms about Loyola and the Society of Jesus," *The Historian* 53 (1991): 685–87; Terence W. O'Reilly, "Melchor Cano and the Spirituality of St. Ignatius Loyola," in *Ignacio de Loyola y su tiempo: Congreso internacional de historia (9–13 Setiembre 1991)*, Juan Plazaola, ed. (Bilbao: Ediciones Mensajero, 1992), 370–78; O'Reilly, "Melchor Cano's *Censura y parecer contra el Instituto de los Padres Jesuitas*: A Transcription of the British Library Manuscript," in *From Ignatius Loyola to John of the Cross: Spirituality and Literature in Sixteenth-Century Spain*, no. 5, Variorum Collected Studies Series, 484 (London: Variorum, 1995), 1–4, 12–22; and Stefania Pastore, *Il Vangelo e la spada: L'inquisizione di Castiglia e i suoi critici (1460–1598)*, "Tribunali della fede," Temi e testi, 46 (Roma: Edizioni di Storia e Letteratura, 2003), 310. On the millennial fervor in Spain, see, e.g., John Leddy Phelan, *The Millennial Kingdom of the Franciscans in the New World*, 2nd ed.

(Berkeley: University of California Press, 1970), 5–28; and John M. McManamon, "Catholic Identity and Anti-Semitism in a Eulogy for Isabel 'the Catholic,'"
Journal of Ecumenical Studies 42 (2007): 198–200, 204–13, 215–16.

2. The text of the *Acta* is cited from the vernacular version in the *Monumenta
Ignatiana*; see *Acta Patris Ignatii*, Dionisio Fernández Zapico and Cándido de
Dalmases, with Pedro de Leturia, eds., Monumenta Historica Societatis Iesu, 66
(Roma: Institutum Historicum Societatis Iesu, 1943), 353–507. English transla-
tions include *The Autobiography of St. Ignatius Loyola with Related Documents*, John
C. Olin, ed., and Joseph F. O'Callaghan, trans. (New York: Harper & Row, 1974);
A Pilgrim's Journey: The Autobiography of Ignatius of Loyola, Joseph N. Tylenda,
trans. (Wilmington, Del.: Michael Glazier, 1985); *Ablaze with God: A Reading of
the Memoirs of Ignatius of Loyola*, Parmananda R. Divarkar, trans. (Anand, India:
Gujarat Sahitya Prakash, 1990), 23–122; "The Autobiography," in *Ignatius of Loyola:
The Spiritual Exercises and Selected Works*, George E. Ganss, ed., and Parmananda
R. Divarkar, trans., The Classics of Western Spirituality (New York: Paulist
Press, 1991), 67–111; *A Pilgrim's Testament: The Memoirs of St. Ignatius of Loyola*,
Parmananda R. Divarkar, trans., Jesuit Primary Sources in English Translation,
13 (St. Louis, Mo.: Institute of Jesuit Sources, 1995); and "Reminiscences (Au-
tobiography)," in *Personal Writings*, Philip Endean, trans. (London: Penguin,
1996), 3–64.

3. On vainglory and narcissism, see, e.g., Donald Capps, *Deadly Sins and Saving
Virtues* (Philadelphia: Fortress Press, 1987), 46–52; Capps, *The Depleted Self: Sin in
a Narcissistic Age* (Minneapolis: Augsburg Fortress Press, 1993), 11–37, 43; Marjorie
O'Rourke Boyle, *Loyola's Acts: The Rhetoric of the Self*, The New Historicism: Studies
in Cultural Poetics, 36 (Berkeley: University of California Press, 1997), 121–23,
154–55; and David A. Boruchoff, "Historiography with License: Isabel, the Catholic
Monarch, and the Kingdom of God," in *Isabel La Católica, Queen of Castile: Critical
Essays*, David A. Boruchoff, ed. (Houndmills, U.K.: Palgrave, 2003), 282 n. 69. In
general, see Lester K. Little, "Pride Goes before Avarice: Social Change and the
Vices in Latin Christendom," *American Historical Review* 76 (1971): 16–49.

4. See Nadal's "Preface" to *Acta*, 356–57 ("ut nobis illa expositio esse posset
loco testamenti et paternae institutionis," 359 ("ut nobis explices, Pater, quemad-
modum Dominus te instituerit"); and the "Preface" of Gonçalves da Câmara to
Acta, 360 ("y que esto era fundar verdaderamente la Compañía"). Nadal used
language that implied an educational value for the text (*institutionis, instituerit*).
Quintilian entitled his treatise on the education of the orator *Institutio oratoria*,
Erasmus entitled his treatise on princely education *Institutio principis Christiani*,
and the full title of the Jesuit plan of studies is *Ratio atque institutio studiorum*.
For Nadal's peculiar role as respected interpreter of Ignatius, see, e.g., John W.
O'Malley, "To Travel to Any Part of the World: Jerónimo Nadal and the Jesuit
Vocation," *Studies in the Spirituality of Jesuits* 16, no. 2 (1984): 3–5.

5. For the text of the "Preface," see *Acta*, 354–63. See further O'Rourke Boyle, *Loyola's Acts*, 5–21.

6. *Acta*, 354: "El año de 53, un viernes a la mañana, 4 de Agosto, víspera de nuestra Sra. de las Nieves, estando el Padre en el huerto junto a la casa o aposento que se dice del Duque." The feast of Our Lady of the Snows commemorated the legend that, around the year 352, the Virgin Mary appeared to a wealthy Roman and to Pope Liberius on the night between 4–5 August in order to tell them to build a church where they found snow on the ground the next morning. That church would become the basilica of Santa Maria Maggiore, eventually dedicated to Mary as "God-bearer" (*theotokos*). See Richard Krautheimer, "The Architecture of Sixtus III: A Fifth-Century Renascence?" in *Studies in Early Christian, Medieval, and Renaissance Art* (New York: New York University Press, 1969), 184, 191–92; Victor W. Turner and Edith L. B. Turner, *Image and Pilgrimage in Christian Culture: Anthropological Perspectives* (New York: Columbia University Press, 1978), 152–54, 166–68; Charles L. Stinger, *The Renaissance in Rome* (Bloomington: Indiana University Press, 1985), 34, 38, 41; and O'Rourke Boyle, *Loyola's Acts*, 55–59.

7. In the *Spiritual Exercises*, no. 43, Ignatius proposed five steps in examining one's conscience: (1) expressing gratitude to God for blessings received; (2) asking for the Spirit's inspiration to recognize sinfulness; (3) reviewing the day to that point, focusing on thoughts, then words, then deeds; (4) asking for forgiveness of sins; and (5) asking for the grace to amend one's life in the future. See Ignatius Loyola, *The Spiritual Exercises of Saint Ignatius: A Literal Translation and a Contemporary Reading*, David L. Fleming, trans. (St. Louis, Mo.: Institute of Jesuit Sources, 1978), 29–30, 63. On the fact that the narrative is not autobiography, see the comments of Françoise Durand, "La première historiographie ignatienne," in *Ignacio de Loyola y su tiempo*, 27–31; and O'Rourke Boyle, *Loyola's Acts*, 1–4.

8. Leonardo R. Silos, "Cardoner in the Life of Saint Ignatius of Loyola," *Archivum historicum Societatis Iesu* 33 (1964): 6–8.

9. The ancient Athenians circumscribed an orator's ethos to his moral believability during the speech. The Romans, by contrast, emphasized a consistency between the values that an orator advocated and the way that he lived in general. During the Italian Renaissance, the Roman sense of ethos became the primary mode of oratorical persuasion. For the classical positions, see George A. Kennedy, *Classical Rhetoric and Its Christian and Secular Tradition from Ancient to Modern Times* (Chapel Hill: University of North Carolina Press, 1980), 68, 80–81. For the Renaissance emphasis on ethos, see John M. McManamon, *Funeral Oratory and the Cultural Ideals of Italian Humanism* (Chapel Hill: University of North Carolina Press, 1989); and McManamon, "Continuity and Change in the

Ideals of Humanism: The Evidence from Florentine Funeral Oratory," in *Life and Death in Fifteenth-Century Florence*, Marcel Tetel, Ronald G. Witt, and Rona Goffen, eds. (Durham, N.C.: Duke University Press, 1989), 68–87.

10. For the possible loss of this early material, see the comments of Fernández Zapico and de Dalmases, *Acta*, 330–31; Juan Manuel Cacho Blecua, "Del gentilhombre mundano al caballero 'a lo divino': Los ideales caballerescos de Ignacio de Loyola," in *Ignacio de Loyola y su tiempo*, 129–35; and John W. O'Malley, *The First Jesuits* (Cambridge, Mass.: Harvard University Press, 1993), 8, 23. On adolescence in the Renaissance, see, e.g., John M. McManamon, *Pierpaolo Vergerio the Elder (ca. 1369–1444): The Humanist as Orator*, Medieval & Renaissance Texts & Studies, 163 (Tempe, Ariz.: Medieval & Renaissance Texts & Studies, 1996), 18–29, 53–54, 94, 172–73; and O'Rourke Boyle, *Loyola's Acts*, 22–24. For Rubio's testimony, see Fidel Fita, "Los tres procesos de S. Ignacio de Loyola en Alcalá de Henares," *Boletín de la Real Academia de la Historia* 33 (1898): 431–33.

11. *Acta*, 363: "Ego, ut vultum eius intuerer, paululum semper appropinquabam, dicente mihi Patre, 'Observa regulam.' " The passage from Gonçalves da Câmara is found only in the Latin translation.

12. *Acta*, 358: "y me empezó a decir toda su vida, y las travesuras de mancebo clara y distintamente. . . . El modo que el Padre tiene de narrar es el que suele en todas las cosas, que es con tanta claridad." See further O'Rourke Boyle, *Loyola's Acts*, 5–11.

13. See Ignacio Echarte, ed., *Concordancia Ignaciana / An Ignatian Concordance* (Bilbao: Ediciones Mensajero, in collaboration with the Institute of Jesuit Sources, St. Louis, Mo., 1996), s.v. *chiaro, claridad, claro* (151, 157–58) [*Praefatio*, 1, 2, 3; *Acta*, 1, 10, 19, 23 (twice), 25, 27, 29, 30, 31, 32, 64, 96, 98].

14. On the role of memory and the mind's eye in medieval composition, see, e.g., Mary Carruthers, *The Book of Memory: A Study of Memory in Medieval Culture*, 2nd ed., Cambridge Studies in Medieval Literature, 70 (Cambridge: Cambridge University Press, 2008), 31–32, 137–43. Ignatius's lifelong practice of meditative prayer would hone those skills. Cf. Stephen Daniels, "Place and the Geographical Imagination," *Geography* 77 (1992): 320–21.

15. *Acta*, 504: "la somma della quale era in mostrare la intentione et simplicità con che havea narrate queste cose, dicendo che era ben certo che non narrava niente di più; et che havea fatte molte offese a nostro Signore dipoi che lo havea cominciato a servire; ma che mai non haveva havuto consenso di peccato mortale."

16. O'Malley, *First Jesuits*, 65, citing an exhortation that Nadal gave at Cologne in 1567. On the step-by-step birth of the text of the *Acta*, see the comments of Fernández Zapico and de Dalmases, *Acta*, 324–41. See further O'Malley, *First Jesuits*, 8–9.

17. O'Malley, *First Jesuits*, 31–32, 66, 330–35, 366–68.

18. Jerónimo Nadal, *Epistolae P. Hieronymi Nadal Societatis Iesu ab anno 1546 ad 1577*, vol. 3, Monumenta Historica Societatis Iesu, 21 (Madrid: Augustinus Avril, 1902), 365, 377, 423–24, 489–90, 505, 518, 534, 538–40. In general, see Philippe Lécrivain, "Ignace de Loyola, un réformateur? Une lecture historique des 'Règles pour avoir le vrai sens de l'Église,'" *Christus* 37, no. 147 (July 1990): 348–52; Terence W. O'Reilly, "Ignatius of Loyola and the Counter-Reformation: The Hagiographic Tradition," *Heythrop Journal* 31 (1990): 439–44, 446–48; Durand, "La première historiographie ignatienne," 23, 33, 35; Pierre-Antoine Fabre, "Ignace de Loyola et Jérôme Nadal: Paternité et filiation chez les premiers jésuites," in *Ignacio de Loyola y su tiempo*, 619–20; Jos E. Vercruysse, "L'historiographie ignatienne aux XVI–XVIII siècles," in *Ignacio de Loyola y su tiempo*, 37–39; and Gloria Guidotti, "Dal 'patto autobiografico' del Loyola alla sua biografia," *Cuadernos de Filología Italiana* 7, número extraordinario, (2000): 267–82, http://www.ucm.es/BUCM/revistas/fll/11339527/articulos/CFIT0000230267A.PDF. Jean Pien acknowledged that he was attempting to remove the *Acta* from the darkness by which it was hidden and return it to the light. For similar efforts to normalize the legacy of Francis of Assisi, or the "Francis question," see Giovanni Miccoli, *Francesco d'Assisi: Realtà e memoria di un'esperienza cristiana* (Torino: Einaudi, 1991).

19. Fabre, "Ignace de Loyola et Jérôme Nadal," 620–30.

20. See, e.g., Mark Rotsaert, "Les premiers contacts de saint Ignace avec l'érasmisme espagnol," *Revue d'histoire de la spiritualité* 49 (1973): 452–60; Terence W. O'Reilly, "Erasmus, Ignatius Loyola, and Orthodoxy," *Journal of Theological Studies*, n.s., 30 (1979): 115–19; Miguel Battlori, "El mito contrarreformista de San Ignacio anti-Lutero," in *Ignacio de Loyola, Magister Artium en París 1528–1535*, Julio Caro Baroja and Antonio Beristain, eds. (San Sebastián: Kutxa, 1991), 87–91; Colin Martin and Geoffrey Parker, *The Spanish Armada*, rev. ed. (Manchester: Mandolin, 1999), 130, 252; Jodi Bilinkoff, "The Many 'Lives' of Pedro de Ribadeneyra," *Renaissance Quarterly* 52 (1999): 182–85; and David Ragazzoni, "Ignazio lettore 'mancato' dell'*Enchiridion*: Possibili reminiscenze erasmiane negli *Esercizi spirituali*?" *Rinascimento*, n.s., 46 (2006): 373–90. For the reclericalization of Catholic ministries from the 1530s on, see esp. Anne Jacobson Schutte, "Periodization of Sixteenth-Century Italian Religious History: The Post-Cantimori Paradigm Shift," *Journal of Modern History* 61 (1989): 275–79.

2. The *Acta* as Mirror of Vainglory

1. See, e.g., the novel by José Luis Urrutia, *Ignacio: Los años de la espada* (Tafalla: Editorial Txalaparta, 2005), 233, where Ignatius, when told that he risks

being killed in a foolhardy defense of the citadel, responds: "Dadme una muerte gloriosa, señor de Asparrot, y no una vida indigna."

2. William W. Meissner, *Ignatius of Loyola: The Psychology of a Saint* (New Haven, Conn.: Yale University Press, 1992), 55. For the wounding at Pamplona and convalescence at Loyola, see *Acta Patris Ignatii*, Dionisio Fernández Zapico and Cándido de Dalmases, with Pedro de Leturia, eds., Monumenta Historica Societatis Iesu, 66 (Roma: Institutum Historicum Societatis Iesu, 1943), 364–79; and Marjorie O'Rourke Boyle, *Loyola's Acts: The Rhetoric of the Self*, The New Historicism: Studies in Cultural Poetics, 36 (Berkeley: University of California Press, 1997), 22–52. See further John W. O'Malley, *The First Jesuits* (Cambridge, Mass.: Harvard University Press, 1993), 23–24, 264–71 (Jesuits, Catholic piety, and the veneration of saints). Fernández Zapico and de Dalmases, *Acta*, 366 n. 7, acknowledge that the text is ambiguous when referring to the persons who carried Ignatius home ("Neque e textu Hispano, nec e versione Latina Coudreti constat clare a quibus Ignatius delatus sit in patriam"). Cándido de Dalmases, *Ignatius of Loyola, Founder of the Jesuits: His Life and Work*, Jerome Aixalá, trans., Modern Scholarly Studies about the Jesuits in English Translations, 6 (St. Louis, Mo.: Institute of Jesuit Sources, 1985), 27, notes that Ignatius favored the verb *señalarse* (to distinguish oneself) and used it in the meditation on the Kingdoms of Christ and Satan in the *Spiritual Exercises*.

3. For the scriptural teaching on vanity in general, see Pierre Miquel, "Gloire (Vaine gloire)," in *Dictionnaire de Spiritualité*, vol. 6, *Gabriel–Guzman* (Paris: Beauchesne, 1967), 495; and Albrecht Oepke, "*kenos, kenoō, kenodoxos, kenodoxia*," in *Theological Dictionary of the New Testament*, Gerhard Kittel and Gerhard Friedrich, eds., and Geoffrey W. Bromiley, trans. (Grand Rapids, Mich.: Eerdmans, 1964–76), 3:659–62. For Qoheleth, see esp. Roland E. Murphy, *The Tree of Life: An Exploration of Biblical Wisdom Literature*, The Anchor Bible Reference Library (New York: Doubleday, 1990), 53–54, 57–60; and cf. Dominique Bertrand, "Ignace de Loyola et la politique," in *Ignacio de Loyola y su tiempo: Congreso internacional de historia (9–13 Setiembre 1991)*, Juan Plazaola, ed. (Bilbao: Ediciones Mensajero, 1992), 705–6, 715–16.

4. *Ep.* 113[19.4].32: "Qui virtutem suam publicari vult non virtuti laborat, sed gloriae." The translation is that of Benedict T. Viviano, "The Gospel According to Matthew," in *The New Jerome Biblical Commentary*, Raymond E. Brown, Joseph A. Fitzmyer, and Roland E. Murphy, eds. (Englewood Cliffs, N.J.: Prentice Hall, 1990), 644.

5. For the seminal contribution of Evagrius, see, e.g., Columba Stewart, "Evagrius Ponticus and the 'Eight Generic *Logismoi*,'" in *In the Garden of Evil: The Vices and Culture in the Middle Ages*, Richard Newhauser, ed., Papers in Mediaeval Studies, 18 (Toronto: Pontifical Institute of Mediaeval Studies, 2005), 30,

32–33. For eastern Christian spiritual writing on vainglory in general, see Miquel, "Gloire (Vaine gloire)," *Dictionnaire de Spiritualité*, 6:494–502. In the West, Jean Gerson also tied vainglory closely to pride; see M. W. F. Stone, "'*Initium omnis peccati est superbia*': Jean Gerson's Analysis of Pride in His Mystical Theology, Pastoral Thought, and Hamartiology," in *In the Garden of Evil*, 316.

6. Chrysostom, *Homilia XXXV in 1 Cor. 14*, in *Patrologia graeca*, J.-P. Migne, ed. (Paris: apud J.-P. Migne editorem, 1862), 61:295–306; and *De inani gloria et de liberis educandis*, Anne-Marie Malingrey, ed. and trans., Sources chrétiennes, 188 (Paris: Éditions du Cerf, 1972). See, e.g., Francis Leduc, "La thème de la vaine gloire chez saint Jean Chrysostome," *Proche-orient chrétien* 19 (1969): 3–32; and Blake Leyerle, *Theatrical Shows and Ascetic Lives: John Chrysostom's Attack on Spiritual Marriage* (Berkeley: University of California Press, 2001), 4–5, 48–54, 62–65.

7. See, e.g., Peter Brown, *The Body and Society: Men, Women, and Sexual Renunciation in Early Christianity* (New York: Columbia University Press, 1988), 238–39; and John Chryssavgis, *John Climacus: From the Egyptian Desert to the Sinaite Mountain* (Aldershot, U.K.: Ashgate, 2004), 29, 42–44, 131–63, 171, 183–87, 213–14.

8. For the triple source of disordered passions, see esp. Donald R. Howard, *The Three Temptations: Medieval Man in Search of the World* (Princeton, N.J.: Princeton University Press, 1966), 43–75. For the language of deadly sins, see, e.g., Morton W. Bloomfield, *The Seven Deadly Sins: An Introduction to the History of a Religious Concept, with Special Reference to Medieval English Literature* (East Lansing: Michigan State University Press, 1952), 44–104.

9. See, e.g., Heidi J. Hornik and Mikeal C. Parsons, *Illuminating Luke*, vol. 2, *The Public Ministry of Christ in Italian Renaissance and Baroque Painting* (Harrisburg, Penn.: T&T Clark International, 2005), 139–41.

10. Jean Kirchmeyer, "Gloire (Vaine gloire): Littérature occidentale," in *Dictionnaire de Spiritualité*, 6:502–5.

11. John B. Morrall, *Gerson and the Great Schism* (Manchester, U.K.: Manchester University Press, 1960), 17–18; and D. Catherine Brown, *Pastor and Laity in the Theology of Jean Gerson* (Cambridge: Cambridge University Press, 1987), 93–94, 128–29.

12. John Cassian, *Cassiani Opera: Collationes XXIIII*, Michael Petschenig and Gottfried Kreuz, eds., Corpus Scriptorum Ecclesiasticorum Latinorum, 13 (Vienna: Verlag der Österreichischen Akademie der Wissenschaften, 2004); Cassian, *Cassiani Opera: De institutis coenobiorum, De incarnatione contra Nestorium*, Michael Petschenig and Gottfried Kreuz, eds., Corpus Scriptorum Ecclesiasticorum Latinorum, 17 (Vienna: Verlag der Österreichischen Akademie der Wissenschaften, 2004). English translations of Cassian's principal works may be found in "The Works of John Cassian," in *Nicene and Post-Nicene Fathers*, 2nd ser., Edgar C. S. Gibson, trans. (New York: Christian Literature Company, 1894; repr. Peabody,

Mass.: Hendrickson, 1994), 11:161–621; *Conferences*, Colm Luibhéid, trans., and Owen Chadwick, intro., The Classics of Western Spirituality (Mahwah, N.J.: Paulist Press, 1985); *The Conferences*, Boniface Ramsey, trans., Ancient Christian Writers, 57 (Mahwah, N.J.: Paulist Press, 1997); *The Monastic Institutes*, Consisting of *On the Training of a Monk* and *The Eight Deadly Sins in Twelve Books*, Jerome Bertram, trans. (London: Saint Austin Press, 1999); and *The Institutes*, Boniface Ramsey, trans., Ancient Christian Writers, 58 (Mahwah, N.J.: Newman Press, 2000). In general, see Philip Rousseau, *Ascetics, Authority, and the Church in the Age of Jerome and Cassian* (Oxford: Oxford University Press, 1978), 169–239; Columba Stewart, *Cassian the Monk*, Oxford Studies in Historical Theology (Oxford: Oxford University Press, 1998), 3–84; and Steven D. Driver, *John Cassian and the Reading of Egyptian Monastic Culture*, Medieval History and Culture, 8 (New York: Routledge, 2002). On Cassian's notion of "discretion," see Rousseau, *Ascetics, Authority, and the Church*, 192–93. For discernment, Ignatius used the Castilian term *discreción*. Cassian's principal treatment of vainglory occurs in book 11 of his *De institutis coenobiorum* (*On the Training for Monks*).

13. *Conferences*, Colm Luibhéid, trans., 64–65.

14. See, e.g., Stewart, *Cassian the Monk*, 66.

15. O'Malley, *First Jesuits*, 270.

16. Juan Manuel Cacho Blecua, "Del gentilhombre mundano al caballero 'a lo divino': Los ideales caballerescos de Ignacio de Loyola," in *Ignacio de Loyola y su tiempo*, 143–46; Georg Eickhoff, "Claraval, Digulleville, Loyola: La alegoría caballeresca de *El peregrino de la vida humana* en los noviciados monástico y jesuítico," in *Ignacio de Loyola y su tiempo*, 874–76; and O'Malley, *First Jesuits*, 241–42, 358. In general, see Dominique Bertrand, *La politique de saint Ignace de Loyola: L'analyse sociale* (Paris: Les Éditions du Cerf, 1985), 189–96.

17. Rebecca Housel, "*Monty Python and the Holy Grail*: Philosophy, Gender, and Society," in *Monty Python and Philosophy: Nudge Nudge, Think Think!*, Gary L. Hardcastle and George A. Reisch, eds., Popular Culture and Philosophy, 19 (Peru, Ill.: Open Court Publishing, 2006), 86–87.

18. O'Rourke Boyle, *Loyola's Acts*, 38–39, 155.

19. James K. Farge, "The University of Paris in the Time of Ignatius of Loyola," in *Ignacio de Loyola y su tiempo*, 225; and Philippe Lécrivain, *Paris au temps d'Ignace de Loyola (1528–1535)* (Paris: Éditions facultés jésuites de Paris, 2006), 123–26.

20. For the journey from Loyola to Montserrat, see *Acta*, 380–89; and O'Rourke Boyle, *Loyola's Acts*, 53–67. See further O'Malley, *First Jesuits*, 24–25, 74–79 (ministry to women and indigenous peoples), 111–14 (ministry of spiritual conversation), 136–52 (confession and casuistry), 159–61 (Jesuits and music), 188–90 (Jesuits and New Christians), and 348 (Jesuits and chastity). On the episode with the Moor, see also Cacho Blecua, "Del gentilhombre mundano," 146–49; and Meissner, *Ignatius of Loyola: The Psychology of a Saint*, 60–65.

21. James Brodrick, *The Origin of the Jesuits* (London: Longmans, Green, 1940; repr. Chicago: Loyola University Press, 1986), 106; and O'Malley, *First Jesuits*, 350. While traveling for Ignatius, Nadal relaxed the prohibition and said that the provincials could use mules on a temporary basis and that some colleges could own them. Nadal admitted that, when traveling for Ignatius, he had experienced scruples for buying, selling, and trading mules.

22. Pedro de Leturia, "Aspetti francescani in Sant'Ignazio di Loyola," in *Estudios Ignacianos*, Ignacio Iparraguirre, ed., Bibliotheca Instituti Historici Societatis Iesu, 10–11 (Roma: Institutum Historicum Societatis Iesu, 1957), 2:420–21; Victor W. Turner and Edith L. B. Turner, *Image and Pilgrimage in Christian Culture: Anthropological Perspectives* (New York: Columbia University Press, 1978), 41–42; William A. Christian, Jr., *Apparitions in Late Medieval and Renaissance Spain* (Princeton, N.J.: Princeton University Press, 1981), 10–26; and O'Rourke Boyle, *Loyola's Acts*, 54–55.

23. In the *Meditations on the Life of Christ* attributed to Bonaventure, the author links the virtues of charity, humility, and patience—summed up in purity of heart—with Jesus's rejections of the devil's invitations in Luke; see Hornik and Parsons, *Illuminating Luke*, 2:23–24.

24. José Luis Orella Unzué, "La provincia de Guipúzcoa y el tema de los judíos en tiempos del joven Iñigo de Loyola (1492–1528)," in *Ignacio de Loyola y su tiempo*, 847–68. For purity of blood in Spain, see, e.g., Henry Kamen, *Inquisition and Society in Spain in the Sixteenth and Seventeenth Centuries* (Bloomington: Indiana University Press, 1985), 114–24; Francisco de Borja de Medina, "Ignacio de Loyola y la 'limpieza de sangre,'" in *Ignacio de Loyola y su tiempo*, 581–82, 587–608; O'Rourke Boyle, *Loyola's Acts*, 60–63; L. P. Harvey, *Muslims in Spain, 1500–1614* (Chicago: University of Chicago Press, 2005), 14–21, 104–10; and Benjamin Ehlers, *Between Christians and Moriscos: Juan de Ribera and Religious Reform in Valencia, 1568–1614* (Baltimore: Johns Hopkins University Press, 2006), 14–17. For honor in Mediterranean culture, see, e.g., Julian Pitt-Rivers, "The Anthropology of Honour," in *The Fate of Shechem, or The Politics of Sex: Essays in the Anthropology of the Mediterranean*, Cambridge Studies and Papers in Social Anthropology, 19 (Cambridge: Cambridge University Press, 1977), 1–13; Samuel Edgerton, Jr., *Pictures and Punishment: Art and Criminal Prosecution during the Florentine Renaissance* (Ithaca, N.Y.: Cornell University Press, 1985), 59–125; David D. Gilmore, "The Shame of Dishonor," in *Honor and Shame and the Unity of the Mediterranean*, David Gilmore, ed. (Washington, D.C.: American Anthropological Association, 1987), 8–16; John K. Chance, "The Anthropology of Honor and Shame: Culture, Values, and Practice," in *Honor and Shame in the World of the Bible*, Victor H. Matthews and Don C. Benjamin, eds., Semeia, 68 (Atlanta: Scholars Press, 1996), 139–43; Halvor Moxnes, "Honor and Shame," in *The Social*

Sciences and New Testament Interpretation, Richard L. Rohrbaugh, ed. (Peabody, Mass.: Hendrickson, 1996), 19–40; and James R. Farr, "Honor, Law, and Custom in Renaissance Europe," in *A Companion to the Worlds of the Renaissance*, Guido Ruggiero, ed., Blackwell Companions to European History (Oxford: Blackwell, 2002), 124–38.

25. Cf. Pitt-Rivers, "Anthropology of Honour," 5: "To leave an affront un-avenged is to leave one's honour in a state of desecration and this is therefore equivalent to cowardice"; and ibid., 8: "The ultimate vindication of honour lies in physical violence and when other means fail the obligation exists, not only in the formal code of honour but in social milieux which admit no such code, to revert to it."

26. See, e.g., Theodor E. Mommsen, "Petrarch and the Story of the Choice of Hercules," *Journal of the Warburg and Courtauld Institutes* 16 (1953): 178–92; G. Karl Galinsky, *The Herakles Theme: The Adaptations of the Hero in Literature from Homer to the Twentieth Century* (Oxford: Basil Blackwell, 1972), 101–8, 137–40, 145, 201–3; and O'Rourke Boyle, *Loyola's Acts*, 2, 30, 63–65. Pythagoras used majuscule upsilon (Y) to illustrate the crossroads of moral choice as one ma-tured from childhood to adolescence; see, e.g., Christiane L. Joost-Gaugier, *Measuring Heaven: Pythagoras and His Influence on Thought and Art in Antiquity and the Middle Ages* (Ithaca, N.Y.: Cornell University Press, 2006), 74–75, 215–18.

27. Brodrick, *Origin of the Jesuits*, 104, 105 (the quotations); and O'Malley, *First Jesuits*, 112.

28. Ignatius and the first Jesuits received so many requests to serve as spiritual directors to women that Ignatius became increasingly cautious about the deco-rum of that apostolate. See, e.g., Charmarie J. Blaisdell, "Calvin's and Loyola's Letters to Women: Politics and Spiritual Counsel in the Sixteenth Century," in *Calviniana: Ideas and Influence of Jean Calvin*, Robert V. Schnucker, ed., Sixteenth Century Essays & Studies, 10 (Kirksville, Mo.: Sixteenth Century Journal Publish-ers, 1988), 246–47; and Robert Aleksander Maryks, *Saint Cicero and the Jesuits: The Influence of the Liberal Arts on the Adoption of Moral Probabilism*, Catholic Christendom, 1300–1700 (Aldershot, U.K.: Ashgate, 2008), 26–30. Women gained a measure of autonomy in the early modern period because they were free to choose a spiritual director. See Patricia Ranft, "A Key to Counter Reformation Women's Activism: The Confessor-Spiritual Director," *Journal of Feminist Studies in Religion* 10, no. 2 (1994): 7–26.

29. Catherine Brault-Noble and Marie-José Marc, "L'Unification religieuse et sociale: La répression des minorités," in *L'Inquisition espagnole, XVe-XIXe siècles*, Bartolomé Bennassar, ed., (Paris: Hachette, 1979), 163–79, 181–83; Ricardo Gar-cía Cárcel, "The Course of the Moriscos up to Their Expulsion," in *The Spanish Inquisition and the Inquisitorial Mind*, Angel Alcalá, ed., Atlantic Studies on Society

in Change, 49 (Boulder, Colo.: Social Science Monographs, 1987), 73–78; Francisco de Borja de Medina, "La Compañía de Jesús y la minoría morisca (1545–1614)," *Archivum historicum Societatis Iesu* 57 (1988): 4–120; Harvey, *Muslims in Spain*, 240; and Lance Gabriel Lazar, *Working in the Vineyard of the Lord: Jesuit Confraternities in Early Modern Italy* (Toronto: University of Toronto Press, 2005), 102–3, 106, 110–14. In general, see Tzvetan Todorov, *The Conquest of America: The Question of the Other*, Richard Howard, trans. (New York: Harper & Row, 1984).

30. Pedro de Leturia, "Damas vascas en la formación y transformación de Iñigo de Loyola," in *Estudios Ignacianos*, Ignacio Iparraguirre, ed., Bibliotheca Instituti Historici Societatis Iesu, 10–11 (Roma: Institutum Historicum Societatis Iesu, 1957), 1:77.

31. See, e.g., Kamen, *Inquisition and Society in Spain*, 101–8; and William Monter, *Frontiers of Heresy: The Spanish Inquisition from the Basque Lands to Sicily*, Cambridge Studies in Early Modern History (Cambridge: Cambridge University Press, 1990), 5–6, 10, 35–37, 125–27, 196–202, 209–17.

32. Medina, "Ignacio de Loyola y la 'limpieza de sangre,'" 608–9; and Robert Aleksander Maryks, *The Jesuit Order as a Synagogue of Jews: Jesuits of Jewish Ancestry and Purity-of-Blood Laws in the Early Society of Jesus*, Studies in Medieval and Reformation Traditions, 146 (Leiden: Brill, 2010), 41–213.

33. See, e.g., Rogelio García Mateo, "Ignacio de Loyola y el mundo caballeresco," in *Ignacio de Loyola, Magister Artium en París 1528–1535*, Julio Caro Baroja and Antonio Beristain, eds. (San Sebastián: Kutxa, 1991), 294–98; and David A. Boruchoff, "Historiography with License: Isabel, the Catholic Monarch, and the Kingdom of God," in *Isabel La Católica, Queen of Castile: Critical Essays*, David A. Boruchoff, ed. (Houndmills, U.K.: Palgrave, 2003), 256–58, 292 n. 123.

34. O'Rourke Boyle, *Loyola's Acts*, 67–69.

35. Marjorie O'Rourke Boyle, "Angels Black and White: Loyola's Spiritual Discernment in Historical Perspective," *Theological Studies* 44 (1983): 248–49; O'Rourke Boyle, "Luther's Rider-Gods: From the Steppe to the Tower," *Journal of Religious History* 13 (1985): 275–76; and Terence W. O'Reilly, "The Spiritual Exercises and the Crisis of Medieval Piety," *The Way*, Supplement, 70 (1991): 108–10.

36. Francesco Petrarca, *Le familiari* 4.1 (26 April 1336 / 1353). An English translation by Hans Nachod, "The Ascent of Mont Ventoux," is published in *The Renaissance Philosophy of Man*, Ernst Cassirer, Paul Oskar Kristeller, and John Herman Randall, Jr., eds. (Chicago: University of Chicago Press, 1948), 36–46. Cf. Jonathan D. Spence, "Matteo Ricci and the Ascent to Peking," in *East Meets West: The Jesuits in China, 1582–1773*, Charles E. Ronan and Bonnie B. C. Oh, eds. (Chicago: Loyola University Press, 1988), 3–18; and O'Rourke Boyle, *Loyola's Acts*, 47–48.

37. O'Malley, *First Jesuits*, 24, notes that Abbot García Jiménez de Cisneros had created a practice at the Benedictine monastery of Montserrat whereby novices spent ten days or more in preparing for a confession of all their past sins. For debate on possible influence of the writings of Cisneros on the spirituality of Ignatius, see, e.g., Anselmo M. Albareda, "Intorno alla scuola di orazione metodica stabilita a Monserrato dall'abate Garsías Jiménez de Cisneros (1493–1510)," *Archivum historicum Societatis Iesu* 25 (1956): 261–99; Terence W. O'Reilly, "The Exercises of Saint Ignatius Loyola and the *Exercitatorio de la vida spiritual*," *Studia monastica* 16 (1974): 305–23; and Manuel Ruiz Jurado, "¿Influyó en S. Ignacio el *Ejercitatorio* de Cisneros?" *Manresa* 51 (1979): 65–75.

38. Lu Ann Homza, *Religious Authority in the Spanish Renaissance*, Johns Hopkins University Studies in Historical and Political Science, 118th ser., 1 (Baltimore: Johns Hopkins University Press, 2000), 150–75; and Roberto Rusconi, *L'ordine dei peccati: La confessione tra Medioevo ed età moderna*, Saggi, 562 (Bologna: Il Mulino, 2002), 26, 33, 42, 89–91, 237, 249–50.

39. In the Vulgate, Rom. 5:20 reads "Ubi autem abundavit delictum superabundavit gratia." Cf. 2 Cor. 9:8, "God is able to provide you with every blessing in abundance." See also Ignacio Echarte, ed., *Concordancia Ignaciana / An Ignatian Concordance* (Bilbao: Ediciones Mensajero, in collaboration with the Institute of Jesuit Sources, St. Louis, Mo., 1996), s.v. *superabundançia* (three times in the *Spiritual Diary*), *superabundantius* (once in the Deliberation of the First Companions) (1213). See also ibid., s.v. *abundançia* (4–6). The word is used once in *Acta*, 48, without reference to grace, but it appears ninety-two times in Ignatius's *Spiritual Diary*, often to characterize the extent of divine generosity or his own consolation and tears. The treatise that Erasmus wrote on the "immense mercy of God" had a particular resonance in Italy from 1524 on. See Silvana Seidel Menchi, *Erasmo in Italia, 1520–1580*, Nuova Cultura, 1 (Torino: Bollati Boringhieri, 1987), 155–67.

40. O'Malley, *First Jesuits*, 139, quotes Xavier in 1549 as recommending that Jesuit confessors should touch the hearts of penitents by emphasizing "the abundant mercy of God"; and ibid., 142, cites Favre in 1544 on the need for Jesuit confessors to avoid pharisaic self-righteousness. Cf. Thomas N. Tentler, *Sin and Confession on the Eve of the Reformation* (Princeton, N.J.: Princeton University Press, 1977), 57–133, 233–344; Lawrence G. Duggan, "Fear and Confession on the Eve of the Reformation," *Archiv für Reformationsgeschichte / Archive for Reformation History* 75 (1984): 158–73; Jean Delumeau, *Sin and Fear: The Emergence of a Western Guilt Culture, 13th–18th Centuries*, Eric Nicholson, trans. (New York: St. Martin's Press, 1990), 189–479; and John Henderson, "Penitence and the Laity in Fifteenth-Century Florence," in *Christianity and the Renaissance: Image and Religious Imagination in the Quattrocento*, Timothy Verdon and John Henderson, eds. (Syracuse, N.Y.: Syracuse University Press, 1990), 229–49.

41. John W. O'Malley, "Renaissance Humanism and the Religious Culture of the First Jesuits," *Heythrop Journal* 31 (1990): 479–80; O'Malley, *First Jesuits*, 139–45; Rusconi, *L'ordine dei peccati*, 254–55, 314–18, 326–29; Robert Aleksander Maryks, "La *consolatio* nel ministero della confessione dei primi gesuiti," in *I Gesuiti e la "Ratio studiorum,"* Manfred Hinz, Roberto Righi, and Danilo Zardin, eds., "Europa delle Corti" Centro studi sulle società di antico regime: Biblioteca del Cinquecento, 113 (Roma: Bulzoni, 2004), 211–27; and Maryks, *Saint Cicero and the Jesuits*, 3–4, 17–26, 79–125.

42. For Ignatius's scrupulosity and flamboyant asceticism at Manresa and later in life, see *Acta*, 388–413; O'Reilly, "The *Spiritual Exercises* and the Crisis," 105–8; Meissner, *Ignatius of Loyola: The Psychology of a Saint*, 69–73, 84–86; and O'Rourke Boyle, *Loyola's Acts*, 69–84, 170–72. See further O'Malley, *First Jesuits*, 25, 152–59 (frequent Communion and priesthood), 341–45 (Jesuit discipline), and 356–60 (Jesuit asceticism, dress, and common prayer). On frequent Communion, see also Michael W. Maher, "How the Jesuits Used Their Congregations to Promote Frequent Communion," in *Confraternities and Catholic Reform in Italy, France, and Spain*, John Patrick Donnelly and Michael W. Maher, eds., Sixteenth Century Essays & Studies, 44 (Kirksville, Mo.: Thomas Jefferson University Press, 1999), 77–81; and Isabella Gagliardi, *Li trofei della croce: L'esperienza gesuata e la società lucchese tra Medioevo ed età moderna*, Centro Alti Studi in Scienze Religiose, 3 (Roma: Edizioni di Storia e Letteratura, 2005), 100–4 (Paolo Maffei). Black clothing at the Spanish court and among Protestants functioned as a protest against the colorful excess of Italian courts; see Jane Schneider, "Peacocks and Penguins: The Political Economy of European Cloth and Colors," *American Ethnologist* 5 (1978): 426–33. For comparison and contrast to Luther's experience of scruples, see David C. Steinmetz, "Luther and Loyola," in *Ignacio de Loyola y su tiempo*, 795–96.

43. O'Rourke Boyle, *Loyola's Acts*, 74.

44. O'Rourke Boyle, *Loyola's Acts*, 77–84. According to Echarte, ed., *Concordancia Ignaciana*, s.v. *agujero* (30), excluding the letters of Ignatius, he used this word only in the *Acta* and only on two occasions (*Acta*, 24, 55).

45. See, e.g., Rhonda L. McDaniel, "Pride Goes before a Fall: Aldhelm's Practical Application of Gregorian and Cassianic Conceptions of *Superbia* and the Eight Principal Vices," in *The Seven Deadly Sins: From Communities to Individuals*, Richard Newhauser, ed., Studies in Medieval and Reformation Traditions: History, Culture, Religion, Ideas, 123 (Leiden: Brill, 2007), 95–96, 101.

46. See, e.g., Willard J. Peterson, "What to Wear? Observation and Participation by Jesuit Missionaries in Late Ming Society," in *Implicit Understandings: Observing, Reporting, and Reflecting on the Encounters between Europeans and Other Peoples in the Early Modern Era*, Stuart B. Schwartz, ed. (Cambridge: Cambridge University Press, 1994), 403–21.

47. O'Malley, *First Jesuits*, 342–43, referring to a 1559 exhortation of Laínez, who in turn was citing Ignatius himself.

48. Echarte, ed., *Concordancia Ignaciana*, s.v. *lacrima, lágrima, lágrimar* (693–700). Excluding his letters, Ignatius used *lágrimas* 255 times, especially in his *Spiritual Diary*. For the use of the two nouns in the *Acta*, see the *Praefatio*, 1; *Acta*, 18, 28 (twice), 33, 98, 100, 101. See further Louis Beirnaert, *Aux frontières de l'acte analytique: La Bible, saint Ignace, Freud, et Lacan* (Paris: Éditions du Seuil, 1987), 205–18; and William A. Christian, Jr., "Provoked Religious Weeping in Early Modern Spain," in *Religion and Emotion: Approaches and Interpretations*, John Corrigan, ed. (Oxford: Oxford University Press, 2004), 33–50.

49. Gagliardi, *Li trofei della croce*, 101.

50. O'Rourke Boyle, *Loyola's Acts*, 84–146. See further O'Malley, *First Jesuits*, 37–50 (content of the *Spiritual Exercises*), 82–84 (Jesuit sense of consolation), 127–33 (the *Spiritual Exercises* as ministry), 163–64 (the *Spiritual Exercises* and mental prayer), and 372–74 (the *Spiritual Exercises* and the conviction that God deals directly with persons).

51. O'Rourke Boyle, *Loyola's Acts*, 85–93.

52. Kenneth Clark, *Civilisation: A Personal View* (New York: Harper & Row, 1970), 175; and O'Rourke Boyle, *Loyola's Acts*, 85–90.

53. See Steinmetz, "Luther and Loyola," 793, who observes that the description "presses rather hard against the boundaries of Chalcedonian orthodoxy."

54. O'Rourke Boyle, *Loyola's Acts*, 100–27. See also Leonardo R. Silos, "Cardoner in the Life of Saint Ignatius of Loyola," *Archivum historicum Societatis Iesu* 33 (1964): 8–15, 38–42. Medieval Western iconography of the Eden serpent portrayed the snake with feet and wings, reshaping the Jewish and eastern Christian interpretation of a serpent who had his legs and feet cut off as punishment for tempting Eve. See Henry Ansgar Kelly, "The Metamorphoses of the Eden Serpent during the Middle Ages and Renaissance," *Viator* 2 (1971): 301–6, 326.

55. On the peacock in medieval bestiaries, see, e.g., T. H. White, ed. and trans., *The Bestiary: A Book of Beasts* (New York: G. P. Putnam's Sons, 1954), 149 (citing Martial *Epigrammata* 13.70); Florence McCulloch, *Mediaeval Latin and French Bestiaries*, University of North Carolina Studies in the Romance Languages and Literatures, 33 (Chapel Hill: University of North Carolina Press, 1962), 153–54; Francis D. Klingender, *Animals in Art and Thought to the End of the Middle Ages*, Evelyn Antal and John Harthan, eds. (Cambridge, Mass.: M.I.T. Press, 1971), 88–89, 271–73, 277, 280, 285–86, 370–71 (citing Aristotle *Historia animalium* 488b); Beryl Rowland, *Birds with Human Souls: A Guide to Bird Symbolism* (Knoxville: University of Tennessee Press, 1978), 127–30; Herbert Friedmann, *A Bestiary for Saint Jerome: Animal Symbolism in European Religious Art* (Washington, D.C.: Smithsonian Institution Press, 1980), 159–60, 284–85 (citing *The Notebooks of Leonardo da Vinci*, Edward MacCurdy, ed., 1078); and John

B. Friedman, "Peacocks and Preachers: Analytic Technique in Marcus of Orvieto's *Liber de moralitatibus*, Vatican lat. MS 5935," in *Beasts and Birds of the Middle Ages: The Bestiary and Its Legacy*, Willene B. Clark and Meredith T. McMunn, eds., Middle Ages Series (Philadelphia: University of Pennsylvania Press, 1989), 186–89, 190–92. Cf. O'Rourke Boyle, *Loyola's Acts*, 122, citing Augustine, *De sermone Domini in monte libros duos*, 2.12.41: "We must particularly point out that vainglory can find a place, not only in the splendor and pomp of worldly wealth, but even in the sordid garment of sackcloth as well, and it is then all the more dangerous because it is a deception under the pretence of service to God." The Byzantine spiritual tradition celebrated monks who returned to the world as "fools for the sake of Christ." They did odd things (e.g., going about naked or paying prostitutes without accepting their services) to prove that virtue conceals itself in silliness. Their good deeds were performed in secret lest they be praised. See Alexander Y. Syrkin, "On the Behavior of the 'Fool for Christ's Sake,'" *History of Religions* 22 (1982): 150–58; and Sergey A. Ivanov, *Holy Fools in Byzantium and Beyond*, Simon Franklin, trans., Oxford Studies in Byzantium (Oxford: Oxford University Press, 2006), 104–34.

56. Meissner, *Ignatius of Loyola: The Psychology of a Saint*, esp. 25–27, 55–60, 105–6, 378–86; and O'Rourke Boyle, *Loyola's Acts*, 1, 127–37. For the Narcissus theme in literature, see, e.g., Rudolph Schevill, *Ovid and the Renascence in Spain*, University of California Publications in Modern Philology, 4, no. 1 (Berkeley: University of California Press, 1913), 148–52, 245–49; Frederick Goldin, *The Mirror of Narcissus in the Courtly Love Lyric* (Ithaca, N.Y.: Cornell University Press, 1967), 20–59; Louise Vinge, *The Narcissus Theme in Western European Literature up to the Early Nineteenth Century*, Robert Dewsnap, Lisbeth Grönlund, Nigel Reeves, and Ingrid Söderberg-Reeves, trans. (Lund: Gleerups, 1967); Kenneth J. Knoespel, *Narcissus and the Invention of Personal History*, Garland Publications in Comparative Literature (New York: Garland, 1985); Maurizio Bettini, *Il ritratto dell'amante*, Saggi, 761 (Torino: Einaudi, 1992); Lynn Enterline, *The Tears of Narcissus: Melancholia and Masculinity in Early Modern Writing* (Stanford, Calif.: Stanford University Press, 1995), 1–18, 168–86. For Narcissus and Freud, see, e.g., Gray Kochhar-Lindgren, *Narcissus Transformed: The Textual Subject in Psychoanalysis and Literature* (University Park: Pennsylvania State University Press, 1993).

57. See, e.g., David A. Salomon, "Forging a New Identity: Narcissism and Imagination in the Mysticism of Ignatius Loyola," *Christianity and Literature* 47 (1998): 195–202; Kenneth L. Becker, *Unlikely Companions: C. G. Jung on the "Spiritual Exercises" of Ignatius of Loyola* (Leominster: Gracewing, 2001), 213, 218, 240–60, 297–307; and Michèle Aumont, *Ignace de Loyola: Seul contre tous . . . et pour tous*, Ouverture philosophique (Paris: L'Harmattan, 2007), 212–24.

58. O'Rourke Boyle, *Loyola's Acts*, 181.

59. O'Malley, *First Jesuits*, 43 (quotation), 373. See also Karl Rahner, *The Dynamic Element in the Church*, W. J. O'Hara, trans., Quaestiones Disputatae, 12 (New York: Herder and Herder, 1964), 89–114; and Terence W. O'Reilly, "Saint Ignatius Loyola and Spanish Erasmianism," *Archivum historicum Societatis Iesu* 43 (1974): 313.

60. *Acta*, 406: "y empeçó a dar grandes gritos a unas señoras, que eran allí venidas por visitalle, que por amor de Dios, quando otra vez le viesen en punto de muerte, que le gritasen a grandes voces, diciéndole pecador, y que se acordase de las ofensas que había hecho a Dios." On the woman who spoke of "my Lord Jesus Christ," see also Noëlle Hausman, "'What Ought I to Do?' *The Pilgrim's Testament*, a Source for the Apostolic Religious Life," *Centrum Ignatianum Spiritualitatis* 20, nos. 1–2 (1990): 29–32. This is the only occasion in the *Acta* where Ignatius used the expression "my Lord." He constantly uses the expression "our Lord." See Echarte, ed., *Concordancia Ignaciana*, s.v. *señor, signore* (1174–75, 1187). For women as charismatic prophets and spiritual directors in early modern Spain, see Jodi Bilinkoff, "A Spanish Prophetess and Her Patrons: The Case of María de Santo Domingo," *Sixteenth-Century Journal* 23 (1992): 21–34. Ignatius may also be defending his controversial friend in Rome, Vittoria Colonna; see, e.g., Massimo Firpo, "Vittoria Colonna, Giovanni Morone, e gli 'spirituali,'" *Rivista di storia e letteratura religiosa* 24 (1988): 211–23, 248–61. Like Ignatius, Vittoria Colonna preferred to describe the church as "the Lord's vineyard"; see Firpo, "Vittoria Colonna," 216, 235–36. For the figure of the old woman in French satire, see Jacques Bailbé, "La thème de la vieille femme dans la poésie satirique du seizième et du début du dix-septième siècles," *Bibliothèque d'humanisme et Renaissance* 26 (1964): 98–119.

61. For the pilgrimage to Jerusalem, see *Acta*, 412–29; and O'Rourke Boyle, *Loyola's Acts*, 147–61, 163–67. See further O'Malley, *First Jesuits*, 25–27, 66–68 (Nadal on journeying for apostolic ministries), 271–72, 362 (Jesuits and the practice of pilgrimage), 298–301 (the fourth vow of the Jesuits for itinerant ministry), 348–51 (Jesuits and the vow of poverty).

62. *The Autobiography of St. Ignatius Loyola with Related Documents*, John C. Olin, ed., and Joseph F. O'Callaghan, trans. (New York: Harper & Row, 1974), 41–42 (*Acta*, 408–10).

63. On medieval pilgrimage and accounts of such travels, see, e.g., Jonathan Sumption, *Pilgrimage: An Image of Mediaeval Religion* (London: Faber & Faber, 1975); Giles Constable, "The Opposition to Pilgrimage in the Middle Ages," *Studia gratiana* 19 (1976): 123–46; Turner and Turner, *Image and Pilgrimage*, 3–39, 140–202, 231–34; Donald R. Howard, *Writers and Pilgrims: Medieval Pilgrimage Narratives and Their Posterity* (Berkeley: University of California Press, 1980), 11–52; and Paul Zumthor, "The Medieval Travel Narrative," Catherine Peebles, trans., *New Literary History* 25 (1994): 810–11, 820.

64. O'Malley, *First Jesuits*, 68. See also Mario Scaduto, "La strada e i primi gesuiti," *Archivum historicum Societatis Iesu* 40 (1971): 323–30, 345–50; John C. Olin, "The Idea of Pilgrimage in the Experience of Ignatius Loyola," *Church History* 48 (1979): 389–97; John W. O'Malley, "To Travel to Any Part of the World: Jerónimo Nadal and the Jesuit Vocation," *Studies in the Spirituality of Jesuits* 16, no. 2 (1984): 5–8, 10–11; and O'Malley, "Five Missions of the Jesuit Charism: Content and Method," *Studies in the Spirituality of Jesuits* 38, no. 4 (2006): 13–14. Scaduto, "La strada," 324, notes the decrepit character of Ignatius's feet at his death, brought on by a lifetime of travel: "i piedi pieni di calli e molto ruvidi per averli tenuti tanto tempo scalzi e per aver fatto tanti viaggi."

65. O'Malley, *First Jesuits*, 271, 301, 362.

66. Cacho Blecua, "Del gentilhombre mundano," 154–55.

67. O'Rourke Boyle, *Loyola's Acts*, 156–60.

68. James K. Farge, *Orthodoxy and Reform in Early Reformation France: The Faculty of Theology of Paris, 1500–1543*, Studies in Medieval and Reformation Thought, 32 (Leiden: Brill, 1985), 28–31.

69. See, e.g., Lester K. Little, *Religious Poverty and the Profit Economy in Medieval Europe* (Ithaca, N.Y.: Cornell University Press, 1978), 8–41, 164–65, 176–83, 201–17; and Michel Mollat du Jourdin, *The Poor in the Middle Ages: An Essay in Social History*, Arthur Goldhammer, trans. (New Haven: Yale University Press, 1986), 193–300.

70. For Ignatius's willingness to use techniques of the free market, see, e.g., Bertrand, *La politique de saint Ignace*, 275–91; and Olwen Hufton, "Persuasion, Promises, and Persistence: Funding the Early Jesuit College," in *I Gesuiti e la "Ratio studiorum,"* 75–76.

71. Ignatius Loyola, *The Spiritual Exercises of Saint Ignatius: A Literal Translation and a Contemporary Reading*, David L. Fleming, trans. (St. Louis, Mo.: Institute of Jesuit Sources, 1978), 84–91.

72. See, e.g., Barbara McClung Hallman, *Italian Cardinals, Reform, and the Church as Property, 1492–1563*, UCLA Center for Medieval and Renaissance Studies, 22 (Berkeley: University of California Press, 1985); and Marco Pellegrini, "A Turning-Point in the History of the Factional System in the Sacred College: The Power of Pope and Cardinals in the Age of Alexander VI," in *Court and Politics in Papal Rome, 1492–1700*, Gianvittorio Signorotto and Maria Antonietta Visceglia, eds., Cambridge Studies in Italian History and Culture (Cambridge: Cambridge University Press, 2002), 17–19, 25–26.

73. Carlo M. Cipolla, *Before the Industrial Revolution: European Society and Economy, 1000–1700*, 2nd ed. (New York: W. W. Norton, 1980), 13–23, esp. 13–14.

74. Gerhart B. Ladner, "*Homo Viator*: Mediaeval Ideas on Alienation and Order," *Speculum* 42 (1967): 233–37, 245–46, 249–51; Sumption, *Pilgrimage*, 126–27, 171–73; Christian K. Zacher, *Curiosity and Pilgrimage: The Literature of Discovery*

in Fourteenth-Century England (Baltimore: Johns Hopkins University Press, 1976), 49–51; and esp. Michel Mollat du Jourdin, "Saint Ignace et les pèlerinages de son temps," in *Ignacio de Loyola y su tiempo*, 161–78.

75. Sumption, *Pilgrimage*, 91. When Willibald visited the chapel of the Ascension in the eighth century, he discovered that it fittingly had no roof. See Michael McCormick, *Origins of the European Economy: Communications and Commerce, A.D. 300–900* (Cambridge: Cambridge University Press, 2001), 132. Constable, "Opposition to Pilgrimage," 152, quotes a warning of Peter the Venerable: "Serving God perpetually in humility and poverty is greater than making a journey to Jerusalem with pride and luxury. While therefore to visit Jerusalem where the Lord's feet stood is good, to look towards the heavens where He is seen face to face is far better."

76. O'Rourke Boyle, *Loyola's Acts*, 19. For discussion by medieval moralists of curiosity as a danger for pilgrims, see Zacher, *Curiosity and Pilgrimage*, 18–41, 51–59. Zacher, ibid., 20, cites the *Sentences* of Peter Lombard, who conjoins "frivolous vanity and harmful curiosity" (*plurimum supervacuae vanitatis et noxiae curiositatis*). Cf. also Brown, *Pastor and Laity*, 161–62, 185–87.

77. Constable, "Opposition to Pilgrimage," 126, 128; and O'Rourke Boyle, *Loyola's Acts*, 166, citing Jerome *Epistolae* 58.2 and Erasmus *Enchiridion militis Christiani* in *Opera omnia*, Jean Leclerc, ed. (Leiden: Pieter van der Aa, 1703–6), 5:38 [English translation of Erasmus, *The Handbook of the Christian Soldier*, by Charles Fantazzi for *The Collected Works of Erasmus* (Toronto: University of Toronto Press, 1988), 66:82].

78. The story has long puzzled commentators. See, e.g., Meissner, *Ignatius of Loyola: The Psychology of a Saint*, 168: "This brief account conceals more than it reveals." O'Rourke Boyle, *Loyola's Acts*, 163, sees an Adam paradigm in Ignatius's fall from the bridge: "The clay and water with which Loyola is caked and soaked upon his emergence from the river associates him with Adam, formed from clay and immersed since original sin in the sea of the world."

79. See the introduction of Jerome Bertram, "John Cassian, a Spiritual Guide for the Laity," to *The Monastic Institutes*, vii–ix. For Cassian's somewhat nuanced attitude toward "the world," see Rousseau, *Ascetics, Authority, and the Church*, 199–220.

80. *Letters and Instructions*, Martin E. Palmer and John W. Padberg, ed. and trans., with John L. McCarthy, ed., Jesuit Primary Sources in English Translations, 23 (St. Louis, Mo.: Institute of Jesuit Sources, 2006), 412–21 (no. 3304). The letter cites Cassian on three occasions. For its context and significance, see, e.g., Bertrand, *La politique de saint Ignace*, 71–95; and O'Malley, *First Jesuits*, 330–33, 351–56.

81. Bertrand, "Ignace de Loyola et la politique," 704–5.

82. Mollat du Jourdin, *Poor in the Middle Ages*, 23, 39–40.

83. Rousseau, *Ascetics, Authority, and the Church*, 194; and Carole Straw, "Gregory, Cassian, and the Cardinal Vices," in *In the Garden of Evil*, 42–43. See John Cassian, *Cassiani Opera: Collationes XXIIII*, Michael Petschenig and Gottfried Kreuz, eds., Corpus Scriptorum Ecclesiasticorum Latinorum, 13 (Vienna: Verlag der Österreichischen Akademie der Wissenschaften, 2004), *Collationes* 4.12.5 (108): "sed horum pugnae aequilibratio iusta succedens sanam et moderatam inter utraque virtutum reseret viam, itinere regio docens militem Christi semper incedere"; and *Collationes* 6.9.3 (162, referring to 2 Cor. 6:7–10): "nec prosperis dumtaxat elatus nec deiectus adversis, sed itinere plano ac via regia semper incedens." In the context of his discussion of vainglory, Cassian uses the expressions "royal road" and "path of virtue," found through discernment in the Spirit. See John Cassian, *Cassiani Opera: De institutis coenobiorum, De incarnatione contra Nestorium*, Michael Petschenig and Gottfried Kreuz, eds., Corpus Scriptorum Ecclesiasticorum Latinorum, 17 (Vienna: Verlag der Österreichischen Akademie der Wissenschaften, 2004), *De institutis* 11.3 (196): "Itaque via regia volentem incedere per arma iustitiae quae a dextris sunt et a sinistris (2 Cor. 6:7) oportet apostolica disciplina transire per gloriam et ignobilitatem, per infamiam et bonam famam (2 Cor. 6:8), et tanta cautione inter tumentes temptationum fluctus gubernante discretione et flante nobis spiritu domini iter dirigere virtutis."

84. Michel Foucault, "The Battle for Chastity," in *Western Sexuality: Practice and Precept in Past and Present Times*, Philippe Ariès and André Béjin, eds., and Anthony Forster, trans., Family, Sexuality, and Social Relations in Past Times (Oxford: Blackwell, 1985), 15–16, 20–25 (quote on 24).

85. For Gregory's definition, see Straw, "Gregory, Cassian, and the Cardinal Vices," 50.

86. Iacobus a Voragine, *Legenda aurea vulgo historica Lombardica dicta*, Johann Georg Theodor Grässe, ed., 3rd ed. (Bratislava: Guilelmus Koebner, 1890), 663, 664, 669. According to Nadal, Ignatius also took notice of the emphasis on vainglory in the life of the hermit Saint Onofrio. See Pedro de Leturia, "El influjo de San Onofre en San Ignacio a base de un texto inédito de Nadal," *Manresa* 2 (1926): 229–30.

87. See, e.g., Yelena Mazour-Matusevich, "Gerson's Legacy," in *A Companion to Jean Gerson*, Brian Patrick McGuire, ed., Brill's Companions to the Christian Tradition, 3 (Leiden: Brill, 2006), 375–82.

88. See, e.g., Bloomfield, *The Seven Deadly Sins*, 87–88 (citing Aquinas), 104; Herbert Grabes, *The Mutable Glass: Mirror-Imagery in Titles and Texts of the Middle Ages and English Renaissance*, Gordon Collier, trans. (Cambridge: Cambridge University Press, 1982), 153–58; Diana Norman, "'Love Justice, You Who Judge the Earth': The Paintings of the Sala dei Nove in the Palazzo Pubblico," in *Siena, Florence, and Padua: Art, Society, and Religion, 1280–1400*, Diana Norman, ed. (New Haven, Conn.: Yale University Press, in association with the Open University, 1995), 2:147–52; Sabine Melchior-Bonnet, *The Mirror: A History*, Katharine

H. Jewett, trans. (London: Routledge, 2001), 192–95; and Straw, "Gregory, Cassian, and the Cardinal Vices," 39, 49–52.

89. See , e.g., Richard J. Goodrich, *Contextualizing Cassian: Aristocrats, Asceticism, and Reformation in Fifth-Century Gaul*, Oxford Early Christian Studies (Oxford: Oxford University Press, 2007), 2–5, 151–207, who argues that Cassian proposed to Gallic aristocrats a radical renunciation of property, social intercourse, and status. On Cassian's educational remedies for ascetic ambition in fifth-century Gaul, see Conrad Leyser, *Authority and Asceticism from Augustine to Gregory the Great* (Oxford: Clarendon Press, 2000), 33–61.

90. *Monumenta Ignatiana*, Series I, *Sancti Ignatii . . . Epistolae et Instructiones* (Madrid: Gabriel Lopez del Horno, 1903–11), 1:99–107 (no. 7); Ignatius Loyola, *Letters of St. Ignatius Loyola*, William J. Young, trans. (Chicago: Loyola University Press, 1959), 18–24; and now *Letters and Instructions*, Palmer and Padberg, ed. and trans., 18–22.

91. See, e.g., Owen Chadwick, "Introduction," in Cassian, *Conferences*, Colm Luibhéid, trans., 2–3, 20–22.

92. In the midst of a schedule of ministries that left no time for other business, Francis Xavier still cherished the daily examination of conscience as essential prayer for the apostle. Paraphrasing the first letter of John, Xavier wondered, "For he who is not good in regard to himself, how can he be good in regard to others?" See Peter Schineller, "In Their Own Words," *Studies in the Spirituality of Jesuits* 38, no. 1 (2006): 16, 22.

93. Echarte, ed., *Concordancia Ignaciana*, s.v. *aprovechar, provecho* (66–68, 1048–49). Ignatius used the verb nine times in the *Acta* (23, 36, 45, 54, 56, 63, 70, 71, 74), and he used it thirty-five times in the *Spiritual Exercises* and forty-two times in the *Constitutions*. He used the noun three times in the *Acta* (11, 55, 59), and he used it thirty times in the *Exercises* and seventeen times in the *Constitutions*. Cf. Mollat du Jourdin, "Saint Ignace et les pèlerinages de son temps," 164.

94. Schineller, "In Their Own Words," 14. See also Echarte, ed., *Concordancia Ignaciana*, s.v. *gloria, vanagloria, vanidad, vano* (566, 1298). To set up his narrative, Ignatius used *vanidades, vano deseo,* and *ganar honra* in the opening lines of the *Acta* (1). Besides one usage in the *Praefatio* (1), *vanagloria* is used only one more time in the *Acta* (36), whereas Ignatius spoke of the "glory of God" in the *Acta* (14, 36, 57, 85). The usage reflects his sense of ongoing conversion. Excluding Ignatius's letters, the term *vanagloria* is used only in the *Acta*.

95. Herbert Moller, "The Social Causation of the Courtly Love Complex," *Comparative Studies in Society and History* 1 (1959): 155–63; Sara T. Nalle, "Literacy and Culture in Early Modern Castile," *Past and Present* no. 125 (Nov. 1989): 80–84, 87–89; and Cacho Blecua, "Del gentilhombre mundano," 141–43.

96. Bartolomé Bennassar, *The Spanish Character: Attitudes and Mentalities from the Sixteenth to the Nineteenth Century*, Benjamin Keen, trans. (Berkeley: University of California Press, 1979), 213–36; Julio Caro Baroja, "Religion, World

Views, Social Classes, and Honor during the Sixteenth and Seventeenth Centuries in Spain," Victoria Hughes, trans., in *Honor and Grace in Anthropology*, John G. Peristiany and Julian Pitt-Rivers, eds., Cambridge Studies in Social and Cultural Anthropology, 76 (Cambridge: Cambridge University Press, 1992), 99–101; and Thomas V. Cohen, "The Lay Liturgy of Affront in Sixteenth-Century Italy," *Journal of Social History* 25 (1992): 860–62.

97. See, e.g., Galinsky, *The Herakles Theme*, 6–7, 56, 101–3, 128, 140, 160–62, 196–200. The Bollandist Jean Pien described Ignatius as "sacer Hercules"; see Jos E. Vercruysse, "L'historiographie ignatienne aux XVI–XVIII siècles," in *Ignacio de Loyola y su tiempo*, 38. Reaching a crossroads in life was a commonplace of *hidalgo* literature; see Cacho Blecua, "Del gentilhombre mundano," 148–49.

98. Jean-Claude Schmitt, "Le suicide au Moyen Âge," *Annales: Économies sociétés civilisations* 31 (1976): 5, 14–16, 18–19.

99. See, e.g., Vinge, *The Narcissus Theme*, 3–19; Knoespel, *Narcissus and the Invention of Personal History*, 9–18; Bettini, *Il ritratto dell'amante*, 113–18; and Tivadar Gorilovics, "Narcissus' Attitude to Death," in *Echoes of Narcissus*, Lieve Spaas, with Trista Selous, eds., Polygons: Cultural Diversities and Intersections, 2 (New York: Bergahn Books, 2000), 263–66.

100. See, e.g., Kochhar-Lindgren, *Narcissus Transformed*, 19–38. In general, see Edward Peters, "*Vir inconstans*: Moral Theology as Palaeopsychology," in *In the Garden of Evil*, 59–73.

101. American Psychiatric Association, *Diagnostic and Statistical Manual of Mental Disorders*, 4th ed. (Washington, D.C.: American Psychiatric Association, 2000), 717. I thank Brother Pat Douglas, S.J., for this reference.

3. The *Acta* as Mirror of Apostolic Religious Life

1. For the journey to Barcelona and the studies at Barcelona and Alcalá, see *Acta Patris Ignatii*, Dionisio Fernández Zapico and Cándido de Dalmases, with Pedro de Leturia, eds., Monumenta Historica Societatis Iesu, 66 (Roma: Institutum Historicum Societatis Iesu, 1943), 428–53; Rafael María Sanz de Diego, "Ignacio de Loyola en Alcalá de Henares (1526–1527): Andanzas de un universitario atípico," in *Ignacio de Loyola y su tiempo: Congreso internacional de historia (9–13 Setiembre 1991)*, Juan Plazaola, ed. (Bilbao: Ediciones Mensajero, 1992), 883–900; and Marjorie O'Rourke Boyle, *Loyola's Acts: The Rhetoric of the Self*, The New Historicism: Studies in Cultural Poetics, 36 (Berkeley: University of California Press, 1997), 167–69. See further John W. O'Malley, *The First Jesuits* (Cambridge, Mass.: Harvard University Press, 1993), 26–28, 85–90 (Jesuit programs of ministry), 115–26 (Jesuits and catechism), 200–15, 225–32, 239–42, 253–64, 374–75 (Jesuit schools and their program of education).

2. Nadal, "Apologia Societatis," in *Monumenta Ignatiana, Fontes narrativi*, 2:68, cited by Miguel Nicolau, "Fisonomía de San Ignacio según sus primeros

compañeros," *Archivum historicum Societatis Iesu* 26 (1957): 262. Ignacio Echarte, ed., *Concordancia Ignaciana / An Ignatian Concordance* (Bilbao: Ediciones Mensajero, in collaboration with the Institute of Jesuit Sources, St. Louis, Mo., 1996), s.v. *estudiar* (505–6), lists the first occurrence in the *Acta*, 50, and twenty-two further occurrences from 54 to 76. When the language shifts to Italian, there are five uses of *studiare* from 80 to 84 (ibid., 1204).

3. The text here is confusing. Gonçalves da Câmara attributes the word "friar" to Ignatius and then glosses the text by offering his belief that the individual in question was a Cistercian monk (*creo que de sant Bernardo*).

4. Victor W. Turner and Edith L. B. Turner, *Image and Pilgrimage in Christian Culture: Anthropological Perspectives* (New York: Columbia University Press, 1978). The comparison of pilgrimage and mysticism is found in ibid., 33, 157.

5. Cf. Turner and Turner, *Image and Pilgrimage*, 239.

6. For the ideal of Jerusalem in the spirituality of Ignatius, see, e.g., Terence W. O'Reilly, "Ignatius of Loyola and the Counter-Reformation: The Hagiographic Tradition," *Heythrop Journal* 31 (1990): 444–46 . Echarte, *Concordancia Ignaciana*, s.v. *Hierusalem* (1425–26), notes twenty-four occurrences of the word, ten of which come after Ignatius returns from his pilgrimage. In the *Acta*, there are also two instances of the form *Jerusalem* (ibid., 1427), and in the *Praefatio* there are two instances of *Jerusalén* (ibid., 1427–28).

7. See, e.g., André Ravier, *Ignatius of Loyola and the Founding of the Society of Jesus*, Maura Daly, Joan Daly, and Carson Daly, trans. (San Francisco: Ignatius Press, 1987), 432–44.

8. Fidel Fita, "Los tres procesos de S. Ignacio de Loyola en Alcalá de Henares," *Boletín de la Real Academia de la Historia* 33 (1898): 441–43 (testimony of Mencía de Benavente, Ana de Benavente, and Leonor de Mena). O'Malley, *First Jesuits*, 119, analyzes Ignatius's only surviving catechism lesson from 1540. The lesson begins with brief advice on confessing and then gives short explanations for matters such as the Ten Commandments, the rules of the church, the deadly sins, the body's five senses, and the corporal and spiritual works of mercy.

9. O'Rourke Boyle, *Loyola's Acts*, 168: "Loyola's election of these courses is regressive, obsolete." For the career of Domingo de Soto, see, e.g., David Brion Davis, *The Problem of Slavery in Western Culture* (Oxford: Oxford University Press, 1966), 187; Anthony Pagden, *The Fall of Natural Man: The American Indian and the Origins of Comparative Ethnology* (Cambridge: Cambridge University Press, 1982), 27–33, 59–60, 69–74, 86, 98–104, 134–35; Henry Kamen, "Toleration and Dissent in Sixteenth-Century Spain: The Alternative Tradition," *Sixteenth Century Journal* 19 (1988): 11–12; E. J. Ashworth, "Traditional Logic," in *The Cambridge History of Renaissance Philosophy*, Charles B. Schmitt and Quentin Skinner, eds. (Cambridge: Cambridge University Press, 1988), 152, 162–63; Michael J. Wilmott and Charles B. Schmitt, "Biobibliographies," in *The Cambridge History of Renaissance Philosophy*, 836; Louis Baeck, *The Mediterranean Tradition in Economic*

Thought (London: Routledge, 1994), 174–80; and M. W. F. Stone, "Making Sense of Thomas Aquinas in the Sixteenth Century: Domingo de Soto on the Natural Desire to See God," in *Platonic Ideas and Concept Formation in Ancient and Medieval Thought*, Gerd van Riel, Caroline Macé, and Leen van Campe, eds. (Leuven: Universitaire Pers, 2004), 217–32. For Soto's lectures on poor relief, see Henry Kamen, *Philip of Spain* (New Haven, Conn.: Yale University Press, 1997), 24.

10. See, e.g., Paul Oskar Kristeller, *Renaissance Thought and Its Sources* (New York: Columbia University Press, 1979); and John W. O'Malley, "Renaissance Humanism and the Religious Culture of the First Jesuits," *The Heythrop Journal* 31 (1990): 471–87.

11. See, e.g., John C. Olin, "Erasmus and St. Ignatius Loyola," in *Six Essays on Erasmus* (New York: Fordham University Press, 1979), 75–92; Mark Rotsaert, "Les premiers contacts de saint Ignace avec l'érasmisme espagnol," *Revue d'histoire de la spiritualité* 49 (1973): 444–50; Terence W. O'Reilly, "Erasmus, Ignatius Loyola, and Orthodoxy," *Journal of Theological Studies*, n.s., 30 (1979): 119–20, 124–27; and David Ragazzoni, "Ignazio lettore 'mancato' dell'*Enchiridion*: Possibili reminiscenze erasmiane negli *Esercizi spirituali*?" *Rinascimento*, n.s., 46 (2006): 373–90. In general, see Erika Rummel, *Erasmus and His Catholic Critics*, 2 vols., Bibliotheca Humanistica & Reformatoria, 45 (Nieuwkoop: De Graaf Publishers, 1989).

12. O'Malley, *First Jesuits*, 213–14.

13. Letter of Pedro de Ribadeneira to King Philip II of Spain, 14 February 1556, in *Monumenta Paedagogica Societatis Iesu*, vol. 1, *1540–1556*, Ladislaus Lukács, ed., 2nd ed., Monumenta Historica Societatis Iesu, 92 (Roma: apud "Monumenta Historica Soc. Iesu," 1965), 475–76: "los que en ella [Compañía] viven no solamente han de tener cuidado de aprovecharse en sus ánimas, mas también han de tener cuenta con sus prójimos . . . todo el bien de la cristiandad y de todo el mundo depende de la buena institución de la juventud . . . para lo cual hay gran falta de virtuosos y letrados maestros que junten el ejemplo con la doctrina . . . viendo nuestro P. Mtro. Ignacio el provecho universal que de esta manera de enseñar ha nacido en todos lugares." Ribadeneira indicates that educating young people requires humility as a less honorable pursuit (*menos honrosa*) but, for that, is no less beneficial (*no menos provechosa*). The letter is also cited in O'Malley, *First Jesuits*, 209.

14. See, e.g., John M. McManamon, *Pierpaolo Vergerio the Elder (ca. 1369–1444): The Humanist as Orator*, Medieval & Renaissance Texts & Studies, 163 (Tempe, Ariz.: Medieval & Renaissance Texts & Studies, 1996), 89–103; and John W. O'Malley, *Four Cultures of the West* (Cambridge, Mass.: Belknap Press of Harvard University Press, 2004), 154–58.

15. O'Malley, *First Jesuits*, 90. In general, see Paul F. Grendler, *Schooling in Renaissance Italy: Literacy and Learning, 1300–1600* (Baltimore: Johns Hopkins University Press, 1989), 363–81, 398–99.

16. See, e.g., Léon Poliakov, *The History of Anti-Semitism*, vol. 2, *From Moham-med to the Marranos*, Natalie Gerardi, trans. (New York: Vanguard Press, 1973), 147–232; Henry Kamen, *Inquisition and Society in Spain in the Sixteenth and Seventeenth Centuries* (Bloomington: Indiana University Press, 1985), 6–61; Stephen Haliczer, "The First Holocaust: The Inquisition and the Converted Jews of Spain and Portugal," in *Inquisition and Society in Early Modern Europe*, Stephen Haliczer, ed. and trans. (Totowa, N.J.: Barnes & Noble Books, 1987), 7–11; Henry Kamen, "The Mediterranean and the Expulsion of Spanish Jews in 1492," *Past and Present* no. 119 (May 1988): 32–55; and Agostino Borromeo, "The Inquisition and Inquisitorial Censorship," in *Catholicism in Early Modern Europe: A Guide to Research*, John W. O'Malley, ed., Reformation Guides to Research, 2 (St. Louis, Mo.: Center for Reformation Research, 1988), 253–67.

17. See, e.g., Luis Fernández Martín, "Iñigo de Loyola y los alumbrados," *Hispania sacra* 35 (1983): 585–92; José C. Nieto, "The Nonmystical Nature of the Sixteenth-Century Alumbrados of Toledo," in *The Spanish Inquisition and the Inquisitorial Mind*, Angel Alcalá, ed., Atlantic Studies on Society in Change, 49 (Boulder, Colo.: Social Science Monographs, 1987), 431–38; Melquíades Andrés, "Alumbrados, Erasmians, 'Lutherans,' and Mystics: The Risk of a More 'Intimate' Spirituality," in *The Spanish Inquisition and the Inquisitorial Mind*, 457–69, 481–82, 488–89; Terence W. O'Reilly, "Melchor Cano and the Spirituality of St. Ignatius Loyola," in *Ignacio de Loyola y su tiempo*, 369–70, 375–76; and Alastair Hamilton, *Heresy and Mysticism in Sixteenth-Century Spain: The* Alumbrados (Cambridge: James Clarke, 1992).

18. Fita, "Los tres procesos," 422–61; John E. Longhurst, "Saint Ignatius at Alcalá, 1526–1527," *Archivum historicum Societatis Iesu* 26 (1957): 252–56; and Fernández Martín, "Iñigo de Loyola y los alumbrados," 643–80. See further Lu Ann Homza, *Religious Authority in the Spanish Renaissance*, Johns Hopkins University Studies in Historical and Political Science, 118th ser., 1 (Baltimore: Johns Hopkins University Press, 2000), 7, who says that the *alumbrados* emerged initially in the context of Franciscan reform but rejected the ecstatic physical manifestations of the Spirit's action popular among Franciscans.

19. See, e.g., Cándido de Dalmases, *Ignatius of Loyola, Founder of the Jesuits: His Life and Work*, Jerome Aixalá, trans., Modern Scholarly Studies about the Jesuits in English Translations, 6 (St. Louis, Mo.: Institute of Jesuit Sources, 1985), 95–105, 111–112, 124–25, 140–42, 151, 157–62, who discusses a well-known letter that Ignatius wrote to King João III of Portugal in 1545 to review his judicial processes; José Luis González Novalín, "La Inquisición y los Jesuitas (s. XVI)," *Anthologica Annua* 37 (1990): 13–23; Antonio Beristain, "La Victimología ante las persecuciones a Ignacio de Loyola y los jesuitas," in *Ignacio de Loyola, Magister Artium en París 1528–1535*, Julio Caro Baroja and Antonio Beristain, eds. (San Sebastián: Kutxa, 1991), 102–7; González Novalín, "Los Jesuitas y la Inquisición

en la época de la implantación de la Compañía," in *Ignacio de Loyola y su tiempo*, 286–91, 300–2; John W. Padberg, "Ignatius and the Popes," in *Ignacio de Loyola y su tiempo*, 687–90; William W. Meissner, *Ignatius of Loyola: The Psychology of a Saint* (New Haven, Conn.: Yale University Press, 1992), 127–37; O'Rourke Boyle, *Loyola's Acts*, 172–75; and Michèle Aumont, *Ignace de Loyola: Seul contre tous . . . et pour tous*, Ouverture philosophique (Paris: L'Harmattan, 2007), 232–39.

20. Homza, *Religious Authority*, 13–17, succinctly describes the formal procedures of the Inquisition and the holding cells inside the tribunals for prisoners during trial. During this third phase, a reformed prostitute named María de la Flor gave the most damaging deposition. She claimed that Ignatius distinguished mortal from venial sins, advised his followers not to reveal some matters to their confessor, and boasted that, because Calixto and he had pronounced a vow of chastity, they could share a bedroom with a young woman and not commit a sin. See also Fita, "Los tres procesos," 444–48; and Hamilton, *Heresy and Mysticism*, 93–97.

21. See, e.g., Acts 5:17–19, 12:3–11, and 16:19–40 (cited below).

22. Echarte, *Concordancia Ignaciana*, s.v. *prender* (1009), lists the multiple occurrences of *el preso / los presos* as "the prisoner(s)," *Acta*, 46, 61 (three times), 66, 67, 69, 70. See also ibid., s.v. *prisión* (1024).

23. Fita, "Los tres procesos," 458–60.

24. For the months in Salamanca, see *Acta*, 452–65. See further O'Malley, *First Jesuits*, 28, 70–71, 272–83 (Jesuits and the Protestant Reformation), 173–74 (Jesuit prison ministry), 43–44, 292–96, 367 (opposition to the Jesuits and the *Spiritual Exercises*), 310–20 (Jesuits and the Inquisition). For humanist currents at Salamanca, see Katherine Elliot van Liere, "After Nebrija: Academic Reformers and the Teaching of Latin in Sixteenth-Century Salamanca," *Sixteenth Century Journal* 34 (2003): 1065–78. Elliot van Liere ascribes humanism's failure to take deeper root to factors like the conservative spirit of the university, its inefficiency, and the well-established careerism and reactionary vigilance of a block of its professors.

25. Echarte, *Concordancia Ignaciana*, lists the occurrences in the *Acta* of *compagnia, compagno, compañero, compañia* (179–80, 193): 1, 35 (four times), 38, 41 (four times), 56, 57, 64 (three times), 66, 67, 69, 79 (two times), 80 (three times), 84, 85 (twice), 86 (twice), 87, 89, 90, 93 (three times), 95 (three times), 96, 97, 98 (twice), 100.

26. Echarte, *Concordancia Ignaciana*, s.v. *aiutare, aiuto, ayuda, ayudar* (30, 83–91). In the *Constitutions*, Ignatius used the expression *ayuda de las ánimas* twelve times and *ayudar a las ánimas / las ánimas* nine times (for twenty-one in total), while he used the expression *ayuda de los próximos* seven times and *ayudar a los próximos / los próximos* nineteen times (for a total of twenty-six).

27. O'Reilly, "Ignatius of Loyola and the Counter-Reformation," 456–57; and Lance Gabriel Lazar, *Working in the Vineyard of the Lord: Jesuit Confraternities in Early Modern Italy* (Toronto: University of Toronto Press, 2005), 108.

28. In 1532, Gian Pietro Carafa lamented the decadence of the church's military orders. In his mind, that decadence had contributed to the recent loss of Rhodes, and he urged Pope Clement VII to back the reform of an unnamed military order. See Carafa, "De Lutheranorum haeresi reprimenda et ecclesia reformanda ad Clementem VII.," in *Concilium Tridentinum: Diariorum, Actorum, Epistularum, Tractatum Nova Collectio,* vol. 12, *Tractatum Pars Prior,* Vincentius Schweitzer, ed. (Freiburg im Breisgau: Herder, 1929; repr. Freiburg im Breisgau: Herder, 1966), 75–77; English translation, "Information Sent to Pope Clement VII by the Bishop of Chieti through Brother Bonaventura of the Franciscan Order [October 4, 1532]," in *Reform Thought in Sixteenth-Century Italy,* Elisabeth G. Gleason, ed. and trans., American Academy of Religion Texts and Translations, 4 (Chico, Calif: Scholars Press, 1981), 77–80.

29. See, e.g., O'Reilly, "Erasmus, Ignatius Loyola, and Orthodoxy," 120–24; Angel Alcalá, "Inquisitorial Control of Humanists and Writers," in *The Spanish Inquisition and the Inquisitorial Mind,* 321–28; Rummel, *Erasmus and His Catholic Critics,* 1:145–78, 2:81–105; and Homza, *Religious Authority,* 49–76, who sees less clear-cut lines between liberal humanists and reactionary Scholastics among the participants at Valladolid. For Diogo de Gouveia's career, see also James K. Farge, *Biographical Register of Paris Doctors of Theology, 1500–1536,* Subsidia Mediaevalia, 10 (Toronto: Pontifical Institute of Mediaeval Studies, 1980), 202–4 (no. 220). He went from fierce criticism of the Jesuits to open support.

30. See, e.g., Robert Aleksander Maryks, *The Jesuit Order as a Synagogue of Jews: Jesuits of Jewish Ancestry and Purity-of-Blood Laws in the Early Society of Jesus,* Studies in Medieval and Reformation Traditions, 146 (Leiden: Brill, 2010), 29–30, 79–86.

31. See, e.g., Terence W. O'Reilly, "Melchor Cano and the Spirituality of St. Ignatius Loyola," in *Ignacio de Loyola y su tiempo,* 371–73, 377–79.

32. James Brodrick, *The Origin of the Jesuits* (London: Longmans, Green, 1940; repr. Chicago: Loyola University Press, 1986), 186–87.

33. Samuel Edgerton, Jr., *Pictures and Punishment: Art and Criminal Prosecution during the Florentine Renaissance* (Ithaca, N.Y.: Cornell University Press, 1985), 126–221.

34. Ignatius to Peter Canisius, 13 August 1554, *Monumenta Ignatiana,* Series I, *Epistolae et instructiones,* Monumenta Historica Societatis Iesu, 34 (Madrid: Gabriel Lopez del Horno, 1908), 7:398–404. Ignatius to Peter Canisius, 13 August 1554, *Monumenta Ignatiana,* Series I, *Epistolae et instructiones,* Monumenta Historica Societatis Iesu, 42 (Madrid: Gabriel Lopez del Horno, 1911), 12:259–62. See further O'Malley, *First Jesuits,* 282–83.

35. Carafa, "De Lutheranorum haeresi reprimenda," in *Concilium Tridentinum,* 12:68 (English translation of Gleason, "Information Sent to Pope Clement VII," 59). For Carafa's inspiration and methods, see Christopher F. Black, *The*

Italian Inquisition (New Haven, Conn.: Yale University Press, 2009), 10–11, 16–17, 20.

36. Pedro de Leturia, "Los 'Recuerdos' presentados por el jesuíta Bobadilla al recién elegido Paulo IV," in *Estudios Ignacianos*, Ignacio Iparraguirre, ed., Bibliotheca Instituti Historici Societatis Iesu, 10–11 (Roma: Institutum Historicum Societatis Iesu, 1957), 1:458 n. 60; and O'Malley, *First Jesuits*, 311–12.

37. Silvana Seidel Menchi, "Origine e origini del Santo Uffizio dell'Inquisizione romana (1542–1559)," in *L'Inquisizione (Atti del Simposio internazionale, Città del Vaticano, 29–31 ottobre 1998)*, Agostino Borromeo, ed., Studi e testi, 417 (Città del Vaticano: Biblioteca Apostolica Vaticana, 2003), 306–8. See also González Novalín, "Los Jesuitas y la Inquisición," 291–300.

38. O'Malley, *First Jesuits*, 314.

39. On the Italian *spirituali*, see, e.g., Elisabeth Gleason, "On the Nature of Sixteenth-Century Italian Evangelism: Scholarship, 1953–1978," *Sixteenth Century Journal* 9, no. 3 (1978): 3–25; and Anne Jacobson Schutte, "Periodization of Sixteenth-Century Italian Religious History: The Post-Cantimori Paradigm Shift," *Journal of Modern History* 61 (1989): 273–75. On acquaintances of Ignatius, see, e.g., Joseph Crehan, "Saint Ignatius and Cardinal Pole," *Archivum historicum Societatis Iesu* 25 (1956): 72–92; Massimo Firpo, "Vittoria Colonna, Giovanni Morone, e gli 'spirituali,'" *Rivista di storia e letteratura religiosa* 24 (1988): 224–48; and Una Roman D'Elia, "Drawing Christ's Blood: Michelangelo, Vittoria Colonna, and the Aesthetics of Reform," *Renaissance Quarterly* 59 (2006): 96–125.

40. J. H. Elliott, *Europe Divided, 1559–1598*, Blackwell Classic Histories of Europe, 2nd ed. (Oxford: Blackwell, 2000), 97. See also Mario Scaduto, "Laínez e l'Indice del 1559: Lullo, Sabunde, Savonarola, Erasmo," *Archivum historicum Societatis Iesu* 24 (1955): 6–8, 12–18.

41. For the dispute between Salmerón and Morone and Paul IV's efforts to use it in his campaign against Pole, Morone, and the spirituali, see, e.g., Dermot Fenlon, *Heresy and Obedience in Tridentine Italy: Cardinal Pole and the Counter Reformation* (Cambridge: Cambridge University Press, 1972), 269–80. In general, see Alister E. McGrath, *Iustitia Dei: A History of the Christian Doctrine of Justification*, 3rd ed. (Cambridge: Cambridge University Press, 2005), 1–357.

42. See, e.g., Jaime Contreras, "The Impact of Protestantism in Spain, 1520–1600," in *Inquisition and Society in Early Modern Europe*, 49–57 (who quotes Bartolomé Bennassar on a pedagogy of fear); Bartolomé Bennassar, "Patterns of the Inquisitorial Mind as the Basis for a Pedagogy of Fear," in *The Spanish Inquisition and the Inquisitorial Mind*, 177–82; Andrés, "Alumbrados, Erasmians, 'Lutherans,' and Mystics," 482–86; O'Malley, *First Jesuits*, 317–20 (who uses the phrase "patent injustice"); Judith Shulevitz, "The Close Reader: The Case of Pius XII," *New York Times Book Review* (8 April 2001): 34; Stefania Pastore, *Il Vangelo e la spada: L'inquisizione di Castiglia e i suoi critici (1460–1598)*, "Tribunali della fede," Temi e

testi, 46 (Roma: Edizioni di Storia e Letteratura, 2003), 229–52; Clive Griffin, *Journeymen-Printers, Heresy, and the Inquisition in Sixteenth-Century Spain* (Oxford: Oxford University Press, 2005), 3–7; and Lu Ann Homza, *The Spanish Inquisition, 1478–1614: An Anthology of Sources* (Indianapolis, Ind.: Hackett Publishing, 2006), 194–95. The classic expression of the survival instincts of institutions is Reinhold Niebuhr, *Moral Man and Immoral Society: A Study in Ethics and Politics*, Library of Theological Ethics (New York: Charles Scribner's Sons, 1932; repr. Louisville, Ky.: Westminster John Knox Press, 2001).

43. For Ignatius's years in Paris, see *Acta*, 464–81; O'Rourke Boyle, *Loyola's Acts*, 113–14, 168, 171–72; Philippe Lécrivain, *Paris au temps d'Ignace de Loyola (1528–1535)* (Paris: Éditions facultés jésuites de Paris, 2006); and Aumont, *Ignace de Loyola*, 165–75. See further O'Malley, *First Jesuits*, 28–32, 52–62 (membership in the first years), 79–84 (qualifications for Jesuit ministries), 215–25, 244–53 (Jesuits, the methods of Paris, and formal theology), 287–92 (opposition to the Jesuits in France). O'Malley, ibid., 28, notes that "[t]he brevity of the account of the Parisian years in his *Autobiography* belies their importance for the future Society of Jesus, and those few pages are remarkable more for what they do not recount than for that what they do."

44. In general, see James K. Farge, *Orthodoxy and Reform in Early Reformation France: The Faculty of Theology of Paris, 1500–1543*, Studies in Medieval and Reformation Thought, 32 (Leiden: Brill, 1985), 11–28, 72–73; and Farge, "The University of Paris in the Time of Ignatius of Loyola," in *Ignacio de Loyola y su tiempo*, 222–38.

45. See, e.g., Gabriel Codina Mir, *Aux sources de la pédagogie des jésuites: Le "Modus parisiensis*," Bibliotheca Instituti Historici Societatis Iesu, 28 (Roma: Institutum Historicum Societatis Iesu, 1968), 99–131, 147–50; William V. Bangert, *A History of the Society of Jesus* (St. Louis, Mo.: Institute of Jesuit Sources, 1972), 27–28; and Gian Paolo Brizzi, "*Studia humanitatis* und Organisation des Unterrichts in den ersten italienischen Kollegien der Gesellschaft Jesu," in *Humanismus im Bildungswesen des 15. und 16. Jahrhunderts*, Wolfgang Reinhard, ed., Deutsche Forschungsgemeinschaft (Weinheim: Acta Humaniora, 1984), 155–70.

46. Farge, "The University of Paris in the Time of Ignatius," 231, thinks that Ignatius moved out of Montaigu in order to room with Favre and Xavier and study under Juan de la Peña, a Spanish regent at the Collège Sainte-Barbe.

47. Paul Oskar Kristeller, "Thomism and the Italian Thought of the Renaissance," in *Medieval Aspects of Renaissance Learning: Three Essays by Paul Oskar Kristeller*, Edward P. Mahoney, ed. and trans., Duke Monographs in Medieval and Renaissance Studies, 1 (Durham, N.C.: Duke University Press, 1974), 27–91; and John W. O'Malley, "The Feast of Thomas Aquinas in Renaissance Rome: A Neglected Document and Its Import," *Rivista di storia della Chiesa in Italia* 35 (1981): 1–27.

48. O'Malley, *First Jesuits*, 247–48. The common medieval form of the saying read "Amicus quidem Plato sed magis amica veritas" and was cited, among others, by Petrarch, "On His Own Ignorance and That of Many Others," in *The Renaissance Philosophy of Man*, Ernst Cassirer, Paul Oskar Kristeller, and John Herman Randall, Jr., eds., and Hans Nachod, trans. (Chicago: University of Chicago Press, 1948), 111. See also W. K. C. Guthrie, *A History of Greek Philosophy*, vol. 6, *Aristotle: An Encounter*, 2nd ed. (Cambridge: Cambridge University Press, 1990), 25–26 n. 2.

49. Leonardo R. Silos, "Cardoner in the Life of Saint Ignatius of Loyola," *Archivum historicum Societatis Iesu* 33 (1964): 29–33; and O'Malley, *First Jesuits*, 243–44, 250–52, 369–70.

50. See, e.g., Anthony Levi, *Renaissance and Reformation: The Intellectual Genesis* (New Haven, Conn.: Yale University Press, 2002), 315–25, who notes Masurier's concern for poor relief in Meaux and his persecution by the theological faculty in Paris.

51. See, e.g., Farge, *Biographical Register of Paris Doctors of Theology*, 73 (no. 81); and Constance Jones Mathers, "Early Spanish Qualms about Loyola and the Society of Jesus," *The Historian* 53 (1991): 680–81.

52. Farge supplies excellent detail on the Faculty's role as consultant and Inquisition in his *Orthodoxy and Reform*, 115–208, 234–38. The Faculty of Theology consulted on theological and ethical matters involving kings, princes, bishops, civil and ecclesiastical institutions, and other individuals. Farge describes more than seventy documented cases of consulting from 1500 to 1536, ranging from Henry VIII's petition for an annulment to a decree for poor relief in the city of Ypres.

53. Farge, *Orthodoxy and Reform*, 204. On Louis de Berquin, see, e.g., Gordon Griffiths, "Berquin, Louis de," in *Contemporaries of Erasmus: A Biographical Register of the Renaissance and Reformation*, vol. 1, *A–E*, P. G. Bietenholz and Thomas B. Deutscher, eds. (Toronto: University of Toronto Press, 1985), 135–40.

54. Farge, *Biographical Register of Paris Doctors of Theology*, 42–43 (no. 42); and Farge, *Orthodoxy and Reform*, 186.

55. For the return to Spain and the reunion in Venice, see *Acta*, 482–97; and O'Rourke Boyle, *Loyola's Acts*, 161–63. See further O'Malley, *First Jesuits*, 32–34, 91–104 (Jesuits and preaching), 161 (Ignatius and Carafa), 171–73 (Jesuits and hospital ministry), 174–78 (Jesuits and the art of dying well), 166–68, 192–99 (Jesuits and confraternities), 205, 256 (Ignatius and Andrea Lippomano of Venice).

56. O'Malley, *First Jesuits*, 58.

57. Fernández Zapico and de Dalmases, *Acta*, 484: "Alli poveri ha fatto dar' ordine come se fosse proveduto publico et ordinariamente." See, e.g., Linda Martz, *Poverty and Welfare in Habsburg Spain: The Example of Toledo*, Cambridge Iberian and Latin American Studies (Cambridge: Cambridge University Press,

1983), 7–15; Valentín Moreno Gallego, "Notas historiográficas al encuentro de Loyola y Vives," in *Ignacio de Loyola y su tiempo*, 901–7; Carter Lindberg, *Beyond Charity: Reformation Initiatives for the Poor* (Minneapolis: Augsburg Press, 1993), 77–84; and Lazar, *Working in the Vineyard*, 25–27.

58. Jones Mathers, "Early Spanish Qualms about Loyola," 682–85; and O'Malley, *First Jesuits*, 92, 100.

59. In general, see Gian Paolo Brizzi and Anna Maria Matteucci, eds., *Dall'isola alla città: I gesuiti a Bologna* (Bologna: Nuova Alfa Editoriale, 1988); and Mario Zanardi, ed., *I gesuiti e Venezia: Momenti e problemi di storia veneziana della Compagnia di Gesù (Atti del Convegno di Studi, Venezia, 2–5 ottobre 1990)* (Padova: Gregoriana Libreria Editrice, 1994).

60. On the Venetian *Scuole Grandi* and new thinking toward the poor, see, e.g., Brian S. Pullan, *Rich and Poor in Renaissance Venice: The Social Institutions of a Catholic State, to 1620* (Cambridge, Mass.: Harvard University Press, 1971), 33–193, 216–38; and Pullan, "The *Scuole Grandi* of Venice: Some Further Thoughts," in *Christianity and the Renaissance: Image and Religious Imagination in the Quattrocento*, Timothy Verdon and John Henderson, eds. (Syracuse, N.Y.: Syracuse University Press, 1990), 272–301. In general, see, e.g., Roberto Rusconi, "Confraternite, compagnie, e devozioni," in *Storia d'Italia: Annali*, vol. 9, *La chiesa e il potere politico dal Medioevo all'età contemporanea*, Giorgio Chittolini and Giovanni Miccoli, eds. (Torino: Einaudi, 1986), 478–94; and Nicholas Terpstra, "Confraternities and Public Charity: Modes of Civic Welfare in Early Modern Italy," in *Confraternities and Catholic Reform in Italy, France, and Spain*, John Patrick Donnelly and Michael W. Maher, eds., Sixteenth Century Essays & Studies, 44 (Kirksville, Mo.: Thomas Jefferson University Press, 1999), 97–121.

61. On Renaissance hospitals, see, e.g., Pullan, *Rich and Poor in Renaissance Venice*, 197–215, 423–28; Martz, *Poverty and Welfare*, 34–44; Katharine Park, *Doctors and Medicine in Early Renaissance Florence* (Princeton, N.J.: Princeton Univ. Press, 1985), 52–53, 87, 90–94, 101–6, 239; Ann G. Carmichael, *Plague and the Poor in Renaissance Florence*, Cambridge History of Medicine (Cambridge: Cambridge University Press, 1986), 51–53, 102–3, 113, 118–21; Michel Mollat du Jourdin, *The Poor in the Middle Ages: An Essay in Social History*, Arthur Goldhammer, trans. (New Haven, Conn.: Yale University Press, 1986), 98–102, 146–53, 262–71, 281–88; Christopher F. Black, *Italian Confraternities in the Sixteenth Century* (Cambridge: Cambridge University Press, 1989), 184–200; Maureen Flynn, *Sacred Charity: Confraternities and Social Welfare in Spain, 1400–1700* (Ithaca, N.Y.: Cornell University Press, 1989), 49–56; Katharine Park, "Healing the Poor: Hospitals and Medical Assistance in Renaissance Florence," in *Medicine and Charity before the Welfare State*, Jonathan Barry and Colin Jones, eds. (London: Routledge, 1991), 26–45; and John Henderson, *The Renaissance Hospital: Healing the Body and Healing the Soul* (New Haven, Conn.: Yale University Press, 2006).

62. See, e.g., Roger Chartier, "Les arts de mourir, 1450–1600," *Annales: Économies sociétés civilisations* 31 (1976): 52–70; and James R. Banker, *Death in the Community: Memorialization and Confraternities in an Italian Commune in the Late Middle Ages* (Athens: University of Georgia Press, 1988), 75–144, 174–86.

63. See, e.g., Pedro de Leturia, "Origine e senso sociale dell'apostolato di Sant'Ignazio di Loyola in Roma," in *Estudios Ignacianos*, Ignacio Iparraguirre, ed., Bibliotheca Instituti Historici Societatis Iesu, 10–11 (Roma: Institutum Historicum Societatis Iesu, 1957), 1:258; Charmarie J. Blaisdell, "Calvin's and Loyola's Letters to Women: Politics and Spiritual Counsel in the Sixteenth Century," in *Calviniana: Ideas and Influence of Jean Calvin*, Robert V. Schnucker, ed., Sixteenth Century Essays & Studies, 10 (Kirksville, Mo.: Sixteenth Century Journal Publishers, 1988), 244–45; Jill Raitt, "Two Spiritual Directors of Women in the Sixteenth Century: St. Ignatius Loyola and St. Teresa of Avila," in *In Laudem Caroli: Renaissance and Reformation Studies for Charles G. Nauert*, James V. Mehl, ed., Sixteenth Century Essays & Studies, 49 (Kirksville, Mo.: Thomas Jefferson University Press, 1998), 218–21; and P. Renée Baernstein, "Reprobates and Courtiers: Lay Masculinities in the Colonna Family, 1520–1584," in *Florence and Beyond: Culture, Society, and Politics in Renaissance Italy. Essays in Honour of John M. Najemy*, David S. Peterson with Daniel E. Bornstein, eds., Essays and Studies, 15 (Toronto: Centre for Reformation and Renaissance Studies, 2008), 294–97.

64. Daniel R. Lesnick, "Civic Preaching in the Early Renaissance: Giovanni Dominici's Florentine Sermons," in *Christianity and the Renaissance: Image and Religious Imagination in the Quattrocento*, Timothy Verdon and John Henderson, eds. (Syracuse, N.Y.: Syracuse University Press, 1990), 210–14, 217–18, 220–21; and Jennifer D. Selwyn, *A Paradise Inhabited by Devils: The Jesuits' Civilizing Mission in Early Modern Naples*, Catholic Christendom, 1300–1700 (Aldershot, U.K.: Ashgate, 2004), 183–209. Renaissance churchmen tried to ameliorate the destructive power of gunpowder weapons by making Saint Barbara their patron. See J. R. Hale, "War and Public Opinion in Renaissance Italy," *Renaissance War Studies* (London: Hambledon Press, 1983), 367; and Hale, "Gunpowder and the Renaissance: An Essay in the History of Ideas," *Renaissance War Studies*, 402.

65. Elisabeth G. Gleason, *Gasparo Contarini: Venice, Rome, and Reform* (Berkeley: University of California Press, 1993), 1–29, 186–256. On the religious environment of Venice, see also Nicolas Davidson, "Il Sant'Uffizio e la tutela del culto a Venezia nel '500," *Studi veneziani*, n.s., 6 (1982): 87–101; John Martin, "Salvation and Society in Sixteenth-Century Venice: Popular Evangelism in a Renaissance City," *Journal of Modern History* 60 (1988): 205–17; and Martin, *Venice's Hidden Enemies: Italian Heretics in a Renaissance City*, Studies on the History of Society and Culture, 16 (Berkeley: University of California Press, 1993), 25–48.

66. Carafa, "De Lutheranorum haeresi reprimenda," in *Concilium Tridenti-num*, 12:67, 68–69, 69–70, 72, 73 (English translation of Gleason, "Information Sent to Pope Clement VII," 57–58, 60–61, 63, 69–70).

67. For Lippomano, see Angelo Martini, "Di chi fu ospite S. Ignazio a Venezia nel 1536?" *Archivum historicum Societatis Iesu* 18 (1949): 255–60; and Martini, "Gli studi teologici di Giovanni de Polanco alle origini della legislazione scolas-tica della Compagnia di Gesù," *Archivum historicum Societatis Iesu* 21 (1952): 229–33. To describe Lippomano, Ignatius used humanist terminology: "mucho docto y bueno." On the new religious orders, including the Theatines, see, e.g., Paul A. Kunkel, *The Theatines in the History of Catholic Reform before the Establishment of Lutheranism* (Washington, D.C.: Catholic University of America Press, 1941), 30–111; John Patrick Donnelly, "Religious Orders of Men, Especially the Society of Jesus," in *Catholicism in Early Modern Europe: A Guide to Research*, 147–55; and Mark A. Lewis, "Recovering the Apostolic Way of Life: The New Clerks Regular of the Sixteenth Century," in *Early Modern Catholicism: Essays in Honour of John W. O'Malley, S.J.*, Kathleen M. Comerford and Hilmar M. Pabel, eds. (Toronto: University of Toronto Press, 2001), 284–90.

68. See Georges Bottereau, "La 'lettre' d'Ignace de Loyola à Gian Pietro Carafa," *Archivum historicum Societatis Iesu* 44 (1975): 139–51; Peter A. Quinn, "Ignatius Loyola and Gian Pietro Carafa: Catholic Reformers at Odds," *Catholic Historical Review* 67 (1981): 388–92; and Meissner, *Ignatius of Loyola: The Psychol-ogy of a Saint*, 168–73. Meissner, 401–4, republished the English translation of the letter by William J. Young, *Letters of St. Ignatius Loyola* (Chicago: Loyola University Press, 1959), 28–31. For the career of Pedro Ortiz, see Farge, *Bio-graphical Register of Paris Doctors of Theology*, 350–53 (no. 371).

69. For the journey to Rome and the vision at La Storta, see *Acta*, 496–507; and O'Rourke Boyle, *Loyola's Acts*, 175–80. See further O'Malley, *First Jesuits*, 18–19 (Ignatius's meaning for "helping souls"), 34–36, 73–74 (decision against benefices), 104–10 (Jesuits and sacred lectures), 134–36, 284–87, 321–28 (Jesuits, Trent, and church reform), 157–59 (Jesuits and priesthood), 178–88 (Jesuit min-istries to prostitutes and orphans). See also O'Malley, "Was Ignatius Loyola a Church Reformer? How to Look at Early Modern Catholicism," *Catholic Histori-cal Review* 77 (1991): 177–93.

70. Charles Chauvin, "La Maison Sainte-Marthe: Ignace et les prostituées de Rome," *Christus* 38, no. 149 (Jan. 1991): 118–25; Chauvin, "Ignace et les courti-sanes: La Maison Sainte Marthe (1542–1548)," in *Ignacio de Loyola y su tiempo*, 551–58; and Lazar, *Working in the Vineyard*, 45–67.

71. Carlo M. Cipolla, *Before the Industrial Revolution: European Society and Economy, 1000–1700*, 2nd ed. (New York: W. W. Norton, 1980), 87. In general, see Achillo Olivieri, "Eroticism and Social Groups in Sixteenth-Century Venice: The Courtesan," in *Western Sexuality: Practice and Precept in Past and Present Times*,

Philippe Ariès and André Béjin, eds., and Anthony Forster, trans., Family, Sexuality, and Social Relations in Past Times (Oxford: Oxford University Press, 1985), 95–102; and Richard C. Trexler, "Florentine Prostitution in the Fifteenth Century: Patrons and Clients," in Dependence in Context in Renaissance Florence, Medieval & Renaissance Texts & Studies, 111 (Binghamton: Center for Medieval and Early Renaissance Studies, State University of New York at Binghamton, 1994), 373–414.

72. Other sources indicate that Ignatius shortened the list of calumniators and named only Francisco de Mudarra and a Barreda or Barrera. Landívar knew Ignatius and Xavier during their time at the University of Paris. See, e.g., Luis Fernández Martín, "Francisco Mudarra, difamador y protegido de San Ignacio, 1538–1555," Archivum historicum Societatis Iesu 62 (1993): 163–67; and Joseph F. Conwell, Impelling Spirit: Revisiting a Founding Experience, 1539, Ignatius of Loyola and His Companions (Chicago: Loyola Press, 1997), 188–98.

73. Marcello Del Piazzo and Cándido de Dalmases, "Il processo sull'ortodossia di S. Ignazio e dei suoi compagni svoltosi a Roma nel 1538: Nuovi documenti," Archivum historicum Societatis Iesu 38 (1969): 431–52. Del Piazzo and de Dalmases published depositions from Pedro Ortiz, from Ambrogio "Catarino" Politi and Lattanzio Tolomei (occasional participants in discussions hosted by Vittoria Colonna in Rome), from Matthieu Ory (secretary to the Inquisition in Paris and then an inquisitor), from Doimo Nascio (encouraged by Carafa to attend the Jesuit lectures), and from Fernando Díez. See also the letters of Ignatius to Isabel Roser (19 Dec. 1538) and Pierre Favre to Diogo de Gouveia (23 Nov. 1538) in Autobiography, John Olin, ed., and Joseph O'Callaghan, trans., 97–105; and Arthur L. Fisher, "A Study in Early Jesuit Government: The Nature and Origins of the Dissent of Nicolás Bobadilla," Viator 10 (1979): 412–13.

74. For the significance of the Roman controversies, see, e.g., O'Rourke Boyle, Loyola's Acts, 174–75; and Meissner, Ignatius of Loyola: The Psychology of a Saint, 177–78, 182. See further O'Malley, First Jesuits, 190–92 (Jesuits and the Roman Jews), 233–39 (Jesuit education in Rome), 296–310 (Jesuits and the papacy), 335–41, 356–62 (spirit and implementation of the Jesuit Constitutions), 375–76 (the leadership of Ignatius).

75. O'Malley, First Jesuits, 296–99. See also O'Malley, "The Fourth Vow in Its Ignatian Context: A Historical Study," Studies in the Spirituality of Jesuits 15, no. 1 (1983): 23–27, 31–34.

76. See, e.g., Víctor Codina, "San Ignacio y Paulo IV: Notas para una teologia del carisma," Manresa 40 (1968): 337–62; Del Piazzo and de Dalmases, "Il processo," 447–48; Quinn, "Ignatius Loyola and Gian Pietro Carafa," 394, 396–400; John W. O'Malley, "The Jesuits, St. Ignatius, and the Counter Reformation: Some Recent Studies and Their Implications for Today," Studies in the Spirituality of Jesuits 14, no. 1 (1982): 19–21; Meissner, Ignatius of Loyola: The Psychology of a Saint, 192–96; and O'Malley, First Jesuits, 306–9.

77. Leturia, "Los 'Recuerdos,'" 1:449–54, 458–59.

78. In the 1532 *Memoriale*, Carafa had expressed his conviction that Franciscans and other religious had become so depraved that they engaged in murder, using poison, knives, swords, and guns. See Carafa, "De Lutheranorum haeresi reprimenda," in *Concilium Tridentinum*, 12:74 (English translation of Gleason, "Information Sent to Pope Clement VII," 74).

79. In general, see Moses A. Shulvass, *The Jews in the World of the Renaissance*, Elvin I. Kose, trans. (Leiden: Brill, 1973), 1–28, 207–14, 266–67, 283–85, 346–59; Kenneth R. Stow, "The Burning of the Talmud in 1553, in the Light of Sixteenth-Century Catholic Attitudes toward the Talmud," *Bibliothèque d'humanisme et Renaissance* 34 (1972): 435–59; James W. Reites, "St. Ignatius of Loyola and the Jews," *Studies in the Spirituality of Jesuits* 13, no. 4 (1981): 2–18; Alessandro Pastore, "Strutture assistenziali fra Chiesa e Stati nell'Italia della Controriforma," in *Storia d'Italia: Annali*, vol. 9, *La chiesa e il potere politico dal Medioevo all'età contemporanea*, Giorgio Chittolini and Giovanni Miccoli, eds. (Torino: Einaudi, 1986), 442–50; Benjamin Ravid, "The Legal Status of the Jews in Venice to 1509," *Proceedings of the American Academy for Jewish Research* 54 (1987): 169–202; Nicolas Davidson, "The Inquisition and the Italian Jews," in *Inquisition and Society in Early Modern Europe*, 19–46; Robert Bonfil, *Jewish Life in Renaissance Italy*, Anthony Oldcorn, trans. (Berkeley: University of California Press, 1994), 19–77, 168–69, 237–39; Kenneth R. Stow, *Theater of Acculturation: The Roman Ghetto in the Sixteenth Century* (Seattle: University of Washington Press, 2001), 39–66; and Eloise Rosenblatt, "Canonizing Edith Stein and Recognizing Catholic Anti-Semitism," in *"Good News" after Auschwitz? Christian Faith within a Post-Holocaust World*, Carol Ann Rittner and John K. Roth, eds. (Macon, Ga.: Mercer University Press, 2001), 56–58. In dealing with the intransigent Silíceo about the question of "New Christians," Ignatius had proposed a compromise whereby Jesuits would not accept New Christians into their college at Alcalá; see Francisco de Borja de Medina, "Ignacio de Loyola y la 'limpieza de sangre,'" in *Ignacio de Loyola y su tiempo*, 599–601.

80. Pierre Bayle, "Loyola," *Dictionnaire historique et critique*, English translation in *Political Writings*, Sally L. Jenkinson, ed., Cambridge Texts in the History of Political Thought (Cambridge: Cambridge University Press, 2000), 154–55, citing Ribadeneira, *Vita Ignatii*, book 3, chapter 9. See further Shlomo Simonsohn, *The Apostolic See and the Jews*, vol. 7, *History*, PIMS Studies and Texts, 109 (Toronto: Pontifical Institute of Mediaeval Studies, 1991), 274–78; and Barbara Sher Tinsley, *Pierre Bayle's Reformation: Conscience and Criticism on the Eve of the Enlightenment* (Cranbury, N.J.: Associated University Presses, 2001), 141–61.

81. O'Reilly, "Ignatius of Loyola and the Counter-Reformation," 458–59 (quote on 459).

82. William Bouwsma, *Venice and the Defense of Republican Liberty*, 41, cited by Martin, "Salvation and Society in Sixteenth-Century Venice," 215–16. See also Martin, ibid., 228–30.

83. Charles Trinkaus, *In Our Image and Likeness: Humanity and Divinity in Italian Humanist Thought*, 2 vols. (Chicago: University of Chicago Press, 1970), 1:230–58; Heidi J. Hornik and Mikeal C. Parsons, *Illuminating Luke*, vol. 2, *The Public Ministry of Christ in Italian Renaissance and Baroque Painting* (Harrisburg, Penn.: T&T Clark International, 2005), 82–102; and John W. O'Malley, "Five Missions of the Jesuit Charism: Content and Method," *Studies in the Spirituality of Jesuits* 38, no. 4 (2006): 28–31.

84. Lewis, "Recovering the Apostolic Way of Life," 290.

85. Carmichael, *Plague and the Poor*, 125; Alessandro Pastore, "Strutture assistenziali fra Chiesa e Stati," 435–41; Anna Foa, "The New and the Old: The Spread of Syphilis (1494–1530)," Carole C. Gallucci, trans., in *Sex and Gender in Historical Perspective*, Edward Muir and Guido Ruggiero, eds., Selections from *Quaderni storici* (Baltimore: Johns Hopkins University Press, 1990), 31–45; and Sante Bortolami, "'Locus magne misericordie': Pellegrinaggi e ospitalità nel Veneto medioevale," in *I percorsi della fede e l'esperienza della carità nel Veneto medioevale (Atti del Convegno, Castello di Monselice, 28 maggio 2000)*, Antonio Rigon, ed. (Monselice: Il Poligrafo, 2002), 111–31.

86. Josef Franz Schütte, *Valignano's Mission Principles for Japan*, vol. 1, *From His Appointment as Visitor until His First Departure from Japan (1573–1582)*, part 2, *The Solution (1580–82)*, John J. Coyne, trans., Modern Scholarly Studies about the Jesuits in English Translations, 5 (St. Louis, Mo.: Institute of Jesuit Sources, 1985), 310–12; and Peter Schineller, "In Their Own Words," *Studies in the Spirituality of Jesuits* 38, no. 1 (2006): 21, 39. Echarte, *Concordancia Ignaciana*, gives twelve occurrences of *hospital* in Acta [18, 19, 56 (twice), 59, 60, 61, 74 (three times), 77 (twice)] and four of *ospedale* (79, 87, 88, 93). See Echarte, *Concordancia Ignaciana*, 631, 884.

87. Martz, *Poverty and Welfare*, 38–41; Stefania Pastore, *Il Vangelo e la spada*, 267–71, 308–17; and Marc Rastoin, "From Windfall to Fall: The *Conversos* in the Society of Jesus," in *Friends on the Way: Jesuits Encounter Contemporary Judaism*, Tom Michel, ed. (New York: Fordham University Press, 2007), 8–27. Pastore suggests that, although Ignatius supported accepting *conversos* as Jesuits, he may have used the amicable relations between Antonio de Aráoz (1515–73) and the Inquisition to shield the Society of Jesus. After hearing Juan de Ávila preach and then speaking with him, Juan de Dios (1495–1550) experienced a religious conversion and founded a famous hospital in Granada. In principle, that hospital was to accept anyone, and it did (beggars, pilgrims, travelers, prostitutes, lepers, syphilitics, elderly, blind, criminals, and the insane, as well as anyone requiring short-term medical attention). See further David Coleman, "Moral Formation

and Social Control in the Catholic Reformation: The Case of San Juan de Ávila," *Sixteenth Century Journal* 26 (1995): 18–27; and Coleman, *Creating Christian Granada: Society and Religious Culture in an Old-World Frontier City, 1492–1600* (Ithaca, N.Y.: Cornell University Press, 2003), 130–43.

88. See esp. Black, *Italian Confraternities*, 190–96.

89. See, e.g., Chauvin, "Ignace et les courtisanes," 552; and Hornik and Parsons, *Illuminating Luke*, 2:111–28.

90. Alonso de Sandoval, *Un tratado sobre la esclavitud ("De instauranda Aethiopum salute")*, Enriqueta Vila Vilar, trans. (Madrid: Alianza Editorial, 1987), 372: "Y no le paresca a nadie indina cosa de Religion, andar buscando un Religioso de casa en casa estas lenguas e interpretes, y despues de hallarlas, llevarlas consigo, aunque sean morenas: pues sabemos, que nuestro santo Padre Ignacio, hazia lo mesmo en la conversion de las mugeres publicas, a quien ni el oficio de general, ni sus canas ni authoridad le retraía, de que no las llevasse el mesmo, aunque fuesse por toda la Ciudad de Roma, adonde se recogiessen y sirviessen a Dios." English translation in Sandoval, *Treatise on Slavery: Selections from "De instauranda Aethiopum salute,"* Nicole von Germeten, trans. (Indianapolis, Ind.: Hackett Publishing, 2008), 103: "It is not undignified for a priest to go from house to house looking for translators. After he finds them, he should not be ashamed to walk with them, even if they are black. Ignatius himself walked with the prostitutes in Rome." See also Lance G. Lazar, " 'E faucibus daemonis': Daughters of Prostitutes, the First Jesuits, and the Compagnia delle Vergini Miserabili di Santa Caterina della Rosa," in *Confraternities and the Visual Arts in Renaissance Italy: Ritual, Spectacle, Image*, Barbara Wisch and Diane Cole Ahl, eds. (Cambridge: Cambridge University Press, 2000), 260–62, 269–70.

91. Mary Elizabeth Perry, " 'Lost Women' in Early Modern Seville: The Politics of Prostitution," *Feminist Studies* 4 (1978): 199–200, 203–6, 211; and Perry, "Magdalens and Jezebels in Counter-Reformation Spain," in *Culture and Control in Counter-Reformation Spain*, Anne J. Cruz and Mary Elizabeth Perry, eds., Hispanic Issues, 7 (Minneapolis: University of Minnesota Press, 1992), 128–32, 134, 137–38. For Roman prostitution, see Jonathan D. Spence, *The Memory Palace of Matteo Ricci* (New York: Penguin Books, 1984), 207–8, who suggests a total of 600–900 prostitutes licensed in Rome and many more in times of famine. On the efforts of Bishop Gabriele Paleotti and philanthropic nobles in Bologna, see Lucia Ferrante, "Honor Regained: Women in the Casa del Soccorso di San Paolo in Sixteenth-Century Bologna," Margaret A. Gallucci, trans., in *Sex and Gender in Historical Perspective*, 46–47, 56–64.

92. Marjorie O'Rourke Boyle, "Angels Black and White: Loyola's Spiritual Discernment in Historical Perspective," *Theological Studies* 44 (1983): 241–57; O'Reilly, "Ignatius of Loyola and the Counter-Reformation," 453–56; and Philippe Lécrivain, "Ignace de Loyola, un réformateur? Une lecture historique des 'Règles

pour avoir le vrai sens de l'Église,'" *Christus* 37, no. 147 (July 1990): 352–60. Cf. Jacob Jervell, *The Theology of the Acts of the Apostles*, New Testament Theology (Cambridge: Cambridge University Press, 1996), 52–54.

93. Seidel Menchi, "Origine e origini del Santo Uffizio," 308–21.

94. See, e.g., Davidson, "The Inquisition and the Italian Jews," 25–26, 35–38; and Stow, "The Burning of the Talmud," 435–42.

95. Shlomo Simonsohn, *The Apostolic See and the Jews*, vol. 6, *Documents: 1546–1555*, PIMS Studies and Texts, 106 (Toronto: Pontifical Institute of Mediaeval Studies, 1990), 2887–90 (no. 3165). The quote from the document on 2889 reads (emphasis mine), "*zelum* officii nostri ad hanc impietatem magis detegendam ac radicitus extirpandam accedere volentes."

96. Davidson, "The Inquisition and the Italian Jews," 30; and Bonfil, *Jewish Life*, 66. On the origins of the term *marrano*, see, e.g., Poliakov, *History of Anti-Semitism*, 2:218–22. For hatred of the *conversos* in Spain, see also Norman Roth, "The Jews of Spain and the Expulsion of 1492," *The Historian* 55 (1992): 22–27.

97. Martin, *Venice's Hidden Enemies*, 64; Spence, *The Memory Palace of Matteo Ricci*, 204; and Echarte, *Concordancia Ignaciana*, s.v. *inquisición* (659), Acta, 59.

4. The *Acta* as Mirror of Luke

1. See, e.g., Joseph A. Fitzmyer, *The Gospel According to Luke: Introduction, Translation, and Notes*, The Anchor Bible, 28–28A (Garden City, N.Y.: Doubleday, 1981–85), 1:164–71.

2. Floyd V. Filson, "The Journey Motif in Luke-Acts," in *Apostolic History and the Gospel: Biblical and Historical Essays Presented to F. F. Bruce on His 60th Birthday*, W. Ward Gasque and Ralph P. Martin, eds. (Grand Rapids, Mich.: Eerdmans, 1970), 68–69; and Michel Mollat du Jourdin, "Saint Ignace et les pèlerinages de son temps," in *Ignacio de Loyola y su tiempo: Congreso internacional de historia (9–13 Setiembre 1991)*, Juan Plazaola, ed. (Bilbao: Ediciones Mensajero, 1992), 171–72.

3. See, e.g., Angelo Martini, "Gli studi teologici di Giovanni de Polanco alle origini della legislazione scolastica della Compagnia di Gesù," *Archivum historicum Societatis Iesu* 21 (1952): 245–46; Gabriel Codina Mir, *Aux sources de la pédagogie des jésuites: Le "Modus parisiensis*," Bibliotheca Instituti Historici Societatis Iesu, 28 (Roma: Institutum Historicum Societatis Iesu, 1968), 44; Terence W. O'Reilly, "The Exercises of Saint Ignatius Loyola and the *Exercitatorio de la vida spiritual*," *Studia monastica* 16 (1974): 306; James K. Farge, *Biographical Register of Paris Doctors of Theology, 1500–1536*, Subsidia Mediaevalia, 10 (Toronto: Pontifical Institute of Mediaeval Studies, 1980), 39–40 (no. 38), 242–43 (no. 268), 304–11 (no. 329), 353–56 (no. 372), 437–41 (no. 473); John W. O'Malley, *The First Jesuits* (Cambridge, Mass.: Harvard University Press, 1993), 114–15, 164, 259; Ignacio Echarte, ed., *Concordancia Ignaciana / An Ignatian Concordance* (Bilbao: Ediciones Mensajero, in collaboration with the Institute of Jesuit Sources, St.

Louis, Mo., 1996), s.v. *Lucas* (1432); and Philippe Lécrivain, *Paris au temps d'Ignace de Loyola (1528–1535)* (Paris: Éditions facultés jésuites de Paris, 2006), 155.

4. In general, see C. C. McCown, "The Geography of Luke's Central Section," *Journal of Biblical Literature* 57 (1938): 51–66; McCown, "Gospel Geography: Fiction, Fact, and Truth," *Journal of Biblical Literature* 60 (1941): 7–9, 14–18, 20; Jindřich Mánek, "The New Exodus in the Books of Luke," *Novum Testamentum* 2 (1958): 10–22; William C. Robinson, Jr., "The Theological Context for Interpreting Luke's Travel Narrative (9:51 ff.)," *Journal of Biblical Literature* 79 (1960): 20–31; Filson, "The Journey Motif in Luke-Acts," 68–77; David H. Gill, "Observations on the Lukan Travel Narrative and Some Related Passages," *Harvard Theological Review* 63 (1970): 199–221; John J. Navone, "The Journey Theme in Luke-Acts," *Bible Today* 58 (Feb. 1972): 616–19; David P. Moessner, "'The Christ Must Suffer': New Light on the Jesus–Peter, Stephen, Paul Parallels in Luke-Acts," *Novum Testamentum* 28 (1986): 238–42; Moessner, *Lord of the Banquet: The Literary and Theological Significance of the Lukan Travel Narrative* (Minneapolis: Augsburg Fortress Press, 1989); James M. Scott, "Luke's Geographical Horizon," in *The Book of Acts in Its First Century Setting*, vol. 2, *The Book of Acts in Its Graeco-Roman Setting*, David W. J. Gill and Conrad Gempf, eds. (Grand Rapids, Mich.: Eerdmans, 1994), 483–544; and Ben Witherington, III, *The Acts of the Apostles: A Socio-Rhetorical Commentary* (Grand Rapids, Mich.: Eerdmans, 1998), 68–76.

5. Loveday Alexander, "'In Journeyings Often': Voyaging in the Acts of the Apostles and in Greek Romance," in *Luke's Literary Achievement: Collected Essays*, Christopher M. Tuckett, ed., *Journal for the Study of the New Testament* Supplement Series, 116 (Sheffield, U.K.: Sheffield Academic Press, 1995), 25–31, 36–37.

6. McCown, "The Geography," 54–56, 59–62; McCown, "Gospel Geography," 15–18; and Fitzmyer, *Gospel According to Luke*, 1:164.

7. See, e.g., P. Simson, "The Drama of the City of God: Jerusalem in St. Luke's Gospel," *Scripture* 15 (1963): 65–80; Fitzmyer, *Gospel According to Luke*, 1:164–68; and Mikeal C. Parsons, "The Place of Jerusalem on the Lukan Landscape: An Exercise in Symbolic Cartography," in *Literary Studies in Luke-Acts: Essays in Honor of Joseph B. Tyson*, Richard P. Thompson and Thomas E. Phillips, eds. (Macon, Ga.: Mercer University Press, 1998), 155–71.

8. McCown, "The Geography," 55; and McCown, "Gospel Geography," 14.

9. John C. Olin, "The Idea of Pilgrimage in the Experience of Ignatius Loyola," *Church History* 48 (1979): 393–95; and Ignasi Salvat, "The Ignatian Experience of 'Service as Worldwide Mission' as Basis for Interpreting the *Constitutions*," *Centrum Ignatianum Spiritualitatis (CIS)* 20, no. 3 (1990): 39–43.

10. See, e.g., Simson, "Drama of the City of God," 67–68; Mark McVann, "Rituals of Status Transformation in Luke-Acts: The Case of Jesus the Prophet," in *The Social World of Luke-Acts: Models for Interpretation*, Jerome H. Neyrey, ed. (Peabody, Mass.: Hendrickson, 1991), 354–55; Fitzmyer, *Gospel According to Luke*, 1:506–18; and Heidi J. Hornik and Mikeal C. Parsons, *Illuminating Luke*, vol. 2,

The Public Ministry of Christ in Italian Renaissance and Baroque Painting (Harrisburg, Penn.: T&T Clark International, 2005), 36–39.

11. See, e.g., Jeffrey L. Staley, " 'With the Power of the Spirit': Plotting the Program and Parallels of Luke 4:14–37 in Luke-Acts," in *Society of Biblical Literature 1993 Seminar Papers*, Eugene H. Lovering, Jr., ed., SBL Seminar Paper Series, 32 (Atlanta: Scholars Press, 1993), 281–91.

12. See, e.g., McCown, "The Geography," 65; Mánek, "The New Exodus," 12–13; Robinson, "Theological Context," 29–31; and Simson, "Drama of the City of God," 68–70.

13. Moessner, " 'The Christ Must Suffer,' " 236–37; and Moessner, *Lord of the Banquet*, 63–65.

14. Simson, "Drama of the City of God," 73; Fitzmyer, *Gospel According to Luke*, 1:823–26 (citing K. L. Schmidt on the lack of progress); 2:1020–21, 1024, 1028–30, 1034–35, 1149, 1152–54; and Moessner, *Lord of the Banquet*, 1–3, 14–33.

15. Moessner, *Lord of the Banquet*, 219.

16. Gill, "Observations on the Lukan Travel Narrative," 212–13; and Fitzmyer, *Gospel According to Luke*, 1:165, 338–39; 2:1242–47, 1251, 1256–57, 1514–15.

17. Bruce J. Malina and Jerome H. Neyrey, "Honor and Shame in Luke-Acts: Pivotal Values of the Mediterranean World," in *The Social World of Luke-Acts*, 48–49, 56; and Fitzmyer, *Gospel According to Luke*, 1:194–95; 2:1587–89.

18. Richard J. Dillon, "Acts of the Apostles," in *The New Jerome Biblical Commentary*, Raymond E. Brown, Joseph A. Fitzmyer, and Roland E. Murphy, eds. (Englewood Cliffs, N.J.: Prentice Hall, 1990), 722. See also Howard Clark Kee, *Good News to the Ends of the Earth: The Theology of Acts* (London: SCM Press, 1990), 42–50; and Witherington, *Acts of the Apostles*, 73–74.

19. Jacob Jervell, *The Theology of the Acts of the Apostles*, New Testament Theology (Cambridge: Cambridge University Press, 1996), 4–5, 12–15, 22–23. Cf. Jerome Kodell, "Luke's Use of *Laos*, 'People,' in the Jerusalem Narrative (Lk. 19:28–24:53)," *Catholic Biblical Quarterly* 31 (1969): 328–43; and J. Bradley Chance, *Jerusalem, the Temple, and the New Age in Luke-Acts* (Macon, Ga.: Mercer University Press, 1988), 35–46.

20. See, e.g., Clark Kee, *Good News*, 50–53; and Jervell, *Theology of the Acts*, 39–43, 129.

21. Marjorie O'Rourke Boyle, *Loyola's Acts: The Rhetoric of the Self*, The New Historicism: Studies in Cultural Poetics, 36 (Berkeley: University of California Press, 1997), 167.

22. See, e.g., Luke 2:4, 22, 41; 3:3; 4:14, 16, 38; 6:1; 7:11; 9:6, 51, 53, 56, 57; 10:1, 38; 13:22, 31, 33, 35; 14:25; 17:11; 18:31, 35, 36; 19:1, 11, 28, 29, 36, 37, 41, 45; 21:37; 24:28.

23. See, e.g., Acts 9:2; 18:25; 19:9, 23; 22:4; 24:14, 22. See further McCown, "The Geography," 53–54; McCown, "Gospel Geography," 15; Robinson, "Theo-

logical Context," 22–27; Filson, "The Journey Motif in Luke-Acts," 70–72, 77; Gill, "Observations on the Lukan Travel Narrative," 200 n. 2; Fitzmyer, *Gospel According to Luke*, 1:241–43; Richard B. Hays, *The Moral Vision of the New Testament: Community, Cross, New Creation; a Contemporary Introduction to New Testament Ethics* (New York: HarperCollins, 1996), 133–34; and Parsons, "Place of Jerusalem," 161.

24. Fitzmyer, *Gospel According to Luke*, 1:168–69.

25. *Letters and Instructions*, Martin E. Palmer and John W. Padberg, ed. and trans., with John L. McCarthy, ed., Jesuit Primary Sources in English Translation, 23 (St. Louis, Mo.: Institute of Jesuit Sources, 2006), 2 (no. 1).

26. Gill, "Observations on the Lukan Travel Narrative," 216–17; and Fitzmyer, *Gospel According to Luke*, 2:1557–60.

27. Richard J. Dillon, *From Eye-Witnesses to Ministers of the Word: Tradition and Composition in Luke 24*, Analecta Biblica, 82 (Roma: Biblical Institute Press, 1978), 136–37, 212–14, 242–43, 268, 272–74; and Fitzmyer, *Gospel According to Luke*, 1:237–39.

28. Jervell, *Theology of the Acts*, 43–52; and Witherington, *Acts of the Apostles*, 24, 59, 70, 72, 129–30.

29. Simson, "Drama of the City of God," 70–77; Gill, "Observations on the Lukan Travel Narrative," 201–4, 207–8, 214; and Fitzmyer, *Gospel According to Luke*, 1:664, 826–27. In general, see Richard N. Longenecker, "Taking up the Cross Daily: Discipleship in Luke-Acts," in *Patterns of Discipleship in the New Testament*, Richard N. Longenecker, ed. (Grand Rapids, Mich.: Eerdmans, 1996), 50–76.

30. John P. Meier, *A Marginal Jew: Rethinking the Historical Jesus*, vol. 2, *Mentor, Message, and Miracles*, The Anchor Bible Reference Library (New York: Doubleday, 1994), 116–77.

31. Letter to Teresa Rejadell (1536), in *Letters and Instructions*, Palmer and Padberg, ed. and trans., 21 (no. 7).

32. See, e.g., Dillon, *From Eye-Witnesses*, 203–20, 323; Fitzmyer, *Gospel According to Luke*, 2:1578–82; and Clark Kee, *Good News*, 99–104.

33. Una Roman D'Elia, "Drawing Christ's Blood: Michelangelo, Vittoria Colonna, and the Aesthetics of Reform," *Renaissance Quarterly* 59 (2006): 98: "non sottrae la grazia né ci asconde / la bella luce l'immortal sostegno / quando emenda il pentir nostro i nostri errori." D'Elia gives a slightly different translation.

34. See, e.g., Leo O'Reilly, *Word and Sign in the Acts of the Apostles: A Study in Lucan Theology*, Analecta Gregoriana, 243 (Roma: Editrice Pontificia Università Gregoriana, 1987), 11–12.

35. Moessner, *Lord of the Banquet*, 2; and Longenecker, "Taking up the Cross Daily," 55–56, 59, 73–74.

36. Dillon, *From Eye-Witnesses*, 114–15, 219; Fitzmyer, *Gospel According to Luke*, 2:1581–82, 1585, 1588; and Hays, *The Moral Vision of the New Testament*, 120–22, 129–32.

37. See, e.g., Gill, "Observations on the Lukan Travel Narrative," 218–19; Dillon, *From Eye-Witnesses*, 139–41, 207–13, 215, 279–81; Fitzmyer, *Gospel According to Luke*, 1:241–51; Moessner, "'The Christ Must Suffer,'" 227–28; Moessner, *Lord of the Banquet*, 304–7, 310–11; and Witherington, *Acts of the Apostles*, 71–73.

38. See, e.g., John R. Donahue, *The Gospel in Parable: Metaphor, Narrative, and Theology in the Synoptic Gospels* (Philadelphia: Fortress Press, 1988), 162–80; Fitzmyer, *Gospel According to Luke*, 1:247–51; and Thomas E. Phillips, "Reading Recent Readings of Issues of Wealth and Poverty in Luke and Acts," *Currents in Biblical Research* 1 (2003): 231–69.

39. Staley, "'With the Power of the Spirit,'" 293.

40. Robinson, "Theological Context," 20–22, 25–27, 28–29; Filson, "The Journey Motif in Luke-Acts," 72–76; Navone, "The Journey Theme," 618–19; Moessner, "'The Christ Must Suffer,'" 254–55; and Alexander, "'In Journeyings Often,'" 21–25.

41. Moessner, *Lord of the Banquet*, 168–71, 274–75, 324; Clark Kee, *Good News*, 95; and Longenecker, "Taking up the Cross Daily," 57–59, 61–62, 71–72.

42. Moessner, *Lord of the Banquet*, 143–44; Malina and Neyrey, "Honor and Shame in Luke-Acts," 50–51; Fitzmyer, *Gospel According to Luke*, 2:883–85; and Hornik and Parsons, *Illuminating Luke*, 2:85–86, 90–91.

43. Fitzmyer, *Gospel According to Luke*, 2:1508–9; and Raymond E. Brown, *The Death of the Messiah: A Commentary on the Passion Narratives in the Four Gospels*, The Anchor Bible Reference Library (New York: Doubleday, 1994), 1:30–31, 2:971–81, 1000–13.

44. Witherington, *Acts of the Apostles*, 70–71, 74–76; and Clark Kee, *Good News*, 105–7.

45. Parsons, "Place of Jerusalem," 157, 162–68; and Scott, "Luke's Geographical Horizon," 499–543.

46. Claude Nicolet, *Space, Geography, and Politics in the Early Roman Empire*, Jerome Lectures, 19 (Ann Arbor: University of Michigan Press, 1991), 15–56, 95–169; and Scott, "Luke's Geographical Horizon," 487–91.

47. See, e.g., Fitzmyer, *Gospel According to Luke*, 1:187–92, 257–58; Moessner, *Lord of the Banquet*, 108–9, 144–45, 275–76; Clark Kee, *Good News*, 42–69; Hays, *The Moral Vision of the New Testament*, 132–33; and Witherington, *Acts of the Apostles*, 55–56, 71, 143–44, 335–39.

48. Arthur L. Fisher, "A Study in Early Jesuit Government: The Nature and Origins of the Dissent of Nicolás Bobadilla," *Viator* 10 (1979): 401 n. 15.

49. Jonathan D. Spence, *The Memory Palace of Matteo Ricci* (New York: Penguin Books, 1984), 131 (woodcut reproduced on 128). Ricci grew up near Loreto, where the famous shrine purportedly preserved the house of the Annunciation and an image of the Virgin painted by Luke; see ibid., 233. Late medieval poets interpreted the Emmaus passage as a story about pilgrims. See Julia Bolton Holloway,

"The Pilgrim in the Poem: Dante, Langland, and Chaucer," *Jerusalem: Essays on Pilgrimage and Literature*, AMS Studies in the Middle Ages, 24 (New York: AMS Press, 1998), 121–41.

50. Clark Kee, *Good News*, 28–41; and Witherington, *Acts of the Apostles*, 21, 72, 173, 835.

51. Robert Aleksander Maryks, "La *consolatio* nel ministero della confessione dei primi gesuiti," in *I Gesuiti e la "Ratio studiorum*," Manfred Hinz, Roberto Righi, and Danilo Zardin, eds., "Europa delle Corti" Centro studi sulle società di antico regime: Biblioteca del Cinquecento, 113 (Roma: Bulzoni, 2004), 227.

52. Fitzmyer, *Gospel According to Luke*, 2:1183–85. See also André Feuillet, "Le pharisien et le publicain (Luc 18, 9–14): La manifestation de la miséricorde divine en Jésus Serviteur souffrant," *Esprit et vie* 91 (1981): 659–63; and John H. Elliott, "Temple versus Household in Luke-Acts: A Contrast in Social Institutions," in *The Social World of Luke-Acts*, 213–15.

53. Dillon, *From Eye-Witnesses*, 240–49; Malina and Neyrey, "Honor and Shame in Luke-Acts," 52, 55, 57–58, 62–63; Fitzmyer, *Gospel According to Luke*, 1:684–88; and James Malcolm Arlandson, *Women, Class, and Society in Early Christianity: Models from Luke-Acts* (Peabody, Mass.: Hendrickson, 1997), 158–62.

54. Echarte, *Concordancia Ignaciana*, s.v. *Lucas* (1432): "*Ej. 282,1* conversión de la Magdalena escribe S. *Lucas* en el 7.° caplo." See, e.g., Marilena Mosco, "La Maddalena: Un'identità velata e violata," in *La Maddalena tra sacro e profano*, M. Mosco, ed. (Firenze: La casa Usher, 1986), 17–23; Victor Saxer, "Santa Maria Maddalena: Dalla storia evangelica alla leggenda e all'arte," in *La Maddalena tra sacro e profano*, 24–28; and Sandra M. Rushing, *The Magdalene Legacy: Exploring the Wounded Icon of Sexuality* (Westport, Conn.: Bergin & Garvey, 1994), 43–59.

5. Ignatius, His *Acta*, and Renaissance Culture

1. Cf. Rafael M. de Hornedo, "La 'vera effigies' de San Ignacio," *Razón y fe* 154 (1956): 203–24.

2. Marjorie O'Rourke Boyle, *Loyola's Acts: The Rhetoric of the Self*, The New Historicism: Studies in Cultural Poetics, 36 (Berkeley: University of California Press, 1997), 168–73.

3. Alasdair C. MacIntyre, *After Virtue: A Study in Moral Theory*, 2nd ed. (Notre Dame, Ind.: University of Notre Dame Press, 1984), 177, 182. I thank Father David Stagaman, S.J., for this reference.

4. M. W. F. Stone, "'*Initium omnis peccati est superbia*': Jean Gerson's Analysis of Pride in His Mystical Theology, Pastoral Thought, and Hamartiology," in *In the Garden of Evil: The Vices and Culture in the Middle Ages*, Richard Newhauser, ed., Papers in Mediaeval Studies, 18 (Toronto: Pontifical Institute of Mediaeval Studies, 2005), 316–17.

5. See, e.g., Régis Boyer, "An Attempt to Define the Typology of Medieval Hagiography," in *Hagiography and Medieval Literature: A Symposium*, Hans Bekker-Nielsen et al., eds. (Odense: Odense University Press, 1981), 27–36; Donald Weinstein and Rudolph M. Bell, *Saints and Society: The Two Worlds of Western Christendom, 1000–1700* (Chicago: University of Chicago Press, 1982), 154–59, 167–79, 211–13, 225, 247–49; Richard Kieckhefer, *Unquiet Souls: Fourteenth-Century Saints and Their Religious Milieu* (Chicago: University of Chicago Press, 1984), 2–3, 8–15, 180–82, 189–201; André Vauchez, "Patronage des saints et religion civique dans l'Italie communale à la fin du Moyen Age," in *Patronage and Public in the Trecento: Proceedings of the St. Lambrecht Symposium, Abtei St. Lambrecht, Styria, 16–19 July 1984*, Vincent Moleta, ed., Biblioteca dell'*Archivum Romanicum*, 202 (Firenze: Olschki, 1986), 59–77; Thomas J. Heffernan, *Sacred Biography: Saints and Their Biographers in the Middle Ages* (Oxford: Oxford University Press, 1988), 15–71; Jean Delumeau, *Sin and Fear: The Emergence of a Western Guilt Culture, 13th–18th Centuries*, Eric Nicholson, trans. (New York: St. Martin's Press, 1990), 9–25; Barbara Abou-El-Haj, *The Medieval Cult of Saints: Formations and Transformations* (Cambridge: Cambridge University Press, 1994), 7–60; Diana Webb, *Patrons and Defenders: The Saints in the Italian City-States*, International Library of Historical Studies, 4 (London: I. B. Tauris, 1996); and André Vauchez, *Sainthood in the Later Middle Ages*, Jean Birrell, trans. (Cambridge: Cambridge University Press, 1997), 387–412.

6. See, e.g., David Burr, *The Spiritual Franciscans: From Protest to Persecution in the Century after Saint Francis* (University Park: Pennsylvania State University Press, 2001).

7. See, e.g., Gillian Rosemary Evans, *Bernard of Clairvaux*, Great Medieval Thinkers (Oxford: Oxford University Press, 2000), 42–56; and John W. O'Malley, *Four Cultures of the West* (Cambridge, Mass.: Belknap Press of Harvard University Press, 2004), 12–15, 144–49. I thank Maria Wagner for the Evans reference.

8. David J. Collins, *Reforming Saints: Saints' Lives and Their Authors in Germany, 1470–1530*, Oxford Studies in Historical Theology (Oxford: Oxford University Press, 2008), 42–43. Collins, 42, notes that imperial bishops who also held secular authority were susceptible to "arrogance and vainglory" (*iactantia et vana gloria*).

9. For late medieval devotion to the passion of Christ, characterized as "ubiquitous," see Richard Kieckhefer, "Major Currents in Late Medieval Devotion," in *Christian Spirituality: High Middle Ages and Reformation*, Jill Raitt, with Bernard McGinn and John Meyendorff, eds., World Spirituality, 17 (London: Routledge & Kegan Paul, 1987), 83–89. See also Claudio Leonardi, "Committenze agiografiche nel Trecento," in *Patronage and Public in the Trecento*, 46–56.

10. See, e.g., Ewert H. Cousins, "Franciscan Roots of Ignatian Meditation," in *Ignatian Spirituality in a Secular Age*, George P. Schner, ed., Studies in Religion Supplements, 15 (Waterloo, Ont.: Wilfrid Laurier University Press, 1984), 53–59.

11. Barbara McClung Hallman, *Italian Cardinals, Reform, and the Church as Property, 1492–1563*, UCLA Center for Medieval and Renaissance Studies, 22 (Berkeley: University of California Press, 1985), 15–16, 62–65; and John W. Padberg, "Ignatius and the Popes," in *Ignacio de Loyola y su tiempo: Congreso internacional de historia (9–13 Setiembre 1991)*, Juan Plazaola, ed. (Bilbao: Ediciones Mensajero, 1992), 691–94.

12. Collins, *Reforming Saints*, 82, fig. 3.1, reproduces Albrecht Dürer's 1515 woodcut of "The Virgin with Saint Bruno," the first printed image of the Carthusians' founder. Bruno stands on the Virgin's left side, and John the Baptist, "a patron of the monastic life in general and the Carthusian order in particular," occupies a parallel position on the Virgin's right.

13. In addition to the seminal studies of O'Malley, see, e.g., Paul Oskar Kristeller, "The Contribution of Religious Orders to Renaissance Thought and Learning," in *Medieval Aspects of Renaissance Learning: Three Essays by Paul Oskar Kristeller*, Edward P. Mahoney, ed. and trans., Duke Monographs in Medieval and Renaissance Studies, 1 (Durham, N.C.: Duke University Press, 1974), 102–6; William J. Bouwsma, "The Spirituality of Renaissance Humanism," in *Christian Spirituality: High Middle Ages and Reformation*, 236–50; and Ronald Modras, *Ignatian Humanism: A Dynamic Spirituality for the 21st Century* (Chicago: Loyola Press, 2004), 51–84.

14. See, e.g., Bo Ivar Reicke, "Instruction and Discussion in the Travel Narrative," *Studia Evangelica: Papers Presented to the International Congress on "The Four Gospels in 1957" Held at Christ Church, Oxford, 1957*, Kurt Aland et al., eds., Texte und Untersuchungen zur Geschichte der altchristlichen Literatur, 73 (Berlin: Akademie-Verlag, 1959), 209–16.

15. Donald R. Howard, *Writers and Pilgrims: Medieval Pilgrimage Narratives and Their Posterity* (Berkeley: University of California Press, 1980), 38–52; and Michel Mollat du Jourdin, "Saint Ignace et les pèlerinages de son temps," in *Ignacio de Loyola y su tiempo*, 166–73.

16. Roland Barthes, *Sade, Fourier, Loyola*, Richard Miller, trans. (New York: Hill and Wang, 1976), 41–44.

17. Marc Fumaroli, "The Fertility and the Shortcomings of Renaissance Rhetoric: The Jesuit Case," in *The Jesuits: Cultures, Sciences, and the Arts, 1540–1773*, J. W. O'Malley, G. A. Bailey, S. J. Harris, and T. F. Kennedy, eds. (Toronto: University of Toronto Press, 1999), 91–99.

18. See, e.g., George A. Kennedy, *Classical Rhetoric and Its Christian and Secular Tradition from Ancient to Modern Times* (Chapel Hill: University of North Carolina Press, 1980), 31–35, 65, 76–77, 90–102; Bruce A. Kimball, *Orators and Philosophers: A History of the Idea of Liberal Education* (New York: Teachers College Press, Columbia University, 1986), 17–19, 26–27, 29–38, 76–79; Paul F. Grendler, *Schooling in Renaissance Italy: Literacy and Learning, 1300–1600* (Baltimore: Johns

Hopkins University Press, 1989), 13–22, 117–41, 221–22, 263–64, 403–10; and O'Malley, *Four Cultures of the West*, 128–33, 149–54.

19. Bernabé Bartolomé Martínez, "Las librerías e imprentas de los jesuitas (1540–1767): Una aportación notable a la cultura española," *Hispania sacra* 40 (1988): 360–64. For the career of Vives in its social and cultural context, see esp. Maurice Kriegel, "Le parcours de Juan Luis Vives: Du milieu judaïsant à l'option érasmienne," *Revue de l'histoire des religions* 215 (1998): 252–80. On the cautious approach to Terence, see, e.g., David McPherson, "Roman Comedy in Renaissance Education: The Moral Question," *Sixteenth Century Journal* 12 (1981): 20–27; and Peter G. McC. Brown, "*The Eunuch* Castrated: Bowdlerization in the Text of the Westminster Latin Play," *International Journal of the Classical Tradition* 15 (2008): 25–26. In a 1585 biography of Ignatius, the Jesuit Giampietro Maffei (1536–1603) gave a Counter-Reformation spin to Ignatius's judicious comments about Terence in the *Constitutions*, no. 469 [George E. Ganss, trans. (St. Louis, Mo.: Institute of Jesuit Sources, 1970), 220], claiming that Ignatius banned the reading of any but a most thoroughly expurgated Terence. See Maffei, *De vita et moribus Ignatii Loiolae qui Societatem Iesu fundavit Libri III* (Köln: apud Maternum Cholinum, 1585), 305–6 (cited and translated by McPherson, "Roman Comedy in Renaissance Education," 27): "Quinetiam in scholis Terentium explicari (ni perpurgatus esset), quamquam optimum Latinitatis auctorem et Romanae comoediae principem, vetuit nominatim, quod eum videlicet parum verecundum ac parum pudicum arbitraretur. Noluit igitur ea lectione puerorum animos imbui ne plus moribus noceret quam prodesset ingeniis."

20. See, e.g., Marcella T. Grendler and Paul F. Grendler, "The Survival of Erasmus in Italy," *Erasmus in English* 8 (1976): 2–5, 8; Marcella and Paul Grendler, "The Erasmus Holdings of Roman and Vatican Libraries," *Erasmus in English* 13 (1984): 5–8; and Miriam Turrini and Annamaria Valenti, "L'educazione religiosa," in *Il catechismo e la grammatica*, vol. 1, *Istruzione e controllo sociale nell'area emiliana e romagnola nel '700*, Gian Paolo Brizzi, ed., Cultura e vita civile nel Settecento (Bologna: Il Mulino, 1985), 352–55, 359–81, 399–401. For the defense of Erasmus in Italy until the time of Paul IV, see also Silvana Seidel Menchi, *Erasmo in Italia, 1520–1580*, Nuova Cultura, 1 (Torino: Bollati Boringhieri, 1987), 270–82.

21. Dominique Julia, "Jésuites et universités: Les logiques d'une politique d'après les textes normatifs," in *Gesuiti e università in Europa (secoli XVI–XVIII) (Atti del Convegno di studi, Parma, 13–15 dicembre 2001)*, Gian Paolo Brizzi and Roberto Greci, eds., Centro interuniversitario per la storia delle università italiane: Studi, 3 (Bologna: Cooperativa Libraria Universitaria Editrice, 2002), 15–22.

22. Andrea Romano, "Il *Messanese Collegium Prototypum Societatis Iesu*," in *Gesuiti e università in Europa (secoli XVI–XVIII)*, 79–80. On imperatives of ideological purity and social control influencing the later *Ratio studiorum*, see, e.g., Gian-Mario Anselmi, "Per un'archeologia della *Ratio*: Dalla 'pedagogia' al 'governo,'"

in *La "Ratio studiorum": Modelli culturali e pratiche educative dei Gesuiti in Italia tra Cinque e Seicento*, Gian Paolo Brizzi, ed., Centro studi "Europa delle Corti": Biblioteca del Cinquecento, 16 (Roma: Bulzoni, 1981), 11–42; Giancarlo Angelozzi, "L'insegnamento dei casi di coscienza nella pratica educativa della Compagnia di Gesù," in *La "Ratio studiorum,"* 121–62; and John W. O'Malley, "How Humanistic Is the Jesuit Tradition? From the 1599 *Ratio Studiorum* to Now," in *Jesuit Education 21: Conference Proceedings on the Future of Jesuit Higher Education, 25–29 June 1999*, Martin R. Tripole, ed. (Philadelphia: Saint Joseph's University Press, 2000), 191–96.

23. Thomas V. Cohen, "Why the Jesuits Joined, 1540–1600," *Historical Papers (The Canadian Historical Association)* 9 (1974): 237–58.

24. Barthes, *Sade, Fourier, Loyola*, 48–68, esp. 66: "We know that to these mistrustings of the image Ignatius responded with a radical imperialism of the image."

25. See, e.g., Pedro de Leturia, "Jerusalén y Roma en los designios de San Ignacio de Loyola," in *Estudios Ignacianos*, Ignacio Iparraguirre, ed., Bibliotheca Instituti Historici Societatis Iesu, 10–11 (Roma: Institutum Historicum Societatis Iesu, 1957), 1:181–83.

26. See, e.g., David M. Robb, "The Iconography of the Annunciation in the Fourteenth and Fifteenth Centuries," *Art Bulletin* 18 (1936): 480–526; John W. O'Malley, *Praise and Blame in Renaissance Rome: Rhetoric, Doctrine, and Reform in the Sacred Orators of the Papal Court, ca. 1450–1521*, Duke Monographs in Medieval and Renaissance Studies, 3 (Durham, N.C.: Duke University Press, 1979), 137–61; Edward Muir, *Civic Ritual in Renaissance Venice* (Princeton, N.J.: Princeton University Press, 1981), 70–72; O'Malley, "The Jesuits, St. Ignatius, and the Counter Reformation: Some Recent Studies and Their Implications for Today," *Studies in the Spirituality of Jesuits* 14, no. 1 (1982): 15–17; Michael Baxandall, *Painting and Experience in Fifteenth-Century Italy: A Primer in the Social History of Pictorial Style*, 2nd ed. (Oxford: Oxford University Press, 1988), 45–56; Nerida Newbigin, "The Word Made Flesh: The *Rappresentazioni* of Mysteries and Miracles in Fifteenth-Century Florence," in *Christianity and the Renaissance: Image and Religious Imagination in the Quattrocento*, Timothy Verdon and John Henderson, eds. (Syracuse, N.Y.: Syracuse University Press, 1990), 367–71; Cyrilla Barr, "Music and Spectacle in Confraternity Drama of Fifteenth-Century Florence: The Reconstruction of a Theatrical Event," in *Christianity and the Renaissance: Image and Religious Imagination in the Quattrocento*, 380–81, 386–87; and Heidi J. Hornik and Mikeal C. Parsons, *Illuminating Luke*, vol. 1, *The Infancy Narrative in Italian Renaissance Painting* (Harrisburg, Penn.: Trinity Press International, 2003), 28–52.

27. Leo Steinberg, *The Sexuality of Christ in Renaissance Art and in Modern Oblivion*, 2nd ed. (Chicago: University of Chicago Press, 1996).

28. See, e.g., Rogelio García Mateo, "La 'Societas Jesu' y el contexto socio-político del s. XVI: Perspectivas para hoy," in *Ignacio de Loyola y su tiempo*, 512–13. Cf. Jacob Jervell, *The Theology of the Acts of the Apostles*, New Testament Theology (Cambridge: Cambridge University Press, 1996), 98–99, 122, who notes that Luke does not deny the sacrificial death of Jesus but "thrusts it into the background" (98).

29. See, e.g., George A. Kennedy, *New Testament Interpretation through Rhetorical Criticism* (Chapel Hill: University of North Carolina Press, 1984), 107–8, 114–40; and Richard B. Hays, *The Moral Vision of the New Testament: Community, Cross, New Creation; a Contemporary Introduction to New Testament Ethics* (New York: HarperCollins, 1996), 112–13, 122–25, 134–35.

30. Paul Zumthor, "The Medieval Travel Narrative," Catherine Peebles, trans., *New Literary History* 25 (1994): 822.

31. See, e.g., Thomas M. Lucas, *Landmarking: City, Church, and Jesuit Urban Strategy* (Chicago: Loyola Press, 1997), 1–153. In the thirteenth and fourteenth centuries, the communes of Siena and Florence had to expand their walls to include within their circuit the mendicant convents.

32. Maria Pia Mannini, "La diffusione del culto in Toscana: Lazzaretti, conventi, case delle Convertite e Malmaritate," in *La Maddalena tra sacro e profano*, Marilena Mosco, ed. (Firenze: La casa Usher, 1986), 60–64; and Romeo De Maio, "Il mito della Maddalena nella Controriforma," in *La Maddalena tra sacro e profano*, 82–83.

33. See, e.g., C. C. McCown, "The Geography of Luke's Central Section," *Journal of Biblical Literature* 57 (1938): 55–56; McCown, "Gospel Geography: Fiction, Fact, and Truth," *Journal of Biblical Literature* 60 (1941): 14–15; Hermann Strathmann, "*polis, polites, politeuomai, politeia, politeuma*," in *Theological Dictionary of the New Testament*, Gerhard Kittel and Gerhard Friedrich, eds., and Geoffrey W. Bromiley, trans. (Grand Rapids, Mich.: Eerdmans, 1964–76), 6:529–30; Jeffrey L. Staley, "'With the Power of the Spirit': Plotting the Program and Parallels of Luke 4:14–37 in Luke-Acts," in *Society of Biblical Literature 1993 Seminar Papers*, Eugene H. Lovering, Jr., ed., SBL Seminar Paper Series, 32 (Atlanta, Ga.: Scholars Press, 1993), 287, 300; and Harvie M. Conn and Manuel Ortiz, *Urban Ministry: The Kingdom, the City, and the People of God* (Downers Grove, Ill.: InterVarsity Press, 2001), 123–25, 127–29. For the civic character of Lukan rhetoric in Acts, see Todd Penner, "Civilizing Discourse: Acts, Declamation, and the Rhetoric of the *Polis*," in *Contextualizing Acts: Lukan Narrative and Greco-Roman Discourse*, Todd Penner and Caroline Vander Stichele, eds., Society of Biblical Literature Symposium Series, 20 (Leiden: Brill, 2004), 72–104.

34. *Acta Patris Ignatii*, Dionisio Fernández Zapico and Cándido de Dalmases, with Pedro de Leturia, eds., Monumenta Historica Societatis Iesu, 66 (Roma: Institutum Historicum Societatis Iesu, 1943), 466. Cf. John W. O'Malley, "To

Travel to Any Part of the World: Jerónimo Nadal and the Jesuit Vocation," *Studies in the Spirituality of Jesuits* 16, no. 2 (1984): 11–13.

35. The Jesuit Reductions (*reducciones*) of Latin America, so-called for the mutually reinforcing goals of "reducere ad Ecclesiam et vitam civilem." See, e.g., Sandra Orienti and Alberto Terruzzi, *Città di fondazione: Le 'reducciones' gesuitiche nel Paraguay tra il XVII e il XVIII secolo* (Firenze: Fratelli Alinari, 1982), 11–47.

36. Adriano Prosperi, "The Missionary," in *Baroque Personae*, Rosario Villari, ed., and Lydia G. Cochrane, trans. (Chicago: University of Chicago Press, 1995), 160–89.

37. Andrew C. Ross, *A Vision Betrayed: The Jesuits in Japan and China, 1542–1742* (Edinburgh: Edinburgh University Press, 1994), 34–40; Ross, "Alessandro Valignano: The Jesuits and Culture in the East," in *The Jesuits: Cultures, Sciences, and the Arts*, 339–41; James W. Reites, "St. Ignatius of Loyola and the Jews," *Studies in the Spirituality of Jesuits* 13, no. 4 (1981): 18–30; Francisco de Borja de Medina, "La Compañía de Jesús y la minoría morisca (1545–1614)," *Archivum historicum Societatis Iesu* 57 (1988): 4–23, 115–16, 120–25; Medina, "Ignacio de Loyola y la 'limpieza de sangre,'" in *Ignacio de Loyola y su tiempo*, 582–87, 608–13; and Robert Aleksander Maryks, *The Jesuit Order as a Synagogue of Jews: Jesuits of Jewish Ancestry and Purity-of-Blood Laws in the Early Society of Jesus*, Studies in Medieval and Reformation Traditions, 146 (Leiden: Brill, 2010), 48–50, 120–22, 145–46, 169–71.

38. Carole Straw, "Gregory, Cassian, and the Cardinal Vices," in *In the Garden of Evil*, 52–54.

39. Michèle Aumont, *Ignace de Loyola: Seul contre tous . . . et pour tous*, Ouverture philosophique (Paris: L'Harmattan, 2007), 212–15.

40. Francis Leduc, "La thème de la vaine gloire chez saint Jean Chrysostome," *Proche-orient chrétien* 19 (1969): 11–13; and Blake Leyerle, *Theatrical Shows and Ascetic Lives: John Chrysostom's Attack on Spiritual Marriage* (Berkeley: University of California Press, 2001), 56.

41. Roberto Rusconi, "Confraternite, compagnie, e devozioni," in *Storia d'Italia: Annali*, vol. 9, *La chiesa e il potere politico dal Medioevo all'età contemporanea*, Giorgio Chittolini and Giovanni Miccoli, eds. (Torino: Einaudi, 1986), 478–94; Maureen Flynn, *Sacred Charity: Confraternities and Social Welfare in Spain, 1400–1700* (Ithaca, N.Y.: Cornell University Press, 1989), 39–74; Michelle M. Fontaine, "A House Divided: The Compagnia de Santa Maria dei Battuti in Modena on the Eve of Catholic Reform," in *Confraternities and Catholic Reform in Italy, France, and Spain*, John Patrick Donnelly and Michael W. Maher, eds., Sixteenth Century Essays & Studies, 44 (Kirksville, Mo.: Thomas Jefferson University Press, 1999), 57–61; and David Michael D'Andrea, *Civic Christianity in Renaissance Italy: The Hospital of Treviso, 1400–1530* (Rochester, N.Y.: University of Rochester Press: Boydell and Brewer, 2007), 58–84.

42. See, e.g., Linda Woodbridge, "Renaissance Bogeymen," in *A Companion to the Worlds of the Renaissance*, Guido Ruggiero, ed., Blackwell Companions to European History (Oxford: Blackwell, 2002), 449–51.

43. Sante Bortolami, " 'Locus magne misericordie': Pellegrinaggi e ospitalità nel Veneto medioevale," in *I percorsi della fede e l'esperienza della carità nel Veneto medioevale (Atti del Convegno, Castello di Monselice, 28 maggio 2000)*, Antonio Rigon, ed. (Monselice: Il Poligrafo, 2002), 125.

44. John Henderson, *The Renaissance Hospital: Healing the Body and Healing the Soul* (New Haven, Conn.: Yale University Press, 2006), 79, 200–10.

45. See, e.g., Robert Bireley, "Early-Modern Catholicism as a Response to the Changing World of the Long Sixteenth Century," *Catholic Historical Review* 95 (2009): 219–39.

46. H. Outram Evennett, *The Spirit of the Counter-Reformation*, John Bossy, ed. (Cambridge: Cambridge University Press, 1968), 26–28, 31–32, 41–42, 73–88, 124. For related discussion, see, e.g., Brian S. Pullan, *Rich and Poor in Renaissance Venice: The Social Institutions of a Catholic State, to 1620* (Cambridge, Mass.: Harvard University Press, 1971), 372–422; Pullan, "Support and Redeem: Charity and Poor Relief in Italian Cities from the Fourteenth to the Seventeenth Century," *Continuity and Change* 3 (1988): 177–208; John Henderson, *Piety and Charity in Late Medieval Florence* (Oxford: Clarendon Press, 1994), 354–410; Nicholas Eckstein, " 'Con Buona Affetione': Confraternities, Charity, and the Poor in Early Cinquecento Florence," in *The Reformation of Charity: The Secular and the Religious in Early Modern Poor Relief*, Thomas Max Safley, ed., Studies in Central European Histories (Boston: Brill, 2003), 47–62; and Brian S. Pullan, "Catholics, Protestants, and the Poor in Early Modern Europe," *Journal of Interdisciplinary History* 35 (2005): 441–46.

47. Ignacio Echarte, ed., *Concordancia Ignaciana / An Ignatian Concordance* (Bilbao: Ediciones Mensajero, in collaboration with the Institute of Jesuit Sources, St. Louis, Mo., 1996), s.v. *amor* (40–41), *caridad, caritas* (131–32). The quotation is from Ignatius Loyola, *Constitutions*, Ganss, trans., 119 (no. 134).

48. William V. Bangert, *A History of the Society of Jesus* (St. Louis, Mo.: Institute of Jesuit Sources, 1972), 49, citing *Sancti Ignatii . . . Epistolae et Instructiones*, 6:91.

49. Alonso de Sandoval, *Un tratado sobre la esclavitud ("De instauranda Aethiopum salute")*, Enriqueta Vila Vilar, trans. (Madrid: Alianza Editorial, 1987), 318–40. English translation in Sandoval, *Treatise on Slavery: Selections from "De instauranda Aethiopum salute,"* Nicole von Germeten, trans. (Indianopolis, Ind.: Hackett, 2008), 88–95.

50. Modras, *Ignatian Humanism*, 45–47, 73.

Bibliography

Abou-El-Haj, Barbara. *The Medieval Cult of Saints: Formations and Transformations*. Cambridge: Cambridge University Press, 1994.

Affholder, Carmen M. "Saint Ignace dans son écriture." *Archivum historicum Societatis Iesu* 29 (1960): 381–98.

Aland, Kurt, et al., eds. *Studia Evangelica: Papers Presented to the International Congress on "The Four Gospels in 1957" Held at Christ Church, Oxford, 1957*. Texte und Untersuchungen zur Geschichte der altchristlichen Literatur, 73. Berlin: Akademie-Verlag, 1959.

Albareda, Anselmo M. "Intorno alla scuola di orazione metodica stabilita a Monserrato dall'abate Garsías Jiménez de Cisneros (1493–1510)." *Archivum historicum Societatis Iesu* 25 (1956): 254–316.

Alcalá, Angel. "Inquisitorial Control of Humanists and Writers." In *The Spanish Inquisition and the Inquisitorial Mind*, Angel Alcalá, ed., 321–59. Atlantic Studies on Society in Change, 49. Boulder, Colo.: Social Science Monographs, 1987.

——, ed. *The Spanish Inquisition and the Inquisitorial Mind*. Atlantic Studies on Society in Change, 49. Boulder, Colo.: Social Science Monographs, 1987.

Alexander, Loveday. "'In Journeyings Often': Voyaging in the Acts of the Apostles and in Greek Romance." In *Luke's Literary Achievement: Collected Essays*, Christopher M. Tuckett, ed., 17–49. *Journal for the Study of the New Testament* Supplement Series, 116. Sheffield, U.K.: Sheffield Academic Press, 1995.

American Psychiatric Association. *Diagnostic and Statistical Manual of Mental Disorders*. 4th ed. Washington, D.C.: American Psychiatric Association, 2000.

Andrés, Melquíades. "Alumbrados, Erasmians, 'Lutherans,' and Mystics: The Risk of a More 'Intimate' Spirituality." In *The Spanish Inquisition and the Inquisitorial Mind*, Angel Alcalá, ed., 457–94. Atlantic Studies on Society in Change, 49. Boulder, Colo.: Social Science Monographs, 1987.

Angelozzi, Giancarlo. "L'insegnamento dei casi di coscienza nella pratica educativa della Compagnia di Gesù." In *La "Ratio studiorum": Modelli culturali e pratiche educative dei Gesuiti in Italia tra Cinque e Seicento*, Gian Paolo Brizzi, ed., 121–62. Centro studi "Europa delle Corti": Biblioteca del Cinquecento, 16. Roma: Bulzoni, 1981.

Anselmi, Gian-Mario. "Per un'archeologia della *Ratio*: Dalla 'pedagogia' al 'governo.'" In *La "Ratio studiorum": Modelli culturali e pratiche educative dei Gesuiti in Italia tra Cinque e Seicento*, Gian Paolo Brizzi, ed., 11–42. Centro studi "Europa delle Corti": Biblioteca del Cinquecento, 16. Roma: Bulzoni, 1981.

Ariès, Philippe, and André Béjin, eds., and Anthony Forster, trans. *Western Sexuality: Practice and Precept in Past and Present Times*. Family, Sexuality, and Social Relations in Past Times. Oxford: Blackwell, 1985.

Arlandson, James Malcolm. *Women, Class, and Society in Early Christianity: Models from Luke-Acts*. Peabody, Mass.: Hendrickson, 1997.

Ashworth, E. J. "Traditional Logic." In *The Cambridge History of Renaissance Philosophy*, Charles B. Schmitt and Quentin Skinner, eds., 143–72. Cambridge: Cambridge University Press, 1988.

Aspe, María-Paz. "Spanish Spirituality's Mid-Sixteenth-Century Change of Course." In *The Spanish Inquisition and the Inquisitorial Mind*, Angel Alcalá, ed., 421–30. Atlantic Studies on Society in Change, 49. Boulder, Colo.: Social Science Monographs, 1987.

Aumont, Michèle. *Ignace de Loyola: Seul contre tous . . . et pour tous*. Ouverture philosophique. Paris: L'Harmattan, 2007.

Baeck, Louis. *The Mediterranean Tradition in Economic Thought*. London: Routledge, 1994.

Baernstein, P. Renée. "Reprobates and Courtiers: Lay Masculinities in the Colonna Family, 1520–1584." In *Florence and Beyond: Culture, Society, and Politics in Renaissance Italy. Essays in Honour of John M. Najemy*, David S. Peterson, with Daniel E. Bornstein, eds., 291–303. Essays and Studies, 15. Toronto: Centre for Reformation and Renaissance Studies, 2008.

Bailbé, Jacques. "La thème de la vieille femme dans la poésie satirique du seizième et du début du dix-septième siècles." *Bibliothèque d'humanisme et Renaissance* 26 (1964): 98–119.

Bangert, William V. *A History of the Society of Jesus*. St. Louis, Mo.: Institute of Jesuit Sources, 1972.

Banker, James R. *Death in the Community: Memorialization and Confraternities in an Italian Commune in the Late Middle Ages*. Athens: University of Georgia Press, 1988.

Barr, Cyrilla. "Music and Spectacle in Confraternity Drama of Fifteenth-Century Florence: The Reconstruction of a Theatrical Event." In *Christianity and the Renaissance: Image and Religious Imagination in the Quattrocento*, Timothy Verdon and John Henderson, eds., 376–404. Syracuse, N.Y.: Syracuse University Press, 1990.

Barry, Jonathan, and Colin Jones, eds. *Medicine and Charity before the Welfare State*. London: Routledge, 1991.

Barthes, Roland. *Sade, Fourier, Loyola*. Richard Miller, trans. New York: Hill and Wang, 1976.

Battlori, Miguel. "El mito contrarreformista de San Ignacio anti-Lutero." In *Ignacio de Loyola, Magister Artium en París 1528–1535*, Julio Caro Baroja and Antonio Beristain, eds., 87–93. San Sebastián: Kutxa, 1991.

Baxandall, Michael. *Painting and Experience in Fifteenth-Century Italy: A Primer in the Social History of Pictorial Style*. 2nd ed. Oxford: Oxford University Press, 1988.

Bayle, Pierre. *Political Writings*. Sally L. Jenkinson, ed. Cambridge Texts in the History of Political Thought. Cambridge: Cambridge University Press, 2000.

Becker, Kenneth L. *Unlikely Companions: C. G. Jung on the "Spiritual Exercises" of Ignatius of Loyola*. Leominster, U.K.: Inigo Enterprises, 2001.

Begheyn, Paul. "Bibliography on the History of the Jesuits: Publications in English, 1900–1993." *Studies in the Spirituality of Jesuits* 28, no. 1 (1996).

Beirnaert, Louis. *Aux frontières de l'acte analytique: La Bible, saint Ignace, Freud, et Lacan*. Paris: Éditions du Seuil, 1987.

Bekker-Nielsen, Hans, et al., eds. *Hagiography and Medieval Literature: A Symposium*. Odense: Odense University Press, 1981.

Bennassar, Bartolomé, ed. *L'Inquisition espagnole, XVe–XIXe siècles*. Paris: Hachette, 1979.

———. "Patterns of the Inquisitorial Mind as the Basis for a Pedagogy of Fear." In *The Spanish Inquisition and the Inquisitorial Mind*, Angel Alcalá, ed., 177–84. Atlantic Studies on Society in Change, 49. Boulder, Colo.: Social Science Monographs, 1987.

———. *The Spanish Character: Attitudes and Mentalities from the Sixteenth to the Nineteenth Century*. Benjamin Keen, trans. Berkeley: University of California Press, 1979.

Beristain, Antonio. "La Victimología ante las persecuciones a Ignacio de Loyola y los jesuitas." In *Ignacio de Loyola, Magister Artium en París 1528–1535*, Julio Caro Baroja and Antonio Beristain, eds., 95–134. San Sebastián: Kutxa, 1991.

Bertram, Jerome. "John Cassian, a Spiritual Guide for the Laity." In John Cassian, *The Monastic Institutes, Consisting of On the Training of a Monk and The Eight Deadly Sins in Twelve Books*, vii–xviii. London: Saint Austin Press, 1999.

Bertrand, Dominique. "Ignace de Loyola et la politique." In *Ignacio de Loyola y su tiempo: Congreso internacional de historia (9–13 Setiembre 1991)*, Juan Plazaola, ed., 701–26. Bilbao: Ediciones Mensajero, 1992.

———. *La politique de saint Ignace de Loyola: L'analyse sociale*. Paris: Les Éditions du Cerf, 1985.

Bettini, Maurizio. *Il ritratto dell'amante*. Saggi, 761. Torino: Einaudi, 1992.

Bietenholz, P. G., and Thomas B. Deutscher, eds. *Contemporaries of Erasmus: A Biographical Register of the Renaissance and Reformation*. Vol. 1, A–E. Toronto: University of Toronto Press, 1985.

Bilinkoff, Jodi. "The Many 'Lives' of Pedro de Ribadeneyra." *Renaissance Quarterly* 52 (1999): 180–96.

———. "A Spanish Prophetess and Her Patrons: The Case of María de Santo Domingo." *Sixteenth Century Journal* 23 (1992): 21–34.

Bireley, Robert. "Early-Modern Catholicism as a Response to the Changing World of the Long Sixteenth Century." *Catholic Historical Review* 95 (2009): 219–39.

Black, Christopher F. *Italian Confraternities in the Sixteenth Century*. Cambridge: Cambridge University Press, 1989.

———. *The Italian Inquisition*. New Haven, Conn.: Yale University Press, 2009.

Blaisdell, Charmarie J. "Calvin's and Loyola's Letters to Women: Politics and Spiritual Counsel in the Sixteenth Century." In *Calviniana: Ideas and Influence of Jean Calvin*, Robert V. Schnucker, ed., 235–53. Sixteenth Century Essays & Studies, 10. Kirksville, Mo.: Sixteenth Century Journal Publishers, 1988.

Bloomfield, Morton W. *The Seven Deadly Sins: An Introduction to the History of a Religious Concept, with Special Reference to Medieval English Literature*. East Lansing: Michigan State University Press, 1952.

Bolton Holloway, Julia. *The Pilgrim and the Book: A Study of Dante, Langland, and Chaucer*. American University Studies, Series IV: English Language and Literature, 42. Rev. ed. New York: Peter Lang, 1992.

———. "The Pilgrim in the Poem: Dante, Langland, and Chaucer." *Jerusalem: Essays on Pilgrimage and Literature*, 121–41. AMS Studies in the Middle Ages, 24. New York: AMS Press, 1998.

Bonfil, Robert. *Jewish Life in Renaissance Italy*. Anthony Oldcorn, trans. Berkeley: University of California Press, 1994.

Borromeo, Agostino. "The Inquisition and Inquisitorial Censorship." In *Catholicism in Early Modern Europe: A Guide to Research*, John W. O'Malley, ed., 253–72. Reformation Guides to Research, 2. St. Louis, Mo.: Center for Reformation Research, 1988.

———, ed. *L'Inquisizione (Atti del Simposio internazionale, Città del Vaticano, 29–31 ottobre 1998)*. Studi e testi, 417. Città del Vaticano: Biblioteca Apostolica Vaticana, 2003.

Bortolami, Sante. " 'Locus magne misericordie': Pellegrinaggi e ospitalità nel Veneto medioevale." In *I percorsi della fede e l'esperienza della carità nel Veneto medioevale (Atti del Convegno, Castello di Monselice, 28 maggio 2000)*, Antonio Rigon, ed., 81–131. Monselice: Il Poligrafo, 2002.

Boruchoff, David A. "Historiography with License: Isabel, the Catholic Monarch, and the Kingdom of God." In *Isabel La Católica, Queen of Castile: Critical Essays*, David A. Boruchoff, ed., 225–94. Houndmills, U.K.: Palgrave, 2003.

———, ed. *Isabel La Católica, Queen of Castile: Critical Essays*. Houndmills, U.K.: Palgrave, 2003.

Bottereau, Georges. "La 'lettre' d'Ignace de Loyola à Gian Pietro Carafa." *Archivum historicum Societatis Iesu* 44 (1975): 139–52.

Bouwsma, William J. "The Spirituality of Renaissance Humanism." In *Christian Spirituality: High Middle Ages and Reformation*, Jill Raitt, with Bernard McGinn and John Meyendorff, eds., 236–51. World Spirituality, 17. London: Routledge & Kegan Paul, 1987.

————. *Venice and the Defense of Republican Liberty: Renaissance Values in the Age of the Counter Reformation*. Berkeley: University of California Press, 1968.

Boyer, Régis. "An Attempt to Define the Typology of Medieval Hagiography." In *Hagiography and Medieval Literature: A Symposium*, Hans Bekker-Nielsen et al., eds., 27–36. Odense: Odense University Press, 1981.

Brault-Noble, Catherine, and Marie-José Marc. "L'Unification religieuse et sociale: La répression des minorités." In *L'Inquisition espagnole, XVe–XIXe siècles*, Bartolomé Bennassar, ed., 139–91. Paris: Hachette, 1979.

Brizzi, Gian Paolo, ed. *Il catechismo e la grammatica*. Vol. 1, *Istruzione e controllo sociale nell'area emiliana e romagnola nel '700*. Cultura e vita civile nel Settecento. Bologna: Il Mulino, 1985.

————, ed. *La "Ratio studiorum": Modelli culturali e pratiche educative dei Gesuiti in Italia tra Cinque e Seicento*. Centro studi "Europa delle Corti": Biblioteca del Cinquecento, 16. Roma: Bulzoni, 1981.

————. *"Studia humanitatis* und Organisation des Unterrichts in den ersten italienischen Kollegien der Gesellschaft Jesu." In *Humanismus im Bildungswesen des 15. und 16. Jahrhunderts*, Wolfgang Reinhard, ed., 155–70. Deutsche Forschungsgemeinschaft. Wenheim: Acta Humaniora, 1984.

Brizzi, Gian Paolo, and Roberto Greci, eds. *Gesuiti e università in Europa (secoli XVI–XVIII) (Atti del Convegno di studi, Parma, 13–15 dicembre 2001)*. Centro interuniversitario per la storia delle università italiane: Studi, 3. Bologna: Cooperativa Libraria Universitaria Editrice, 2002.

Brizzi, Gian Paolo, and Anna Maria Matteucci, eds. *Dall'isola alla città: I gesuiti a Bologna*. Bologna: Nuova Alfa Editoriale, 1988.

Brodrick, James. *The Origin of the Jesuits*. London: Longmans, Green, 1940. Repr. Chicago: Loyola University Press, 1986.

Brown, D. Catherine. *Pastor and Laity in the Theology of Jean Gerson*. Cambridge: Cambridge University Press, 1987.

Brown, Peter. *The Body and Society: Men, Women, and Sexual Renunciation in Early Christianity*. New York: Columbia University Press, 1988.

Brown, Peter G. McC. "*The Eunuch* Castrated: Bowdlerization in the Text of the Westminster Latin Play." *International Journal of the Classical Tradition* 15 (2008): 16–28.

Brown, Raymond E. *The Death of the Messiah: A Commentary on the Passion Narratives in the Four Gospels*. 2 vols. The Anchor Bible Reference Library. New York: Doubleday, 1994.

Brown, Raymond E., Joseph A. Fitzmyer, and Roland E. Murphy, eds. *The New Jerome Biblical Commentary*. Englewood Cliffs, N.J.: Prentice Hall, 1990.

Burr, David. *The Spiritual Franciscans: From Protest to Persecution in the Century after Saint Francis*. University Park: Pennsylvania State University Press, 2001.

Cacho Blecua, Juan Manuel. "Del gentilhombre mundano al caballero 'a lo divino': Los ideales caballerescos de Ignacio de Loyola." In *Ignacio de Loyola y su tiempo: Congreso internacional de historia (9–13 Setiembre 1991)*, Juan Plazaola, ed., 129–59. Bilbao: Ediciones Mensajero, 1992.

Capps, Donald. *Deadly Sins and Saving Virtues*. Philadelphia: Fortress Press, 1987.

———. *The Depleted Self: Sin in a Narcissistic Age*. Minneapolis: Augsburg Fortress Press, 1993.

Carafa, Gian Pietro. "De Lutheranorum haeresi reprimenda et ecclesia reformanda ad Clementem VII.." In *Concilium Tridentinum: Diariorum, Actorum, Epistularum, Tractatum Nova Collectio*. Vol. 12, *Tractatum Pars Prior*, Vincentius Schweitzer, ed., 67–77. Freiburg im Breisgau: Herder, 1929. Repr. Freiburg im Breisgau: Herder, 1966.

———. "Information Sent to Pope Clement VII by the Bishop of Chieti through Brother Bonaventura of the Franciscan Order [October 4, 1532]." In *Reform Thought in Sixteenth-Century Italy*, Elisabeth G. Gleason, ed. and trans., 57–80. American Academy of Religion Texts and Translations, 4. Chico, Calif.: Scholars Press, 1981.

Carmichael, Ann G. *Plague and the Poor in Renaissance Florence*. Cambridge History of Medicine. Cambridge: Cambridge University Press, 1986.

Caro Baroja, Julio. "Religion, World Views, Social Classes, and Honor during the Sixteenth and Seventeenth Centuries in Spain." Victoria Hughes, trans. In *Honor and Grace in Anthropology*, John G. Peristiany and Julian Pitt-Rivers, eds., 91–102. Cambridge Studies in Social and Cultural Anthropology, 76. Cambridge: Cambridge University Press, 1992.

Carruthers, Mary. *The Book of Memory: A Study of Memory in Medieval Culture*. 2nd ed. Cambridge Studies in Medieval Literature, 70. Cambridge: Cambridge University Press, 2008.

Carter, Charles H., ed. *From the Renaissance to the Counter-Reformation: Essays in Honor of Garrett Mattingly*. New York: Random House, 1965.

Cassian, John. *Cassiani Opera: Collationes XXIIII*. Michael Petschenig and Gottfried Kreuz, eds. Corpus Scriptorum Ecclesiasticorum Latinorum, 13. Vienna: Verlag der Österreichischen Akademie der Wissenschaften, 2004.

———. *Cassiani Opera: De institutis coenobiorum, De incarnatione contra Nestorium*. Michael Petschenig and Gottfried Kreuz, eds. Corpus Scriptorum Ecclesiasticorum Latinorum, 17. Vienna: Verlag der Österreichischen Akademie der Wissenschaften, 2004.

———. *Conferences.* Colm Luibhéid, trans., and Owen Chadwick, intro. Classics of Western Spirituality. Mahwah, N.J.: Paulist Press, 1985.

———. *The Conferences.* Boniface Ramsey, trans. Ancient Christian Writers, 57. Mahwah, N.J.: Paulist Press, 1997.

———. *The Institutes.* Boniface Ramsey, trans. Ancient Christian Writers, 58. Mahwah, N.J.: Newman Press, 2000.

———. *The Monastic Institutes,* Consisting of *On the Training of a Monk* and *The Eight Deadly Sins in Twelve Books.* Jerome Bertram, trans. London: Saint Austin Press, 1999.

———. "The Works of John Cassian." In *Nicene and Post-Nicene Fathers,* Edgar C. S. Gibson, trans., 2nd ser., 11:161–621. New York: Christian Literature Company, 1894. Repr. Peabody, Mass.: Hendrickson, 1994.

Cassirer, Ernst, Paul Oskar Kristeller, and John Herman Randall, Jr., eds., and Hans Nachod, trans. *The Renaissance Philosophy of Man.* Chicago: University of Chicago Press, 1948.

Cesareo, Francesco C. "Review Essay: The Complex Nature of Catholicism in the Renaissance." *Renaissance Quarterly* 54 (2001): 1561–73.

Chadwick, Owen. "Introduction." In John Cassian, *Conferences,* Colm Luibhéid, trans., 1–36. Classics of Western Spirituality. Mahwah, N.J.: Paulist Press, 1985.

Chance, J. Bradley. *Jerusalem, the Temple, and the New Age in Luke-Acts.* Macon, Ga.: Mercer University Press, 1988.

Chance, John K. "The Anthropology of Honor and Shame: Culture, Values, and Practice." In *Honor and Shame in the World of the Bible,* Victor H. Matthews and Don C. Benjamin, eds., 139–51. Semeia, 68. Atlanta: Scholars Press, 1996.

Chartier, Roger. "Les arts de mourir, 1450–1600." *Annales: Économies sociétés civilisations* 31 (1976): 51–75.

Chauvin, Charles. "Ignace et les courtisanes: La Maison Sainte Marthe (1542–1548)." In *Ignacio de Loyola y su tiempo: Congreso internacional de historia (9–13 Setiembre 1991),* Juan Plazaola, ed., 551–62. Bilbao: Ediciones Mensajero, 1992.

———. "La Maison Sainte-Marthe: Ignace et les prostituées de Rome." *Christus* 38, no. 149 (Jan. 1991): 117–26.

Chittolini, Giorgio, and Giovanni Miccoli, eds. *Storia d'Italia: Annali.* Vol. 9, *La chiesa e il potere politico dal Medioevo all'età contemporanea.* Torino: Einaudi, 1986.

Christian, William A., Jr. *Apparitions in Late Medieval and Renaissance Spain.* Princeton, N.J.: Princeton University Press, 1981.

———. "Provoked Religious Weeping in Early Modern Spain." In *Religion and Emotion: Approaches and Interpretations,* John Corrigan, ed., 33–50. Oxford: Oxford University Press, 2004.

Chryssavgis, John. *John Climacus: From the Egyptian Desert to the Sinaite Mountain.* Aldershot, U.K.: Ashgate, 2004.

Cipolla, Carlo M. *Before the Industrial Revolution: European Society and Economy, 1000–1700.* 2nd ed. New York: W. W. Norton, 1980.

Clark, Kenneth. *Civilisation: A Personal View.* New York: Harper & Row, 1970.

Clark, Willene B., and Meredith T. McMunn, eds. *Beasts and Birds of the Middle Ages: The Bestiary and Its Legacy.* Middle Ages Series. Philadelphia: University of Pennsylvania Press, 1989.

Clark Kee, Howard. *Good News to the Ends of the Earth: The Theology of Acts.* London: SCM Press, 1990.

Codina, Víctor. "San Ignacio y Paulo IV: Notas para una teologia del carisma." *Manresa* 40 (1968): 337–62.

Codina Mir, Gabriel. *Aux sources de la pédagogie des jésuites: Le "Modus parisiensis."* Bibliotheca Instituti Historici Societatis Iesu, 28. Roma: Institutum Historicum Societatis Iesu, 1968.

Cohen, Thomas V. "The Lay Liturgy of Affront in Sixteenth-Century Italy." *Journal of Social History* 25 (1992): 857–77.

———. "Why the Jesuits Joined, 1540–1600." *Historical Papers (The Canadian Historical Association)* 9 (1974): 237–58.

Coleman, David. *Creating Christian Granada: Society and Religious Culture in an Old-World Frontier City, 1492–1600.* Ithaca, N.Y.: Cornell University Press, 2003.

———. "Moral Formation and Social Control in the Catholic Reformation: The Case of San Juan de Ávila." *Sixteenth Century Journal* 26 (1995): 17–30.

Collins, David J. *Reforming Saints: Saints' Lives and Their Authors in Germany, 1470–1530.* Oxford Studies in Historical Theology. Oxford: Oxford University Press, 2008.

Comerford, Kathleen M., and Hilmar M. Pabel, eds. *Early Modern Catholicism: Essays in Honour of John W. O'Malley, S. J.* Toronto: University of Toronto Press, 2001.

Conn, Harvie M., and Manuel Ortiz. *Urban Ministry: The Kingdom, the City, and the People of God.* Downers Grove, Ill.: InterVarsity Press, 2001.

Constable, Giles. "Opposition to Pilgrimage in the Middle Ages." *Studia gratiana* 19 (1976): 123–46.

Contreras, Jaime. "The Impact of Protestantism in Spain, 1520–1600." In *Inquisition and Society in Early Modern Europe,* Stephen Haliczer, ed. and trans., 47–63. Totowa, N.J.: Barnes & Noble Books, 1987.

Conwell, Joseph F. *Impelling Spirit: Revisiting a Founding Experience, 1539, Ignatius of Loyola and His Companions.* Chicago: Loyola Press, 1997.

Corrigan, John, ed. *Religion and Emotion: Approaches and Interpretations.* Oxford: Oxford University Press, 2004.

Cousins, Ewert H. "Franciscan Roots of Ignatian Meditation." In *Ignatian Spirituality in a Secular Age,* George P. Schner, ed., 51–64. Studies in Religion Supplements, 15. Waterloo, Ont.: Wilfrid Laurier University Press, 1984.

Crehan, Joseph. "Saint Ignatius and Cardinal Pole." *Archivum historicum Societatis Iesu* 25 (1956): 72–98.

Cruz, Anne J., and Mary Elizabeth Perry, eds. *Culture and Control in Counter-Reformation Spain*. Hispanic Issues, 7. Minneapolis: University of Minnesota Press, 1992.

Dalmases, Cándido de. *Ignatius of Loyola, Founder of the Jesuits: His Life and Work*. Jerome Aixalá, trans. Modern Scholarly Studies about the Jesuits in English Translations, 6. St. Louis, Mo.: Institute of Jesuit Sources, 1985.

D'Andrea, David Michael. *Civic Christianity in Renaissance Italy: The Hospital of Treviso, 1400–1530*. Rochester, N.Y.: University of Rochester Press, 2007.

Daniels, Stephen. "Place and the Geographical Imagination." *Geography* 77 (1992): 310–22.

Davidson, Nicolas. "Il Sant'Uffizio e la tutela del culto a Venezia nel '500." *Studi veneziani*, n.s., 6 (1982): 87–101.

———. "The Inquisition and the Italian Jews." In *Inquisition and Society in Early Modern Europe*, Stephen Haliczer, ed. and trans., 19–46. Totowa, N.J.: Barnes & Noble Books, 1987.

Davis, David Brion. *The Problem of Slavery in Western Culture*. Oxford: Oxford University Press, 1966.

D'Elia, Una Roman. "Drawing Christ's Blood: Michelangelo, Vittoria Colonna, and the Aesthetics of Reform." *Renaissance Quarterly* 59 (2006): 90–129.

Del Piazzo, Marcello, and Cándido de Dalmases. "Il processo sull'ortodossia di S. Ignazio e dei suoi compagni svoltosi a Roma nel 1538: Nuovi documenti." *Archivum historicum Societatis Iesu* 38 (1969): 431–53.

Delumeau, Jean. *Sin and Fear: The Emergence of a Western Guilt Culture, 13th–18th Centuries*. Eric Nicholson, trans. New York: St. Martin's Press, 1990.

De Maio, Romeo. "Il mito della Maddalena nella Controriforma." In *La Maddalena tra sacro e profano*, Marilena Mosco, ed., 82–83. Firenze: La casa Usher, 1986.

Dillon, Richard J. "Acts of the Apostles." In *The New Jerome Biblical Commentary*, Raymond E. Brown, Joseph A. Fitzmyer, and Roland E. Murphy, eds., 722–67. Englewood Cliffs, N.J.: Prentice Hall, 1990.

———. *From Eye-Witnesses to Ministers of the Word: Tradition and Composition in Luke 24*. Analecta Biblica, 82. Roma: Biblical Institute Press, 1978.

Ditchfield, Simon. "Of Missions and Models: The Jesuit Enterprise (1540–1773) Reassessed in Recent Literature." *Catholic Historical Review* 93 (2007): 325–43.

Donahue, John R. *The Gospel in Parable: Metaphor, Narrative, and Theology in the Synoptic Gospels*. Philadelphia: Fortress Press, 1988.

Donnelly, John Patrick. "Religious Orders of Men, Especially the Society of Jesus." In *Catholicism in Early Modern Europe: A Guide to Research*, John W. O'Malley, ed., 147–62. Reformation Guides to Research, 2. St. Louis, Mo.: Center for Reformation Research, 1988.

Donnelly, John Patrick, and Michael W. Maher, eds. *Confraternities and Catholic Reform in Italy, France, and Spain.* Sixteenth Century Essays & Studies, 44. Kirksville, Mo.: Thomas Jefferson University Press, 1999.

Driver, Steven D. *John Cassian and the Reading of Egyptian Monastic Culture.* Medieval History and Culture, 8. New York: Routledge, 2002.

Duggan, Lawrence G. "Fear and Confession on the Eve of the Reformation." *Archiv für Reformationsgeschichte / Archive for Reformation History* 75 (1984): 153–75.

Durand, Françoise. "La première historiographie ignatienne." In *Ignacio de Loyola y su tiempo: Congreso internacional de historia (9–13 Setiembre 1991)*, Juan Plazaola, ed., 23–36. Bilbao: Ediciones Mensajero, 1992.

Echarte, Ignacio, ed. *Concordancia Ignaciana / An Ignatian Concordance.* Bilbao: Ediciones Mensajero, in collaboration with the Institute of Jesuit Sources, St. Louis, Mo., 1996.

Eckstein, Nicholas. "'Con Buona Affetione': Confraternities, Charity, and the Poor in Early Cinquecento Florence." In *The Reformation of Charity: The Secular and the Religious in Early Modern Poor Relief*, Thomas Max Safley, ed., 47–62. Studies in Central European Histories. Boston: Brill, 2003.

Edgerton, Samuel, Jr. *Pictures and Punishment: Art and Criminal Prosecution During the Florentine Renaissance.* Ithaca, N.Y.: Cornell University Press, 1985.

Ehlers, Benjamin. *Between Christians and Moriscos: Juan de Ribera and Religious Reform in Valencia, 1568–1614.* Baltimore: Johns Hopkins University Press, 2006.

Eickhoff, Georg. "Claraval, Digulleville, Loyola: La alegoría caballeresca de *El peregrino de la vida humana* en los noviciados monástico y jesuítico." In *Ignacio de Loyola y su tiempo: Congreso internacional de historia (9–13 Setiembre 1991)*, Juan Plazaola, ed., 869–81. Bilbao: Ediciones Mensajero, 1992.

Elliott, J. H. *Europe Divided, 1559–1598.* 2nd ed. Blackwell Classic Histories of Europe. Oxford: Blackwell, 2000.

Elliott, John H. "Temple versus Household in Luke-Acts: A Contrast in Social Institutions." In *The Social World of Luke-Acts: Models for Interpretation*, Jerome H. Neyrey, ed., 211–40. Peabody, Mass.: Hendrickson, 1991.

Elliot van Liere, Katherine. "After Nebrija: Academic Reformers and the Teaching of Latin in Sixteenth-Century Salamanca." *Sixteenth Century Journal* 34 (2003): 1065–1105.

Endean, Philip. "Who Do You Say Ignatius Is? Jesuit Fundamentalism and Beyond." *Studies in the Spirituality of Jesuits* 19, no. 5 (1987).

Enterline, Lynn. *The Tears of Narcissus: Melancholia and Masculinity in Early Modern Writing.* Stanford, Calif.: Stanford University Press, 1995.

Erasmus, Desiderius. *Enchiridion militis Christiani*. In *Opera omnia*, Jean Leclerc, ed., 5:1–65. Leiden: Pieter van der Aa, 1703–6.

———. *The Handbook of the Christian Soldier*. In *The Collected Works of Erasmus*, Charles Fantazzi, trans. and ann., 66:1–127. Toronto: University of Toronto Press, 1988.

Evans, Gillian Rosemary. *Bernard of Clairvaux*. Great Medieval Thinkers. Oxford: Oxford University Press, 2000.

Evennett, H. Outram. *The Spirit of the Counter-Reformation*. John Bossy, ed. Cambridge: Cambridge University Press, 1968.

Fabre, Pierre-Antoine. "Ignace de Loyola et Jérôme Nadal: Paternité et filiation chez les premiers jésuites." In *Ignacio de Loyola y su tiempo: Congreso internacional de historia (9–13 Setiembre 1991)*, Juan Plazaola, ed., 617–33. Bilbao: Ediciones Mensajero, 1992.

Farge, James K. *Biographical Register of Paris Doctors of Theology, 1500–1536*. Subsidia Mediaevalia, 10. Toronto: Pontifical Institute of Mediaeval Studies, 1980.

———. *Orthodoxy and Reform in Early Reformation France: The Faculty of Theology of Paris, 1500–1543*. Studies in Medieval and Reformation Thought, 32. Leiden: Brill, 1985.

———. "The University of Paris in the Time of Ignatius of Loyola." In *Ignacio de Loyola y su tiempo: Congreso internacional de historia (9–13 Setiembre 1991)*, Juan Plazaola, ed., 221–43. Bilbao: Ediciones Mensajero, 1992.

Farr, James R. "Honor, Law, and Custom in Renaissance Europe." In *A Companion to the Worlds of the Renaissance*, Guido Ruggiero, ed., 124–38. Blackwell Companions to European History. Oxford: Blackwell, 2002.

Fenlon, Dermot. *Heresy and Obedience in Tridentine Italy: Cardinal Pole and the Counter Reformation*. Cambridge: Cambridge University Press, 1972.

Fernández Martín, Luis. "Francisco Mudarra, difamador y protegido de San Ignacio, 1538–1555." *Archivum historicum Societatis Iesu* 62 (1993): 161–73.

———. "Iñigo de Loyola y los alumbrados." *Hispania sacra* 35 (1983): 585–680.

Ferrante, Lucia. "Honor Regained: Women in the Casa del Soccorso di San Paolo in Sixteenth-Century Bologna." Margaret A. Gallucci, trans. In *Sex and Gender in Historical Perspective*, Edward Muir and Guido Ruggiero, eds., 46–72. Selections from *Quaderni storici*. Baltimore: Johns Hopkins University Press, 1990.

Feuillet, André. "Le pharisien et le publicain (Luc 18, 9–14): La manifestation de la miséricorde divine en Jésus Serviteur souffrant." *Esprit et vie* 91 (1981): 657–65.

Filson, Floyd V. "The Journey Motif in Luke-Acts." In *Apostolic History and the Gospel: Biblical and Historical Essays Presented to F. F. Bruce on His 60th Birthday*, W. Ward Gasque and Ralph P. Martin, eds., 68–77. Grand Rapids, Mich.: William B. Eerdmans, 1970.

Firpo, Massimo. "Vittoria Colonna, Giovanni Morone, e gli 'spirituali.'" *Rivista di storia e letteratura religiosa* 24 (1988): 211–61.

Fisher, Arthur L. "A Study in Early Jesuit Government: The Nature and Origins of the Dissent of Nicolás Bobadilla." *Viator* 10 (1979): 397–431.

Fita, Fidel. "Los tres procesos de San Ignacio de Loyola en Alcalá de Henares: Estudio crítico." *Boletín de la Real Academia de la Historia* 33 (1898): 422–61.

Fitzmyer, Joseph A. *The Gospel According to Luke: Introduction, Translation, and Notes.* The Anchor Bible, 28–28A. Garden City, N.Y.: Doubleday, 1981–85.

Flynn, Maureen. *Sacred Charity: Confraternities and Social Welfare in Spain, 1400–1700.* Ithaca, N.Y.: Cornell University Press, 1989.

Foa, Anna. "The New and the Old: The Spread of Syphilis (1494–1530)." Carole C. Gallucci, trans. In *Sex and Gender in Historical Perspective*, Edward Muir and Guido Ruggiero, eds., 26–45. Selections from *Quaderni storici*. Baltimore: Johns Hopkins University Press, 1990.

Fois, Mario. "La giustificazione cristiana degli studi umanistici da parte di Ignazio di Loyola e le sue consequenze nei gesuiti posteriori." In *Ignacio de Loyola y su tiempo: Congreso internacional de historia (9–13 Setiembre 1991)*, Juan Plazaola, ed., 405–40. Bilbao: Ediciones Mensajero, 1992.

Fontaine, Michelle M. "A House Divided: The Compagnia de Santa Maria dei Battuti in Modena on the Eve of Catholic Reform." In *Confraternities and Catholic Reform in Italy, France, and Spain*, John Patrick Donnelly and Michael W. Maher, eds., 55–73. Sixteenth Century Essays & Studies, 44. Kirksville, Mo.: Thomas Jefferson University Press, 1999.

Foucault, Michel. "The Battle for Chastity." In *Western Sexuality: Practice and Precept in Past and Present Times*, Philippe Ariès and André Béjin, eds., and Anthony Forster, trans., 14–25. Family, Sexuality, and Social Relations in Past Times. Oxford: Blackwell, 1985.

Friedman, John B. "Peacocks and Preachers: Analytic Technique in Marcus of Orvieto's *Liber de moralitatibus*, Vatican lat. MS 5935." In *Beasts and Birds of the Middle Ages: The Bestiary and Its Legacy*, Willene B. Clark and Meredith T. McMunn, eds., 179–96. Middle Ages Series. Philadelphia: University of Pennsylvania Press, 1989.

Friedmann, Herbert. *A Bestiary for Saint Jerome: Animal Symbolism in European Religious Art.* Washington, D.C.: Smithsonian Institution Press, 1980.

Fumaroli, Marc. "The Fertility and the Shortcomings of Renaissance Rhetoric: The Jesuit Case." In *The Jesuits: Cultures, Sciences, and the Arts, 1540–1773*, J. W. O'Malley, G. A. Bailey, S. J. Harris, and T. F. Kennedy, eds., 90–106. Toronto: University of Toronto Press, 1999.

Gagliardi, Isabella. *Li trofei della croce: L'esperienza gesuata e la società lucchese tra Medioevo ed età moderna.* Centro Alti Studi in Scienze Religiose, 3. Roma: Edizioni di Storia e Letteratura, 2005.

Galinsky, G. Karl. *The Herakles Theme: The Adaptations of the Hero in Literature from Homer to the Twentieth Century.* Oxford: Basil Blackwell, 1972.

García Cárcel, Ricardo. "The Course of the Moriscos up to Their Expulsion." In *The Spanish Inquisition and the Inquisitorial Mind*, Angel Alcalá, ed., 73–86. Atlantic Studies on Society in Change, 49. Boulder, Colo.: Social Science Monographs, 1987.

García Mateo, Rogelio. "Ignacio de Loyola y el mundo caballeresco." In *Ignacio de Loyola, Magister Artium en París 1528–1535*, Julio Caro Baroja and Antonio Beristain, eds., 293–302. San Sebastián: Kutxa, 1991.

———. "La 'Societas Jesu' y el contexto socio-político del s. XVI: Perspectivas para hoy." In *Ignacio de Loyola y su tiempo: Congreso internacional de historia (9–13 Setiembre 1991)*, Juan Plazaola, ed., 505–50. Bilbao: Ediciones Mensajero, 1992.

Gasque, W. Ward, and Ralph P. Martin, eds. *Apostolic History and the Gospel: Biblical and Historical Essays Presented to F. F. Bruce on His 60th Birthday.* Grand Rapids, Mich.: William B. Eerdmans, 1970.

Gill, David H. "Observations on the Lukan Travel Narrative and Some Related Passages." *Harvard Theological Review* 63 (1970): 199–221.

Gill, David W. J., and Conrad Gempf, eds. *The Book of Acts in Its First Century Setting.* Vol. 2, *The Book of Acts in Its Graeco-Roman Setting.* Grand Rapids, Mich.: Eerdmans, 1994.

Gilmore, David D., ed. *Honor and Shame and the Unity of the Mediterranean.* Washington, D.C.: American Anthropological Association, 1987.

———. "The Shame of Dishonor." In *Honor and Shame and the Unity of the Mediterranean*, David Gilmore, ed., 8–16. Washington, D.C.: American Anthropological Association, 1987.

Gleason, Elisabeth G. *Gasparo Contarini: Venice, Rome, and Reform.* Berkeley: University of California Press, 1993.

———. "On the Nature of Sixteenth-Century Italian Evangelism: Scholarship, 1953–1978." *Sixteenth Century Journal* 9, no. 3 (1978): 3–26.

Goldin, Frederick. *The Mirror of Narcissus in the Courtly Love Lyric.* Ithaca, N.Y.: Cornell University Press, 1967.

González Novalín, José Luis. "La Inquisición y los Jesuitas (s. XVI)." *Anthologica Annua* 37 (1990): 11–56.

———. "Los Jesuitas y la Inquisición en la época de la implantación de la Compañía." In *Ignacio de Loyola y su tiempo: Congreso internacional de historia (9–13 Setiembre 1991)*, Juan Plazaola, ed., 285–303. Bilbao: Ediciones Mensajero, 1992.

Goodrich, Richard J. *Contextualizing Cassian: Aristocrats, Asceticism, and Reformation in Fifth-Century Gaul.* Oxford Early Christian Studies. Oxford: Oxford University Press, 2007.

Gorilovics, Tivadar. "Narcissus' Attitude to Death." In *Echoes of Narcissus*, Lieve Spaas, with Trista Selous, eds., 263–70. Polygons: Cultural Diversities and Intersections, 2. New York: Bergahn Books, 2000.

Grabes, Herbert. *The Mutable Glass: Mirror-Imagery in Titles and Texts of the Middle Ages and English Renaissance*. Gordon Collier, trans. Cambridge: Cambridge University Press, 1982.

Grendler, Marcella T., and Paul F. Grendler. "The Erasmus Holdings of Roman and Vatican Libraries." *Erasmus in English* 13 (1984): 2–29.

———. "The Survival of Erasmus in Italy." *Erasmus in English* 8 (1976): 2–12.

Grendler, Paul F. *Schooling in Renaissance Italy: Literacy and Learning, 1300–1600*. Baltimore: Johns Hopkins University Press, 1989.

Griffin, Clive. *Journeymen-Printers, Heresy, and the Inquisition in Sixteenth-Century Spain*. Oxford: Oxford University Press, 2005.

Griffiths, Gordon. "Berquin, Louis de." In *Contemporaries of Erasmus: A Biographical Register of the Renaissance and Reformation*. Vol. 1, *A–E*, P. G. Bietenholz and Thomas B. Deutscher, eds., 135–40. Toronto: University of Toronto Press, 1985.

Guidotti, Gloria. "Dal 'patto autobiografico' del Loyola alla sua biografia." *Cuadernos de Filología Italiana* 7, número extraordinario, (2000): 267–82, http://www.ucm.es/BUCM/revistas/fll/11339527/articulos/CFIT0000230267A.PDF.

Guthrie, W. K. C. *A History of Greek Philosophy*. Vol. 6, *Aristotle: An Encounter*. 2nd ed. Cambridge: Cambridge University Press, 1990.

Hale, J. R. "Gunpowder and the Renaissance: An Essay in the History of Ideas." In *From the Renaissance to the Counter-Reformation: Essays in Honor of Garrett Mattingly*, Charles H. Carter, ed., 113–44. New York: Random House, 1965. Repr. in *Renaissance War Studies*, 389–420. London: Hambledon Press, 1983.

———. "War and Public Opinion in Renaissance Italy." In *Italian Renaissance Studies*, E. F. Jacob, ed., 94–122. London: Faber, 1960. Repr. in *Renaissance War Studies*, 359–87. London: Hambledon Press, 1983.

Haliczer, Stephen. "The First Holocaust: The Inquisition and the Converted Jews of Spain and Portugal." In *Inquisition and Society in Early Modern Europe*, Stephen Haliczer, ed. and trans., 7–18. Totowa, N.J.: Barnes & Noble Books, 1987.

———, ed. and trans. *Inquisition and Society in Early Modern Europe*. Totowa, N.J.: Barnes & Noble Books, 1987.

Hamilton, Alastair. *Heresy and Mysticism in Sixteenth-Century Spain: The Alumbrados*. Cambridge: James Clarke, 1992.

Hardcastle, Gary L., and George A. Reisch, eds. *Monty Python and Philosophy: Nudge Nudge, Think Think!* Popular Culture and Philosophy, 19. Peru, Ill.: Open Court Publishing, 2006.

Harvey, L. P. *Muslims in Spain, 1500–1614*. Chicago: University of Chicago Press, 2005.

Hausman, Noëlle. "'What Ought I to Do?' *The Pilgrim's Testament*, a Source for the Apostolic Religious Life." *Centrum Ignatianum Spiritualitatis (CIS)* 20, nos. 1–2 (1990): 13–38.

Hays, Richard B. *The Moral Vision of the New Testament: Community, Cross, New Creation; a Contemporary Introduction to New Testament Ethics.* New York: HarperCollins, 1996.

Heffernan, Thomas J. *Sacred Biography: Saints and Their Biographers in the Middle Ages.* Oxford: Oxford University Press, 1988.

Henderson, John. "Penitence and the Laity in Fifteenth-Century Florence." In *Christianity and the Renaissance: Image and Religious Imagination in the Quattrocento*, Timothy Verdon and John Henderson, eds., 229–49. Syracuse, N.Y.: Syracuse University Press, 1990.

——. *Piety and Charity in Late Medieval Florence.* Oxford: Clarendon Press, 1994.

——. *The Renaissance Hospital: Healing the Body and Healing the Soul.* New Haven, Conn.: Yale University Press, 2006.

Hinz, Manfred, Roberto Righi, and Danilo Zardin, eds. *I Gesuiti e la "Ratio studiorum."* "Europa delle Corti" Centro studi sulle società di antico regime: Biblioteca del Cinquecento, 113. Roma: Bulzoni, 2004.

Homza, Lu Ann. *Religious Authority in the Spanish Renaissance.* Johns Hopkins University Studies in Historical and Political Science, 118th ser., 1. Baltimore: Johns Hopkins University Press, 2000.

——, ed. and trans. *The Spanish Inquisition, 1478–1614: An Anthology of Sources.* Indianapolis, Ind.: Hackett Publishing, 2006.

Hornedo, Rafael M. de. "La 'vera effigies' de San Ignacio." *Razón y fe* 154 (1956): 203–24.

Hornik, Heidi J., and Mikeal C. Parsons. *Illuminating Luke.* Vol. 1, *The Infancy Narrative in Italian Renaissance Painting.* Harrisburg, Penn.: Trinity Press International, 2003; Vol. 2, *The Public Ministry of Christ in Italian Renaissance and Baroque Painting.* New York: T&T Clark International, 2005.

Housel, Rebecca. "*Monty Python and the Holy Grail*: Philosophy, Gender, and Society." In *Monty Python and Philosophy: Nudge Nudge, Think Think!*, Gary L. Hardcastle and George A. Reisch, eds., 83–92. Popular Culture and Philosophy, 19. Peru, Ill.: Open Court Publishing, 2006.

Howard, Donald R. *The Three Temptations: Medieval Man in Search of the World.* Princeton, N.J.: Princeton University Press, 1966.

——. *Writers and Pilgrims: Medieval Pilgrimage Narratives and Their Posterity.* Berkeley: University of California Press, 1980.

Hufton, Olwen. "Persuasion, Promises, and Persistence: Funding the Early Jesuit College." In *I Gesuiti e la "Ratio studiorum*," Manfred Hinz, Roberto Righi, and Danilo Zardin, eds., 75–95. "Europa delle Corti" Centro studi sulle società di antico regime: Biblioteca del Cinquecento, 113. Roma: Bulzoni, 2004.

Hurtubise, Pierre. "Rome au temps d'Ignace de Loyola." In *Ignacio de Loyola y su tiempo: Congreso internacional de historia (9–13 Setiembre 1991)*, Juan Plazaola, ed., 441–71. Bilbao: Ediciones Mensajero, 1992.

Iacobus a Voragine. *Legenda aurea vulgo historica Lombardica dicta.* Johann Georg Theodor Grässe, ed. 3rd ed. Bratislava: Guilelmus Koebner, 1890.

Ignatius Loyola. *Ablaze with God: A Reading of the Memoirs of Ignatius of Loyola.* Parmananda R. Divarkar, trans. Anand, India: Gujarat Sahitya Prakash, 1990.

——. *Acta patris Ignatii.* Dionisio Fernández Zapico and Cándido de Dalmases, with Pedro de Leturia, eds., 331–57. Monumenta Historica Societatis Iesu, 66. Roma: Institutum Historicum Societatis Iesu, 1943.

——. *The Autobiography of St. Ignatius Loyola with Related Documents.* Joseph F. O'Callaghan, trans., and John C. Olin, ed. New York: Harper & Row, 1974.

——. *The Constitutions of the Society of Jesus.* George E. Ganss, trans., with an Introduction and a Commentary. St. Louis, Mo.: Institute of Jesuit Sources, 1970.

——. *Ignatius of Loyola: The Spiritual Exercises and Selected Works.* George E. Ganss, ed. Classics of Western Spirituality. New York: Paulist Press, 1991.

——. *Letters and Instructions.* Martin E. Palmer and John W. Padberg, ed. and trans., with John L. McCarthy, ed. Jesuit Primary Sources in English Translation, 23. St. Louis, Mo.: Institute of Jesuit Sources, 2006.

——. *Letters of St. Ignatius Loyola.* William J. Young, trans. Chicago: Loyola University Press, 1959.

——. *Monumenta Ignatiana.* Series I, *Sancti Ignatii . . . Epistolae et Instructiones.* 12 vols. Madrid: Gabriel Lopez del Horno, 1903–11.

——. *A Pilgrim's Journey: The Autobiography of Ignatius of Loyola.* Joseph N. Tylenda, trans. Wilmington, Del.: Michael Glazier, 1985.

——. *A Pilgrim's Testament: The Memoirs of St. Ignatius of Loyola.* Parmananda R. Divarkar, trans. Jesuit Primary Sources in English Translation, 13. St. Louis, Mo.: Institute of Jesuit Sources, 1995.

——. "Reminiscences (Autobiography)." In *Personal Writings*, Philip Endean, trans., 3–64. London: Penguin, 1996.

——. *The Spiritual Exercises of Saint Ignatius: A Literal Translation and a Contemporary Reading.* David L. Fleming, trans. St. Louis, Mo.: Institute of Jesuit Sources, 1978.

Iparraguirre, Ignacio. *Orientaciones bibliográficas sobre San Ignacio de Loyola.* 2nd ed. Subsidia ad historiam Societatis Iesu, 1. Roma: Institutum Historicum Societatis Iesu, 1965.

Ivanov, Sergey A. *Holy Fools in Byzantium and Beyond.* Simon Franklin, trans. Oxford Studies in Byzantium. Oxford: Oxford University Press, 2006.

Jackson Lualdi, Katharine, and Anne T. Thayer, eds. *Penitence in the Age of Reformations.* St. Andrews Studies in Reformation History. Aldershot, U.K.: Ashgate, 2000.

Jacob, E. F., ed. *Italian Renaissance Studies*. London: Faber, 1960.

Jervell, Jacob. *The Theology of the Acts of the Apostles*. New Testament Theology. Cambridge: Cambridge University Press, 1996.

John Chrysostom. *De inani gloria et de liberis educandis*. Anne-Marie Malingrey, ed. and trans. Sources chrétiennes, 188. Paris: Éditions du Cerf, 1972.

———. *Homilia XXXV in 1 Cor. 14*. In *Patrologia graeca*, J.-P. Migne, ed., 61:295–306. Paris: apud J.-P. Migne editorem, 1862.

Jones Mathers, Constance. "Early Spanish Qualms about Loyola and the Society of Jesus." *The Historian* 53 (1991): 679–90.

Joost-Gaugier, Christiane L. *Measuring Heaven: Pythagoras and His Influence on Thought and Art in Antiquity and the Middle Ages*. Ithaca, N.Y.: Cornell University Press, 2006.

Julia, Dominique. "Jésuites et universités: Les logiques d'une politique d'après les textes normatifs." In *Gesuiti e università in Europa (secoli XVI–XVIII) (Atti del Convegno di studi, Parma, 13–15 dicembre 2001)*, Gian Paolo Brizzi and Roberto Greci, eds., 13–36. Centro interuniversitario per la storia delle università italiane: Studi, 3. Bologna: Cooperativa Libraria Universitaria Editrice, 2002.

Kamen, Henry. *Inquisition and Society in Spain in the Sixteenth and Seventeenth Centuries*. Bloomington: Indiana University Press, 1985.

———. "The Mediterranean and the Expulsion of Spanish Jews in 1492." *Past and Present*, no. 119 (May 1988): 30–55.

———. *Philip of Spain*. New Haven, Conn.: Yale University Press, 1997.

———. "Toleration and Dissent in Sixteenth-Century Spain: The Alternative Tradition." *Sixteenth Century Journal* 19 (1988): 3–23.

Kelly, Henry Ansgar. "The Metamorphoses of the Eden Serpent during the Middle Ages and Renaissance." *Viator* 2 (1971): 301–28.

Kennedy, George A. *Classical Rhetoric and Its Christian and Secular Tradition from Ancient to Modern Times*. Chapel Hill: University of North Carolina Press, 1980.

———. *New Testament Interpretation through Rhetorical Criticism*. Chapel Hill: University of North Carolina Press, 1984.

Kieckhefer, Richard. "Major Currents in Late Medieval Devotion." In *Christian Spirituality: High Middle Ages and Reformation*, Jill Raitt, with Bernard McGinn and John Meyendorff, eds., 75–108. World Spirituality, 17. London: Routledge & Kegan Paul, 1987.

———. *Unquiet Souls: Fourteenth-Century Saints and Their Religious Milieu*. Chicago: University of Chicago Press, 1984.

Kimball, Bruce A. *Orators and Philosophers: A History of the Idea of Liberal Education*. New York: Teachers College Press, Columbia University, 1986.

Kirchmeyer, Jean. "Gloire (Vaine gloire): Littérature occidentale." In *Dictionnaire de Spiritualité*. Vol. 6, *Gabriel–Guzman*, 502–5. Paris: Beauchesne, 1967.

Kittel, Gerhard, and Gerhard Friedrich, eds. *Theological Dictionary of the New Testament*. Geoffrey W. Bromiley, trans. Grand Rapids, Mich.: Eerdmans, 1964–76.

Klingender, Francis D. *Animals in Art and Thought to the End of the Middle Ages*. Evelyn Antal and John Harthan, eds. Cambridge, Mass.: M.I.T. Press, 1971.

Knoespel, Kenneth J. *Narcissus and the Invention of Personal History*. Garland Publications in Comparative Literature. New York: Garland, 1985.

Kochhar-Lindgren, Gray. *Narcissus Transformed: The Textual Subject in Psychoanalysis and Literature*. University Park: Pennsylvania State University Press, 1993.

Kodell, Jerome. "Luke's Use of *Laos*, 'People,' in the Jerusalem Narrative (Lk. 19:28–24:53)." *Catholic Biblical Quarterly* 31 (1969): 327–43.

Krautheimer, Richard. "The Architecture of Sixtus III: A Fifth-Century Renascence?" *Studies in Early Christian, Medieval, and Renaissance Art*, 181–96. New York: New York University Press, 1969.

Kriegel, Maurice. "Le parcours de Juan Luis Vives: Du milieu judaïsant à l'option érasmienne." *Revue de l'histoire des religions* 215 (1998): 249–81.

Kristeller, Paul Oskar. "The Contribution of Religious Orders to Renaissance Thought and Learning." In *Medieval Aspects of Renaissance Learning: Three Essays by Paul Oskar Kristeller*, Edward P. Mahoney, ed. and trans., 95–158. Duke Monographs in Medieval and Renaissance Studies, 1. Durham, N.C.: Duke University Press, 1974.

——. *Medieval Aspects of Renaissance Learning: Three Essays by Paul Oskar Kristeller*. Edward P. Mahoney, ed. Duke Monographs in Medieval and Renaissance Studies, 1. Durham, N.C.: Duke University Press, 1974.

——. *Renaissance Thought and Its Sources*. New York: Columbia University Press, 1979.

——. "Thomism and the Italian Thought of the Renaissance." In *Medieval Aspects of Renaissance Learning: Three Essays by Paul Oskar Kristeller*, Edward P. Mahoney, ed. and trans., 27–91. Duke Monographs in Medieval and Renaissance Studies, 1. Durham, N.C.: Duke University Press, 1974.

Kunkel, Paul A. *The Theatines in the History of Catholic Reform before the Establishment of Lutheranism*. Washington, D.C.: Catholic University of America Press, 1941.

Ladner, Gerhart B. "*Homo Viator*: Mediaeval Ideas on Alienation and Order." *Speculum* 42 (1967): 233–59.

Lazar, Lance Gabriel. " 'E faucibus daemonis': Daughters of Prostitutes, the First Jesuits, and the Compagnia delle Vergini Miserabili di Santa Caterina della Rosa." In *Confraternities and the Visual Arts in Renaissance Italy: Ritual, Spectacle, Image*, Barbara Wisch and Diane Cole Ahl, eds., 259–79. Cambridge: Cambridge University Press, 2000.

———. *Working in the Vineyard of the Lord: Jesuit Confraternities in Early Modern Italy*. Toronto: University of Toronto Press, 2005.

Lécrivain, Philippe. "Ignace de Loyola, un réformateur? Une lecture historique des 'Règles pour avoir le vrai sens de l'Église.'" *Christus* 37, no. 147 (July 1990): 348–60.

———. *Paris au temps d'Ignace de Loyola (1528–1535)*. Paris: Éditions facultés jésuites de Paris, 2006.

Leduc, Francis. "La thème de la vaine gloire chez saint Jean Chrysostome." *Proche-orient chrétien* 19 (1969): 3–32.

Leonardi, Claudio. "Committenze agiografiche nel Trecento." In *Patronage and Public in the Trecento: Proceedings of the St. Lambrecht Symposium, Abtei St. Lambrecht, Styria, 16–19 July 1984*, Vincent Moleta, ed., 37–58. Biblioteca dell'*Archivum Romanicum*, 202. Firenze: Olschki, 1986.

———. "L'esperienza di Dio in Giovanni Cassiano e Salviano di Marsiglia." In *Medioevo Latino: La cultura dell'Europa cristiana*, 25–47. Millenio Medievale, 40 (Strumenti e studi, n.s., 2). Firenze: SISMEL—Edizioni del Galluzzo, 2004.

Lesnick, Daniel R. "Civic Preaching in the Early Renaissance: Giovanni Dominici's Florentine Sermons." In *Christianity and the Renaissance: Image and Religious Imagination in the Quattrocento*, Timothy Verdon and John Henderson, eds., 208–25. Syracuse, N.Y.: Syracuse University Press, 1990.

Leturia, Pedro de. "Aspetti francescani in Sant'Ignazio di Loyola." In *Estudios Ignacianos*, Ignacio Iparraguirre, ed., 2:419–23. Bibliotheca Instituti Historici Societatis Iesu, 10–11. Roma: Institutum Historicum Societatis Iesu, 1957.

———. "Damas vascas en la formación y transformación de Iñigo de Loyola." In *Estudios Ignacianos*, Ignacio Iparraguirre, ed., 1:69–85. Bibliotheca Instituti Historici Societatis Iesu, 10–11. Roma: Institutum Historicum Societatis Iesu, 1957.

———. "El influjo de San Onofre en San Ignacio a base de un texto inédito de Nadal." *Manresa* 2 (1926): 224–38. Repr. in *Estudios Ignacianos*, Ignacio Iparraguirre, ed., 1:97–111. Bibliotheca Instituti Historici Societatis Iesu, 10–11. Roma: Institutum Historicum Societatis Iesu, 1957.

———. "Jerusalén y Roma en los designios de San Ignacio de Loyola." In *Estudios Ignacianos*, Ignacio Iparraguirre, ed., 1:181–200. Bibliotheca Instituti Historici Societatis Iesu, 10–11. Roma: Institutum Historicum Societatis Iesu, 1957.

———. "Los 'Recuerdos' presentados por el jesuíta Bobadilla al recién elegido Paulo IV." In *Estudios Ignacianos*, Ignacio Iparraguirre, ed., 1:447–59. Bibliotheca Instituti Historici Societatis Iesu, 10–11. Roma: Institutum Historicum Societatis Iesu, 1957.

———. "Origine e senso sociale dell'apostolato di Sant'Ignazio di Loyola in Roma." In *Estudios Ignacianos*, Ignacio Iparraguirre, ed., 1:257–83. Bibliotheca

Instituti Historici Societatis Iesu, 10–11. Roma: Institutum Historicum Societatis Iesu, 1957.

Levi, Anthony. *Renaissance and Reformation: The Intellectual Genesis*. New Haven, Conn.: Yale University Press, 2002.

Lewis, Mark A. "Recovering the Apostolic Way of Life: The New Clerks Regular of the Sixteenth Century." In *Early Modern Catholicism: Essays in Honour of John W. O'Malley, S.J.*, Kathleen M. Comerford and Hilmar M. Pabel, eds., 280–96. Toronto: University of Toronto Press, 2001.

Leyerle, Blake. *Theatrical Shows and Ascetic Lives: John Chrysostom's Attack on Spiritual Marriage*. Berkeley: University of California Press, 2001.

Leyser, Conrad. *Authority and Asceticism from Augustine to Gregory the Great*. Oxford: Clarendon Press, 2000.

Lindberg, Carter. *Beyond Charity: Reformation Initiatives for the Poor*. Minneapolis: Augsburg Press, 1993.

Little, Lester K. "Pride Goes before Avarice: Social Change and the Vices in Latin Christendom." *American Historical Review* 76 (1971): 16–49.

———. *Religious Poverty and the Profit Economy in Medieval Europe*. Ithaca, N.Y.: Cornell University Press, 1978.

Longenecker, Richard N., ed. *Patterns of Discipleship in the New Testament*. Grand Rapids, Mich.: Eerdmans, 1996.

———. "Taking up the Cross Daily: Discipleship in Luke-Acts." In *Patterns of Discipleship in the New Testament*, Richard N. Longenecker, ed., 50–76. Grand Rapids, Mich.: Eerdmans, 1996.

Longhurst, John E. "Saint Ignatius at Alcalá, 1526–1527." *Archivum historicum Societatis Iesu* 26 (1957): 252–56.

Lovering, Eugene H., Jr., ed. *Society of Biblical Literature 1993 Seminar Papers*. SBL Seminar Paper Series, 32. Atlanta: Scholars Press, 1993.

Lucas, Thomas M. *Landmarking: City, Church, and Jesuit Urban Strategy*. Chicago: Loyola Press, 1997.

Lukács, Ladislaus, ed. *Monumenta Paedagogica Societatis Iesu*. Vol. 1, *1540–1556*. 2nd ed. Monumenta Historica Societatis Iesu, 92. Roma: apud "Monumenta Historica Soc. Iesu," 1965.

MacCulloch, Diarmaid, Mary Laven, and Eamon Duffy. "Recent Trends in the Study of Christianity in Sixteenth-Century Europe." *Renaissance Quarterly* 59 (2006): 697–731.

MacIntyre, Alasdair C. *After Virtue: A Study in Moral Theory*. 2nd ed. Notre Dame, Ind.: University of Notre Dame Press, 1984.

Maffei, Giampietro. *De vita et moribus Ignatii Loiolae qui Societatem Iesu fundavit Libri III*. Köln: apud Maternum Cholinum, 1585.

Maher, Michael W. "How the Jesuits Used Their Congregations to Promote Frequent Communion." In *Confraternities and Catholic Reform in Italy, France, and*

Spain, John Patrick Donnelly and Michael W. Maher, eds., 75–95. Sixteenth Century Essays & Studies, 44. Kirksville, Mo.: Thomas Jefferson University Press, 1999.

Mahoney, Edward P., ed. and trans. *Medieval Aspects of Renaissance Learning: Three Essays by Paul Oskar Kristeller*. Duke Monographs in Medieval and Renaissance Studies, 1. Durham, N.C.: Duke University Press, 1974.

Malina, Bruce J., and Jerome H. Neyrey. "Honor and Shame in Luke-Acts: Pivotal Values of the Mediterranean World." In *The Social World of Luke-Acts: Models for Interpretation*, Jerome H. Neyrey, ed., 25–65. Peabody, Mass.: Hendrickson, 1991.

Mánek, Jindřich. "The New Exodus in the Books of Luke." *Novum Testamentum* 2 (1958): 8–23.

Mannini, Maria Pia. "La diffusione del culto in Toscana: Lazzaretti, conventi, case delle Convertite e Malmaritate." In *La Maddalena tra sacro e profano*, Marilena Mosco, ed., 60–64. Firenze: La casa Usher, 1986.

Martin, Colin, and Geoffrey Parker. *The Spanish Armada*. Rev. ed. Manchester: Mandolin, 1999.

Martin, John. "Salvation and Society in Sixteenth-Century Venice: Popular Evangelism in a Renaissance City." *Journal of Modern History* 60 (1988): 205–33.

———. *Venice's Hidden Enemies: Italian Heretics in a Renaissance City*. Studies on the History of Society and Culture, 16. Berkeley: University of California Press, 1993.

Martínez, Bernabé Bartolomé. "Las librerías e imprentas de los jesuitas (1540–1767): Una aportación notable a la cultura española." *Hispania sacra* 40 (1988): 315–88.

Martini, Angelo. "Di chi fu ospite S. Ignazio a Venezia nel 1536?" *Archivum historicum Societatis Iesu* 18 (1949): 253–60.

———. "Gli studi teologici di Giovanni de Polanco alle origini della legislazione scolastica della Compagnia di Gesù." *Archivum historicum Societatis Iesu* 21 (1952): 225–81.

Martz, Linda. *Poverty and Welfare in Habsburg Spain: The Example of Toledo*. Cambridge Iberian and Latin American Studies. Cambridge: Cambridge University Press, 1983.

Maryks, Robert Aleksander. *The Jesuit Order as a Synagogue of Jews: Jesuits of Jewish Ancestry and Purity-of-Blood Laws in the Early Society of Jesus*. Studies in Medieval and Reformation Traditions, 146. Leiden: Brill, 2010.

———. "La *consolatio* nel ministero della confessione dei primi gesuiti." In *I Gesuiti e la "Ratio studiorum,"* Manfred Hinz, Roberto Righi, and Danilo Zardin, eds., 211–27. "Europa delle Corti" Centro studi sulle società di antico regime: Biblioteca del Cinquecento, 113. Roma: Bulzoni, 2004.

————. *Saint Cicero and the Jesuits: The Influence of the Liberal Arts on the Adoption of Moral Probabilism.* Catholic Christendom, 1300–1700. Aldershot, U.K.: Ashgate, 2008.

Matthews, Victor H., and Don C. Benjamin, eds. *Honor and Shame in the World of the Bible.* Semeia, 68. Atlanta: Scholars Press, 1996.

Mazour-Matusevich, Yelena. "Gerson's Legacy." In *A Companion to Jean Gerson,* Brian Patrick McGuire, ed., 357–99. Brill's Companions to the Christian Tradition, 3. Leiden: Brill, 2006.

McClung Hallman, Barbara. *Italian Cardinals, Reform, and the Church as Property, 1492–1563.* UCLA Center for Medieval and Renaissance Studies, 22. Berkeley: University of California Press, 1985.

McCormick, Michael. *Origins of the European Economy: Communications and Commerce, A.D. 300–900.* Cambridge: Cambridge University Press, 2001.

McCown, C. C. "The Geography of Luke's Central Section." *Journal of Biblical Literature* 57 (1938): 51–66.

————. "Gospel Geography: Fiction, Fact, and Truth." *Journal of Biblical Literature* 60 (1941): 1–25.

McCulloch, Florence. *Mediaeval Latin and French Bestiaries.* University of North Carolina Studies in the Romance Languages and Literatures, 33. Chapel Hill: University of North Carolina Press, 1962.

McDaniel, Rhonda L. "Pride Goes before a Fall: Aldhelm's Practical Application of Gregorian and Cassianic Conceptions of *Superbia* and the Eight Principal Vices." In *The Seven Deadly Sins: From Communities to Individuals,* Richard Newhauser, ed., 95–109. Studies in Medieval and Reformation Traditions: History, Culture, Religion, Ideas, 123. Leiden: Brill, 2007.

McGrath, Alister E. *Iustitia Dei: A History of the Christian Doctrine of Justification.* 3rd ed. Cambridge: Cambridge University Press, 2005.

McKendrick, Melveena. *Theatre in Spain, 1490–1700.* Cambridge: Cambridge University Press, 1989.

McManamon, John M. "Catholic Identity and Anti-Semitism in a Eulogy for 'Isabel the Catholic.'" *Journal of Ecumenical Studies* 42 (2007): 196–216.

————. "Continuity and Change in the Ideals of Humanism: The Evidence from Florentine Funeral Oratory." In *Life and Death in Fifteenth-Century Florence,* Marcel Tetel, Ronald G. Witt, and Rona Goffen, eds., 68–87. Durham, N.C.: Duke University Press, 1989.

————. *Funeral Oratory and the Cultural Ideals of Italian Humanism.* Chapel Hill: University of North Carolina Press, 1989.

————. *Pierpaolo Vergerio the Elder (ca. 1369–1444): The Humanist as Orator.* Medieval & Renaissance Texts & Studies, 163. Tempe, Ariz.: Medieval & Renaissance Texts & Studies, 1996.

McPherson, David. "Roman Comedy in Renaissance Education: The Moral Question." *Sixteenth Century Journal* 12 (1981): 19–30.

McVann, Mark. "Rituals of Status Transformation in Luke-Acts: The Case of Jesus the Prophet." In *The Social World of Luke-Acts: Models for Interpretation*, Jerome H. Neyrey, ed., 333–60. Peabody, Mass.: Hendrickson, 1991.

Medina, Francisco de Borja de. "Ignacio de Loyola y la 'limpieza de sangre.'" In *Ignacio de Loyola y su tiempo: Congreso internacional de historia (9–13 Setiembre 1991)*, Juan Plazaola, ed., 579–615. Bilbao: Ediciones Mensajero, 1992.

———. "La Compañía de Jesús y la minoría morisca (1545–1614)." *Archivum historicum Societatis Iesu* 57 (1988): 3–136.

Mehl, James V., ed. *In Laudem Caroli: Renaissance and Reformation Studies for Charles G. Nauert*. Sixteenth Century Essays & Studies, 49. Kirksville, Mo.: Thomas Jefferson University Press, 1998.

Meier, John P. *A Marginal Jew: Rethinking the Historical Jesus*. Vol. 2, *Mentor, Message, and Miracles*. The Anchor Bible Reference Library. New York: Doubleday, 1994.

Meissner, William W. *Ignatius of Loyola: The Psychology of a Saint*. New Haven, Conn.: Yale University Press, 1992.

Melchior-Bonnet, Sabine. *The Mirror: A History*. Katharine H. Jewett, trans. London: Routledge, 2001.

Miccoli, Giovanni. *Francesco d'Assisi: Realtà e memoria di un'esperienza cristiana*. Torino: Einaudi, 1991.

Michel, Tom, ed. *Friends on the Way: Jesuits Encounter Contemporary Judaism*. New York: Fordham University Press, 2007.

Miquel, Pierre. "Gloire (Vaine gloire)." In *Dictionnaire de Spiritualité*. Vol. 6, *Gabriel–Guzman*, 494–502. Paris: Beauchesne, 1967.

Modras, Ronald. *Ignatian Humanism: A Dynamic Spirituality for the 21st Century*. Chicago: Loyola Press, 2004.

Moessner, David P. "'The Christ Must Suffer': New Light on the Jesus–Peter, Stephen, Paul Parallels in Luke-Acts." *Novum Testamentum* 28 (1986): 220–56.

———. *Lord of the Banquet: The Literary and Theological Significance of the Lukan Travel Narrative*. Minneapolis: Augsburg Fortress Press, 1989.

Moleta, Vincent, ed. *Patronage and Public in the Trecento: Proceedings of the St. Lambrecht Symposium, Abtei St. Lambrecht, Styria, 16–19 July 1984*. Biblioteca dell'*Archivum Romanicum*, 202. Firenze: Olschki, 1986.

Mollat du Jourdin, Michel. *The Poor in the Middle Ages: An Essay in Social History*. Arthur Goldhammer, trans. New Haven, Conn.: Yale University Press, 1986.

———. "Saint Ignace et les pèlerinages de son temps." In *Ignacio de Loyola y su tiempo: Congreso internacional de historia (9–13 Setiembre 1991)*, Juan Plazaola, ed., 161–78. Bilbao: Ediciones Mensajero, 1992.

Moller, Herbert. "The Social Causation of the Courtly Love Complex." *Comparative Studies in Society and History* 1 (1959): 137–63.

Mommsen, Theodor E. "Petrarch and the Story of the Choice of Hercules." *Journal of the Warburg and Courtauld Institutes* 16 (1953): 178–92.

Monter, William. *Frontiers of Heresy: The Spanish Inquisition from the Basque Lands to Sicily.* Cambridge Studies in Early Modern History. Cambridge: Cambridge University Press, 1990.

Moreno Gallego, Valentín. "Notas historiográficas al encuentro de Loyola y Vives." In *Ignacio de Loyola y su tiempo: Congreso internacional de historia (9–13 Setiembre 1991),* Juan Plazaola, ed., 901–7. Bilbao: Ediciones Mensajero, 1992.

Morgan, Ronald J. "Jesuit Confessors, African Slaves, and the Practice of Confession in Seventeenth-Century Cartagena." In *Penitence in the Age of Reformations,* Katharine Jackson Lualdi and Anne T. Thayer, eds., 222–39. St. Andrews Studies in Reformation History. Aldershot, U.K.: Ashgate, 2000.

Morrall, John B. *Gerson and the Great Schism.* Manchester, U.K.: Manchester University Press, 1960.

Mosco, Marilena, ed. *La Maddalena tra sacro e profano.* Firenze: La casa Usher, 1986.

———. "La Maddalena: Un'identità velata e violata." In *La Maddalena tra sacro e profano,* M. Mosco, ed., 17–23. Firenze: La casa Usher, 1986.

Moxnes, Halvor. "Honor and Shame." In *The Social Sciences and New Testament Interpretation,* Richard L. Rohrbaugh, ed., 19–40. Peabody, Mass.: Hendrickson, 1996.

Muir, Edward. *Civic Ritual in Renaissance Venice.* Princeton, N.J.: Princeton University Press, 1981.

Muir, Edward, and Guido Ruggiero, eds. *Sex and Gender in Historical Perspective.* Selections from *Quaderni storici.* Baltimore: Johns Hopkins University Press, 1990.

Murphy, Roland E. *The Tree of Life: An Exploration of Biblical Wisdom Literature.* The Anchor Bible Reference Library. New York: Doubleday, 1990.

Nadal, Jerónimo. *Epistolae P. Hieronymi Nadal Societatis Iesu ab anno 1546 ad 1577.* 4 vols. Monumenta Historica Societatis Iesu, 13, 15, 21, 27. Madrid: Augustinus Avrial, 1898–1905.

Nalle, Sara T. "Literacy and Culture in Early Modern Castile." *Past and Present,* no. 125 (Nov. 1989): 65–96.

Navone, John J. "The Journey Theme in Luke-Acts." *Bible Today* 58 (Feb. 1972): 616–19.

Newbigin, Nerida. "The Word Made Flesh: The *Rappresentazioni* of Mysteries and Miracles in Fifteenth-Century Florence." In *Christianity and the Renaissance:*

Image and Religious Imagination in the Quattrocento, Timothy Verdon and John Henderson, eds., 361–75. Syracuse, N.Y.: Syracuse University Press, 1990.

Newhauser, Richard, ed. *In the Garden of Evil: The Vices and Culture in the Middle Ages*. Papers in Mediaeval Studies, 18. Toronto: Pontifical Institute of Mediaeval Studies, 2005.

———, ed. *The Seven Deadly Sins: From Communities to Individuals*. Studies in Medieval and Reformation Traditions: History, Culture, Religion, Ideas, 123. Leiden: Brill, 2007.

Neyrey, Jerome H., ed. *The Social World of Luke-Acts: Models for Interpretation*. Peabody, Mass.: Hendrickson, 1991.

Nicolau, Miguel. "Fisonomía de San Ignacio según sus primeros compañeros." *Archivum historicum Societatis Iesu* 26 (1957): 257–69.

Nicolet, Claude. *Space, Geography, and Politics in the Early Roman Empire*. Jerome Lectures, 19. Ann Arbor, Mich.: University of Michigan Press, 1991.

Niebuhr, Reinhold. *Moral Man and Immoral Society: A Study in Ethics and Politics*. Library of Theological Ethics. New York: Charles Scribner's Sons, 1932. Repr. Louisville, Ky.: Westminster John Knox Press, 2001.

Nieto, José C. "The Nonmystical Nature of the Sixteenth-Century Alumbrados of Toledo." In *The Spanish Inquisition and the Inquisitorial Mind*, Angel Alcalá, ed., 431–56. Atlantic Studies on Society in Change, 49. Boulder, Colo.: Social Science Monographs, 1987.

Norman, Diana. "'Love Justice, You Who Judge the Earth': The Paintings of the Sala dei Nove in the Palazzo Pubblico." In *Siena, Florence, and Padua: Art, Society, and Religion, 1280–1400*, Diana Norman, ed., 2:145–68. New Haven, Conn.: Yale University Press, in association with the Open University, 1995.

Oepke, Albrecht. "*kenos, kenoō, kenodoxos, kenodoxia*." In *Theological Dictionary of the New Testament*, Gerhard Kittel and Gerhard Friedrich, eds., and Geoffrey W. Bromiley, trans., 3:659–62. Grand Rapids, Mich.: Eerdmans, 1964–76.

Olin, John C. "Erasmus and St. Ignatius Loyola." *Six Essays on Erasmus*, 75–92. New York: Fordham University Press, 1979.

———. "The Idea of Pilgrimage in the Experience of Ignatius Loyola." *Church History* 48 (1979): 387–97.

Olivieri, Achillo. "Eroticism and Social Groups in Sixteenth-Century Venice: The Courtesan." In *Western Sexuality: Practice and Precept in Past and Present Times*, Philippe Ariès and André Béjin, eds., and Anthony Forster, trans., 95–102. Family, Sexuality, and Social Relations in Past Times. Oxford: Oxford University Press, 1985.

O'Malley, John W., ed. *Catholicism in Early Modern Europe: A Guide to Research*. Reformation Guides to Research, 2. St. Louis, Mo.: Center for Reformation Research, 1988.

———. "The Feast of Thomas Aquinas in Renaissance Rome: A Neglected Document and Its Import." *Rivista di storia della Chiesa in Italia* 35 (1981): 1–27.

———. *The First Jesuits.* Cambridge, Mass.: Harvard University Press, 1993.

———. "Five Missions of the Jesuit Charism: Content and Method." *Studies in the Spirituality of Jesuits* 38, no. 4 (2006).

———. *Four Cultures of the West.* Cambridge, Mass.: Belknap Press of Harvard University Press, 2004.

———. "The Fourth Vow in Its Ignatian Context: A Historical Study." *Studies in the Spirituality of Jesuits* 15, no. 1 (1983).

———. "The Historiography of the Society of Jesus: Where Does It Stand Today?" In *The Jesuits: Cultures, Sciences, and the Arts, 1540–1773*, J. W. O'Malley, G. A. Bailey, S. J. Harris, and T. F. Kennedy, eds., 3–37. Toronto: University of Toronto Press, 1999.

———. "How Humanistic Is the Jesuit Tradition? From the 1599 *Ratio Studiorum* to Now." In *Jesuit Education 21: Conference Proceedings on the Future of Jesuit Higher Education, 25–29 June 1999*, Martin R. Tripole, ed., 189–201. Philadelphia: Saint Joseph's University Press, 2000.

———. "The Jesuits, St. Ignatius, and the Counter Reformation: Some Recent Studies and Their Implications for Today." *Studies in the Spirituality of Jesuits* 14, no. 1 (1982).

———. *Praise and Blame in Renaissance Rome: Rhetoric, Doctrine, and Reform in the Sacred Orators of the Papal Court, ca. 1450–1521.* Duke Monographs in Medieval and Renaissance Studies, 3. Durham, N.C.: Duke University Press, 1979.

———. "Renaissance Humanism and the Religious Culture of the First Jesuits." *The Heythrop Journal* 31 (1990): 471–87.

———. "To Travel to Any Part of the World: Jerónimo Nadal and the Jesuit Vocation." *Studies in the Spirituality of Jesuits* 16, no. 2 (1984).

———. "Was Ignatius Loyola a Church Reformer? How to Look at Early Modern Catholicism." *Catholic Historical Review* 77 (1991): 177–93.

O'Malley, John W., G. A. Bailey, S. J. Harris, and T. F. Kennedy, eds. *The Jesuits: Cultures, Sciences, and the Arts, 1540–1773.* Toronto: University of Toronto Press, 1999.

O'Reilly, Leo. *Word and Sign in the Acts of the Apostles: A Study in Lucan Theology.* Analecta Gregoriana, 243. Roma: Editrice Pontificia Università Gregoriana, 1987.

O'Reilly, Terence W. "Erasmus, Ignatius Loyola, and Orthodoxy." *Journal of Theological Studies*, n.s., 30 (1979): 115–27.

———. "The Exercises of Saint Ignatius Loyola and the *Exercitatorio de la vida spiritual.*" *Studia monastica* 16 (1974): 301–23.

———. *From Ignatius Loyola to John of the Cross: Spirituality and Literature in Sixteenth-Century Spain.* Variorum Collected Studies Series, 484. London: Variorum, 1995.

———. "Ignatius of Loyola and the Counter-Reformation: The Hagiographic Tradition." *Heythrop Journal* 31 (1990): 439–70.

———. "Melchor Cano and the Spirituality of St. Ignatius Loyola." In *Ignacio de Loyola y su tiempo: Congreso internacional de historia (9–13 Setiembre 1991),* Juan Plazaola, ed., 369–80. Bilbao: Ediciones Mensajero, 1992.

———. "Melchor Cano's *Censura y parecer contra el Instituto de los Padres Jesuitas*: A Transcription of the British Library Manuscript." In *From Ignatius Loyola to John of the Cross: Spirituality and Literature in Sixteenth-Century Spain,* no. 5, 1–22. Variorum Collected Studies Series, 484. London: Variorum, 1995.

———. "Saint Ignatius Loyola and Spanish Erasmianism." *Archivum historicum Societatis Iesu* 43 (1974): 301–21.

———. "The *Spiritual Exercises* and the Crisis of Medieval Piety." *The Way,* Supplement, 70 (1991): 101–13.

Orella Unzué, José Luis. "La provincia de Guipúzcoa y el tema de los judíos en tiempos del joven Iñigo de Loyola (1492–1528)." In *Ignacio de Loyola y su tiempo: Congreso internacional de historia (9–13 Setiembre 1991),* Juan Plazaola, ed., 847–68. Bilbao: Ediciones Mensajero, 1992.

Orienti, Sandra, and Alberto Terruzzi. *Città di fondazione: Le 'reducciones' gesuitiche nel Paraguay tra il XVII e il XVIII secolo.* Firenze: Fratelli Alinari, 1982.

O'Rourke Boyle, Marjorie. "Angels Black and White: Loyola's Spiritual Discernment in Historical Perspective." *Theological Studies* 44 (1983): 241–57.

———. *Loyola's Acts: The Rhetoric of the Self.* The New Historicism: Studies in Cultural Poetics, 36. Berkeley: University of California Press, 1997.

———. "Luther's Rider-Gods: From the Steppe to the Tower." *Journal of Religious History* 13 (1985): 260–82.

Pacini, Gian Piero. "I Crociferi e le comunità ospedaliere lungo le vie dei pellegrinaggi nel Veneto medioevale secoli XII–XIV." In *I percorsi della fede e l'esperienza della carità nel Veneto medioevale (Atti del Convegno, Castello di Monselice, 28 maggio 2000),* Antonio Rigon, ed., 155–72. Monselice: Il Poligrafo, 2002.

Padberg, John W. "Ignatius and the Popes." In *Ignacio de Loyola y su tiempo: Congreso internacional de historia (9–13 Setiembre 1991),* Juan Plazaola, ed., 683–99. Bilbao: Ediciones Mensajero, 1992.

Pagden, Anthony. *The Fall of Natural Man: The American Indian and the Origins of Comparative Ethnology.* Cambridge: Cambridge University Press, 1982.

Park, Katharine. *Doctors and Medicine in Early Renaissance Florence.* Princeton, N.J.: Princeton University Press, 1985.

———. "Healing the Poor: Hospitals and Medical Assistance in Renaissance Florence." In *Medicine and Charity before the Welfare State*, Jonathan Barry and Colin Jones, eds., 26–45. London: Routledge, 1991.

Parsons, Mikeal C. "The Place of Jerusalem on the Lukan Landscape: An Exercise in Symbolic Cartography." In *Literary Studies in Luke-Acts: Essays in Honor of Joseph B. Tyson*, Richard P. Thompson and Thomas E. Phillips, eds., 155–71. Macon, Ga.: Mercer University Press, 1998.

Pastore, Alessandro. "Strutture assistenziali fra Chiesa e Stati nell'Italia della Controriforma." In *Storia d'Italia: Annali*. Vol. 9, *La chiesa e il potere politico dal Medioevo all'età contemporanea*, Giorgio Chittolini and Giovanni Miccoli, eds., 431–65. Torino: Einaudi, 1986.

Pastore, Stefania. *Il Vangelo e la spada: L'inquisizione di Castiglia e i suoi critici (1460–1598)*. "Tribunali della fede," Temi e testi, 46. Roma: Edizioni di Storia e Letteratura, 2003.

Pellegrini, Marco. "A Turning-Point in the History of the Factional System in the Sacred College: The Power of Pope and Cardinals in the Age of Alexander VI." In *Court and Politics in Papal Rome, 1492–1700*, Gianvittorio Signorotto and Maria Antonietta Visceglia, eds., 8–30. Cambridge Studies in Italian History and Culture. Cambridge: Cambridge University Press, 2002.

Penner, Todd. "Civilizing Discourse: Acts, Declamation, and the Rhetoric of the *Polis*." In *Contextualizing Acts: Lukan Narrative and Greco-Roman Discourse*, Todd Penner and Caroline Vander Stichele, eds., 65–104. Society of Biblical Literature Symposium Series, 20. Leiden: Brill, 2004.

Pérez-Mallaína, Pablo E. *Spain's Men of the Sea: Daily Life on the Indies Fleets in the Sixteenth Century*. Carla Rahn Phillips, trans. Baltimore: Johns Hopkins University Press, 2005.

Peristiany, John G., and Julian Pitt-Rivers, eds. *Honor and Grace in Anthropology*. Cambridge Studies in Social and Cultural Anthropology, 76. Cambridge: Cambridge University Press, 1992.

Perry, Mary Elizabeth. "'Lost Women' in Early Modern Seville: The Politics of Prostitution." *Feminist Studies* 4 (1978): 195–214.

———. "Magdalens and Jezebels in Counter-Reformation Spain." In *Culture and Control in Counter-Reformation Spain*, Anne J. Cruz and Mary Elizabeth Perry, eds., 124–44. Hispanic Issues, 7. Minneapolis: University of Minnesota Press, 1992.

Peters, Edward. "*Vir inconstans*: Moral Theology as Palaeopsychology." In *In the Garden of Evil: The Vices and Culture in the Middle Ages*, Richard Newhauser, ed., 59–73. Papers in Mediaeval Studies, 18. Toronto: Pontifical Institute of Mediaeval Studies, 2005.

Peterson, David S., with Daniel E. Bornstein, eds. *Florence and Beyond: Culture, Society, and Politics in Renaissance Italy. Essays in Honour of John M. Najemy*.

Essays and Studies, 15. Toronto: Centre for Reformation and Renaissance Studies, 2008.

Peterson, Willard J. "What to Wear? Observation and Participation by Jesuit Missionaries in Late Ming Society." In *Implicit Understandings: Observing, Reporting, and Reflecting on the Encounters between Europeans and Other Peoples in the Early Modern Era*, Stuart B. Schwartz, ed., 403–21. Cambridge: Cambridge University Press, 1994.

Petrarca, Francesco. "The Ascent of Mont Ventoux." In *The Renaissance Philosophy of Man*, Ernst Cassirer, Paul Oskar Kristeller, and John Herman Randall, Jr., eds., and Hans Nachod, trans., 36–46. Chicago: University of Chicago Press, 1948.

———. "On His Own Ignorance and That of Many Others." In *The Renaissance Philosophy of Man*, Ernst Cassirer, Paul Oskar Kristeller, and John Herman Randall, Jr., eds., and Hans Nachod, trans., 49–133. Chicago: University of Chicago Press, 1948.

Phelan, John Leddy. *The Millennial Kingdom of the Franciscans in the New World.* 2nd ed. Berkeley: University of California Press, 1970.

Phillips, Thomas E. "Reading Recent Readings of Issues of Wealth and Poverty in Luke and Acts." *Currents in Biblical Research* 1 (2003): 231–69.

Pitt-Rivers, Julian. "The Anthropology of Honour." In *The Fate of Shechem, or The Politics of Sex: Essays in the Anthropology of the Mediterranean*, 1–17. Cambridge Studies and Papers in Social Anthropology, 19. Cambridge: Cambridge University Press, 1977.

Plazaola, Juan, ed. *Ignacio de Loyola y su tiempo: Congreso internacional de historia (9–13 Setiembre 1991).* Bilbao: Ediciones Mensajero, 1992.

Polgár, László. *Bibliographie sur l'histoire de la Compagnie de Jésus, 1901–1980.* 3 vols. Roma: Institutum Historicum Societatis Iesu, 1981–90.

Poliakov, Léon. *The History of Anti-Semitism.* Vol. 2, *From Mohammed to the Marranos.* Natalie Gerardi, trans. New York: Vanguard Press, 1973.

Prosperi, Adriano. "The Missionary." In *Baroque Personae*, Rosario Villari, ed., and Lydia G. Cochrane, trans., 160–94. Chicago: University of Chicago Press, 1995.

Pullan, Brian S. "Catholics, Protestants, and the Poor in Early Modern Europe." *Journal of Interdisciplinary History* 35 (2005): 441–56.

———. *Rich and Poor in Renaissance Venice: The Social Institutions of a Catholic State, to 1620.* Cambridge, Mass.: Harvard University Press, 1971.

———. "The *Scuole Grandi* of Venice: Some Further Thoughts." In *Christianity and the Renaissance: Image and Religious Imagination in the Quattrocento*, Timothy Verdon and John Henderson, eds., 272–301. Syracuse, N.Y.: Syracuse University Press, 1990.

———. "Support and Redeem: Charity and Poor Relief in Italian Cities from the Fourteenth to the Seventeenth Century." *Continuity and Change* 3 (1988): 177–208.

Quinn, Peter A. "Ignatius Loyola and Gian Pietro Carafa: Catholic Reformers at Odds." *Catholic Historical Review* 67 (1981): 386–400.

Ragazzoni, David. "Ignazio lettore 'mancato' dell'*Enchiridion*: Possibili reminiscenze erasmiane negli *Esercizi spirituali*?" *Rinascimento*, n.s., 46 (2006): 373–90.

Rahner, Karl. *The Dynamic Element in the Church*. W. J. O'Hara, trans. Quaestiones Disputatae, 12. New York: Herder and Herder, 1964.

Rahn Phillips, Carla. *Six Galleons for the King of Spain: Imperial Defense in the Early Seventeenth Century*. Baltimore: Johns Hopkins University Press, 1986.

Raitt, Jill. "Two Spiritual Directors of Women in the Sixteenth Century: St. Ignatius Loyola and St. Teresa of Avila." In *In Laudem Caroli: Renaissance and Reformation Studies for Charles G. Nauert*, James V. Mehl, ed., 213–32. Sixteenth Century Essays & Studies, 49. Kirksville, Mo.: Thomas Jefferson University Press, 1998.

Raitt, Jill, with Bernard McGinn and John Meyendorff, eds. *Christian Spirituality: High Middle Ages and Reformation*. World Spirituality, 17. London: Routledge & Kegan Paul, 1987.

Raitz von Frentz, Emmerich. "Ludolphe le Chartreux et les Exercises de S. Ignace de Loyola." *Revue d'ascétique et de mystique* 25 (1949): 375–88.

Ranft, Patricia. "A Key to Counter Reformation Women's Activism: The Confessor-Spiritual Director." *Journal of Feminist Studies in Religion* 10, no. 2 (1994): 7–26.

Rastoin, Marc. "From Windfall to Fall: The *Conversos* in the Society of Jesus." In *Friends on the Way: Jesuits Encounter Contemporary Judaism*, Tom Michel, ed., 8–27. New York: Fordham University Press, 2007.

Ravid, Benjamin. "The Legal Status of the Jews in Venice to 1509." *Proceedings of the American Academy for Jewish Research* 54 (1987): 169–202.

Ravier, André. *Ignatius of Loyola and the Founding of the Society of Jesus*. Maura Daly, Joan Daly, and Carson Daly, trans. San Francisco: Ignatius Press, 1987.

Reicke, Bo Ivar. "Instruction and Discussion in the Travel Narrative." *Studia Evangelica: Papers Presented to the International Congress on "The Four Gospels in 1957" Held at Christ Church, Oxford, 1957*, Kurt Aland et al., eds., 206–16. Texte und Untersuchungen zur Geschichte der altchristlichen Literatur, 73. Berlin: Akademie-Verlag, 1959.

Reinhard, Wolfgang, ed. *Humanismus im Bildungswesen des 15. und 16. Jahrhunderts*. Deutsche Forschungsgemeinschaft. Wenheim: Acta Humaniora, 1984.

Reites, James W. "St. Ignatius of Loyola and the Jews." *Studies in the Spirituality of Jesuits* 13, no. 4 (1981).

Rey, Eusebio. "San Ignacio de Loyola y el problema de los cristianos nuevos." *Razón y fe* 153 (1956): 173–204.

Riel, Gerd van, Caroline Macé, and Leen van Campe, eds. *Platonic Ideas and Concept Formation in Ancient and Medieval Thought.* Leuven: Universitaire Pers, 2004.

Rigon, Antonio, ed. *I percorsi della fede e l'esperienza della carità nel Veneto medioevale (Atti del Convegno, Castello di Monselice, 28 maggio 2000).* Monselice: Il Poligrafo, 2002.

Rittner, Carol Ann, and John K. Roth, eds. *"Good News" after Auschwitz? Christian Faith within a Post-Holocaust World.* Macon, Ga.: Mercer University Press, 2001.

Robb, David M. "The Iconography of the Annunciation in the Fourteenth and Fifteenth Centuries." *Art Bulletin* 18 (1936): 480–526.

Robinson, William C., Jr. "The Theological Context for Interpreting Luke's Travel Narrative (9:51 ff.)." *Journal of Biblical Literature* 79 (1960): 20–31.

Rohrbaugh, Richard L., ed. *The Social Sciences and New Testament Interpretation.* Peabody, Mass.: Hendrickson, 1996.

Romano, Andrea. "Il *Messanese Collegium Prototypum Societatis Iesu.*" In *Gesuiti e università in Europa (secoli XVI–XVIII) (Atti del Convegno di studi, Parma, 13–15 dicembre 2001),* Gian Paolo Brizzi and Roberto Greci, eds., 79–94. Centro interuniversitario per la storia delle università italiane: Studi, 3. Bologna: Cooperativa Libraria Universitaria Editrice, 2002.

Ronan, Charles E., and Bonnie B. C. Oh, eds. *East Meets West: The Jesuits in China, 1582–1773.* Chicago: Loyola University Press, 1988.

Rosenblatt, Eloise. "Canonizing Edith Stein and Recognizing Catholic Anti-Semitism." In *"Good News" after Auschwitz?: Christian Faith within a Post-Holocaust World,* Carol Ann Rittner and John K. Roth, eds., 45–68. Macon, Ga.: Mercer University Press, 2001.

Ross, Andrew C. "Alessandro Valignano: The Jesuits and Culture in the East." In *The Jesuits: Cultures, Sciences, and the Arts, 1540–1773,* J. W. O'Malley, G. A. Bailey, S. J. Harris, and T. F. Kennedy, eds., 336–51. Toronto: University of Toronto Press, 1999.

———. *A Vision Betrayed: The Jesuits in Japan and China, 1542–1742.* Edinburgh: Edinburgh University Press, 1994.

Roth, Norman. "The Jews of Spain and the Expulsion of 1492." *The Historian* 55 (1992): 17–30.

Rotsaert, Mark. "Les premiers contacts de saint Ignace avec l'érasmisme espagnol." *Revue d'histoire de la spiritualité* 49 (1973): 443–64.

Rousseau, Philip. *Ascetics, Authority, and the Church in the Age of Jerome and Cassian.* Oxford: Oxford University Press, 1978.

Rowland, Beryl. *Birds with Human Souls: A Guide to Bird Symbolism.* Knoxville: University of Tennessee Press, 1978.

Ruggiero, Guido, ed. *A Companion to the Worlds of the Renaissance*. Blackwell Companions to European History. Oxford: Blackwell, 2002.

Ruiz Jurado, Manuel "¿Influyó en S. Ignacio el *Ejercitatorio* de Cisneros?" *Manresa* 51 (1979): 65–75.

———. *Orientaciones bibliográficas sobre San Ignacio de Loyola*. Vol. 2, *1965–76*. Subsidia ad historiam Societatis Iesu, 8. Roma: Institutum Historicum Societatis Iesu, 1977; Vol. 3, *1977–89*. Subsidia ad historiam Societatis Iesu, 10. Roma: Institutum Historicum Societatis Iesu, 1990.

Rummel, Erika. *Erasmus and His Catholic Critics*. 2 vols. Bibliotheca Humanistica & Reformatoria, 45. Nieuwkoop: De Graaf Publishers, 1989.

Rusconi, Roberto. "Confraternite, compagnie, e devozioni." In *Storia d'Italia: Annali*. Vol. 9, *La chiesa e il potere politico dal Medioevo all'età contemporanea*, Giorgio Chittolini and Giovanni Miccoli, eds., 467–506. Torino: Einaudi, 1986.

———. *L'ordine dei peccati: La confessione tra Medioevo ed età moderna*. Saggi, 562. Bologna: Il Mulino, 2002.

Rushing, Sandra M. *The Magdalene Legacy: Exploring the Wounded Icon of Sexuality*. Westport, Conn.: Bergin & Garvey, 1994.

Safley, Thomas Max, ed. *The Reformation of Charity: The Secular and the Religious in Early Modern Poor Relief*. Studies in Central European Histories. Boston: Brill, 2003.

Salomon, David A. "Forging a New Identity: Narcissism and Imagination in the Mysticism of Ignatius Loyola." *Christianity and Literature* 47 (1998): 195–212.

Salvat, Ignasi. "The Ignatian Experience of 'Service as Worldwide Mission' as Basis for Interpreting the *Constitutions*." *Centrum Ignatianum Spiritualitatis (CIS)* 20, no. 3 (1990): 39–49.

Sandoval, Alonso de. *Treatise on Slavery: Selections from "De instauranda Aethiopum salute*." Nicole von Germeten, trans. Indianapolis, Ind.: Hackett, 2008.

———. *Un tratado sobre la esclavitud ("De instauranda Aethiopum salute")*. Enriqueta Vila Vilar, trans. Madrid: Alianza Editorial, 1987.

Sanz de Diego, Rafael M. "Ignacio de Loyola en Alcalá de Henares (1526–1527): Andanzas de un universitario atípico." In *Ignacio de Loyola y su tiempo: Congreso internacional de historia (9–13 Setiembre 1991)*, Juan Plazaola, ed., 883–900. Bilbao: Ediciones Mensajero, 1992.

Saxer, Victor. "Santa Maria Maddalena: Dalla storia evangelica alla leggenda e all'arte." In *La Maddalena tra sacro e profano*, Marilena Mosco, ed., 24–28. Firenze: La casa Usher, 1986.

Scaduto, Mario. "Laínez e l'Indice del 1559: Lullo, Sabunde, Savonarola, Erasmo." *Archivum historicum Societatis Iesu* 24 (1955): 3–32.

———. "La strada e i primi gesuiti." *Archivum historicum Societatis Iesu* 40 (1971): 323–90.

Schevill, Rudolph. *Ovid and the Renascence in Spain*. University of California Publications in Modern Philology, 4, no. 1. Berkeley: University of California Press, 1913.

Schineller, Peter. "In Their Own Words." *Studies in the Spirituality of Jesuits* 38, no. 1 (2006).

Schmitt, Charles B., and Quentin Skinner, eds. *The Cambridge History of Renaissance Philosophy*. Cambridge: Cambridge University Press, 1988.

Schmitt, Jean-Claude. "Le suicide au Moyen Âge." *Annales: Économies sociétés civilisations* 31 (1976): 3–28.

Schneider, Jane. "Peacocks and Penguins: The Political Economy of European Cloth and Colors." *American Ethnologist* 5 (1978): 413–47.

Schner, George P., ed. *Ignatian Spirituality in a Secular Age*. Studies in Religion Supplements, 15. Waterloo, Ont.: Wilfrid Laurier University Press, 1984.

Schnucker, Robert V., ed. *Calviniana: Ideas and Influence of Jean Calvin*. Sixteenth Century Essays & Studies, 10. Kirksville, Mo.: Sixteenth Century Journal Publishers, 1988.

Schutte, Anne Jacobson. "Periodization of Sixteenth-Century Italian Religious History: The Post-Cantimori Paradigm Shift." *Journal of Modern History* 61 (1989): 269–84.

Schütte, Josef Franz. *Valignano's Mission Principles for Japan*. Vol. 1, *From His Appointment as Visitor until His First Departure from Japan (1573–1582)*. Part 2, *The Solution (1580–82)*. John J. Coyne, trans. Modern Scholarly Studies about the Jesuits in English Translations, 5. St. Louis, Mo.: Institute of Jesuit Sources, 1985.

Schwartz, Stuart B., ed. *Implicit Understandings: Observing, Reporting, and Reflecting on the Encounters between Europeans and Other Peoples in the Early Modern Era*. Cambridge: Cambridge University Press, 1994.

Schweitzer, Vincentius, ed. *Concilium Tridentinum: Diariorum, Actorum, Epistularum, Tractatum Nova Collectio*. Vol. 12, *Tractatum Pars Prior*. Freiburg im Breisgau: Herder, 1929. Repr. Freiburg im Breisgau: Herder, 1966.

Scott, James M. "Luke's Geographical Horizon." In *The Book of Acts in Its First Century Setting*. Vol. 2, *The Book of Acts in Its Graeco-Roman Setting*, David W. J. Gill and Conrad Gempf, eds., 483–544. Grand Rapids, Mich.: Eerdmans, 1994.

Seidel Menchi, Silvana. *Erasmo in Italia, 1520–1580*. Nuova Cultura, 1. Torino: Bollati Boringhieri, 1987.

———. "Origine e origini del Santo Uffizio dell'Inquisizione romana (1542–1559)." In *L'Inquisizione (Atti del Simposio internazionale, Città del Vaticano, 29–31 ottobre 1998)*, Agostino Borromeo, ed., 291–321. Studi e testi, 417. Città del Vaticano: Biblioteca Apostolica Vaticana, 2003.

Selwyn, Jennifer D. *A Paradise Inhabited by Devils: The Jesuits' Civilizing Mission in Early Modern Naples*. Catholic Christendom, 1300–1700. Aldershot, U.K.: Institutum Historicum Societatis Iesu, 2004.

Sher Tinsley, Barbara. *Pierre Bayle's Reformation: Conscience and Criticism on the Eve of the Enlightenment*. Cranbury, N.J.: Associated University Presses, 2001.

Shulevitz, Judith. "The Close Reader: The Case of Pius XII." *New York Times Book Review* (8 April 2001): 34.

Shulvass, Moses A. *The Jews in the World of the Renaissance*. Elvin I. Kose, trans. Leiden: Brill, 1973.

Signorotto, Gianvittorio, and Maria Antonietta Visceglia, eds. *Court and Politics in Papal Rome, 1492–1700*. Cambridge Studies in Italian History and Culture. Cambridge: Cambridge University Press, 2002.

Silos, Leonardo R. "Cardoner in the Life of Saint Ignatius of Loyola." *Archivum historicum Societatis Iesu* 33 (1964): 3–43.

Simonsohn, Shlomo. *The Apostolic See and the Jews*. Vol. 6, *Documents: 1546–1555*. PIMS Studies and Texts, 106. Toronto: Pontifical Institute of Mediaeval Studies, 1990.

———. *The Apostolic See and the Jews*. Vol. 7, *History*. PIMS Studies and Texts, 109. Toronto: Pontifical Institute of Mediaeval Studies, 1991.

Simson, P. "The Drama of the City of God: Jerusalem in St. Luke's Gospel." *Scripture* 15 (1963): 65–80.

Spaas, Lieve, with Trista Selous, eds. *Echoes of Narcissus*. Polygons: Cultural Diversities and Intersections, 2. New York: Bergahn Books, 2000.

Spence, Jonathan D. "Matteo Ricci and the Ascent to Peking." In *East Meets West: The Jesuits in China, 1582–1773*, Charles E. Ronan and Bonnie B. C. Oh, eds., 3–18. Chicago: Loyola University Press, 1988.

———. *The Memory Palace of Matteo Ricci*. New York: Penguin Books, 1984.

Staley, Jeffrey L. " 'With the Power of the Spirit': Plotting the Program and Parallels of Luke 4:14–37 in Luke-Acts." In *Society of Biblical Literature 1993 Seminar Papers*, Eugene H. Lovering, Jr., ed., 281–302. SBL Seminar Paper Series, 32. Atlanta: Scholars Press, 1993.

Steinberg, Leo. *The Sexuality of Christ in Renaissance Art and in Modern Oblivion*. 2nd ed. Chicago: University of Chicago Press, 1996.

Steinmetz, David C. "Luther and Loyola." In *Ignacio de Loyola y su tiempo: Congreso internacional de historia (9–13 Setiembre 1991)*, Juan Plazaola, ed., 791–800. Bilbao: Ediciones Mensajero, 1992.

Stewart, Columba. *Cassian the Monk*. Oxford Studies in Historical Theology. Oxford: Oxford University Press, 1998.

———. "Evagrius Ponticus and the 'Eight Generic *Logismoi*.' " In *In the Garden of Evil: The Vices and Culture in the Middle Ages*, Richard Newhauser, ed., 3–34. Papers in Mediaeval Studies, 18. Toronto: Pontifical Institute of Mediaeval Studies, 2005.

Stinger, Charles L. *The Renaissance in Rome.* Bloomington: Indiana University Press, 1985.

Stone, M. W. F. "'*Initium omnis peccati est superbia*': Jean Gerson's Analysis of Pride in His Mystical Theology, Pastoral Thought, and Hamartiology." In *In the Garden of Evil: The Vices and Culture in the Middle Ages*, Richard Newhauser, ed., 293–323. Papers in Mediaeval Studies, 18. Toronto: Pontifical Institute of Mediaeval Studies, 2005.

———. "Making Sense of Thomas Aquinas in the Sixteenth Century: Domingo de Soto on the Natural Desire to See God." In *Platonic Ideas and Concept Formation in Ancient and Medieval Thought*, Gerd van Riel, Caroline Macé, and Leen van Campe, eds., 211–32. Leuven: Universitaire Pers, 2004.

Stow, Kenneth R. "The Burning of the Talmud in 1553, in the Light of Sixteenth-Century Catholic Attitudes toward the Talmud." *Bibliothèque d'humanisme et Renaissance* 34 (1972): 435–59.

———. *Theater of Acculturation: The Roman Ghetto in the Sixteenth Century.* Seattle: University of Washington Press, 2001.

Strathmann, Hermann. "*polis, polites, politeuomai, politeia, politeuma*." In *Theological Dictionary of the New Testament*, Gerhard Kittel and Gerhard Friedrich, eds., and Geoffrey W. Bromiley, trans., 6:516–35. Grand Rapids, Mich.: Eerdmans, 1964–76.

Straw, Carole. "Gregory, Cassian, and the Cardinal Vices." In *In the Garden of Evil: The Vices and Culture in the Middle Ages*, Richard Newhauser, ed., 35–58. Papers in Mediaeval Studies, 18. Toronto: Pontifical Institute of Mediaeval Studies, 2005.

Sumption, Jonathan. *Pilgrimage: An Image of Mediaeval Religion.* London: Faber & Faber, 1975.

Syrkin, Alexander Y. "On the Behavior of the 'Fool for Christ's Sake.'" *History of Religions* 22 (1982): 150–71.

Tentler, Thomas N. *Sin and Confession on the Eve of the Reformation.* Princeton, N.J.: Princeton University Press, 1977.

Terpstra, Nicholas. "Confraternities and Public Charity: Modes of Civic Welfare in Early Modern Italy." In *Confraternities and Catholic Reform in Italy, France, and Spain*, John Patrick Donnelly and Michael W. Maher, eds., 97–121. Sixteenth Century Essays & Studies, 44. Kirksville, Mo.: Thomas Jefferson University Press, 1999.

Tetel, Marcel, Ronald G. Witt, and Rona Goffen, eds. *Life and Death in Fifteenth-Century Florence.* Durham, N.C.: Duke University Press, 1989.

Thompson, Richard P., and Thomas E. Phillips, eds. *Literary Studies in Luke-Acts: Essays in Honor of Joseph B. Tyson.* Macon, Ga.: Mercer University Press, 1998.

Todorov, Tzvetan. *The Conquest of America: The Question of the Other.* Richard Howard, trans. New York: Harper & Row, 1984.

Trexler, Richard C. "Florentine Prostitution in the Fifteenth Century: Patrons and Clients." In *Dependence in Context in Renaissance Florence*, 373–414. Medieval & Renaisssance Texts & Studies, 111. Binghamton: Center for Medieval and Early Renaissance Studies, State University of New York at Binghamton, 1994.

Trinkaus, Charles. *In Our Image and Likeness: Humanity and Divinity in Italian Humanist Thought*. 2 vols. Chicago: University of Chicago Press, 1970.

Tripole, Martin R., ed. *Jesuit Education 21: Conference Proceedings on the Future of Jesuit Higher Education, 25–29 June 1999*. Philadelphia: Saint Joseph's University Press, 2000.

Tuckett, Christopher M., ed. *Luke's Literary Achievement: Collected Essays. Journal for the Study of the New Testament* Supplement Series, 116. Sheffield, U.K.: Sheffield Academic Press, 1995.

Turner, Victor W., and Edith Turner. *Image and Pilgrimage in Christian Culture: Anthropological Perspectives*. New York: Columbia University Press, 1978.

Turrini, Miriam, and Annamaria Valenti. "L'educazione religiosa." In *Il catechismo e la grammatica*. Vol. 1, *Istruzione e controllo sociale nell'area emiliana e romagnola nel '700*, Gian Paolo Brizzi, ed., 347–423. Cultura e vita civile nel Settecento. Bologna: Il Mulino, 1985.

Urrutia, José Luis. *Ignacio: Los años de la espada*. Tafalla: Editorial Txalaparta, 2005.

Vauchez, André. "Patronage des saints et religion civique dans l'Italie communale à la fin du Moyen Age." In *Patronage and Public in the Trecento: Proceedings of the St. Lambrecht Symposium, Abtei St. Lambrecht, Styria, 16–19 July 1984*, Vincent Moleta, ed., 59–80. Biblioteca dell'*Archivum Romanicum*, 202. Firenze: Olschki, 1986.

———. *Sainthood in the Later Middle Ages*. Jean Birrell, trans. Cambridge: Cambridge University Press, 1997.

Vercruysse, Jos E. "L'historiographie ignatienne aux XVI–XVIII siècles." In *Ignacio de Loyola y su tiempo: Congreso internacional de historia (9–13 Setiembre 1991)*, Juan Plazaola, ed., 37–54. Bilbao: Ediciones Mensajero, 1992.

Verdon, Timothy, and John Henderson, eds. *Christianity and the Renaissance: Image and Religious Imagination in the Quattrocento*. Syracuse, N.Y.: Syracuse University Press, 1990.

Villari, Rosario, ed., and Lydia G. Cochrane, trans. *Baroque Personae*. Chicago: University of Chicago Press, 1995.

Vinge, Louise. *The Narcissus Theme in Western European Literature up to the Early Nineteenth Century*. Robert Dewsnap, Lisbeth Grönlund, Nigel Reeves, and Ingrid Söderberg-Reeves, trans. Lund: Gleerups, 1967.

Viviano, Benedict T. "The Gospel According to Matthew." In *The New Jerome Biblical Commentary*, Raymond E. Brown, Joseph A. Fitzmyer, and Roland E. Murphy, eds., 630–74. Englewood Cliffs, N.J.: Prentice Hall, 1990.

Webb, Diana. *Patrons and Defenders: The Saints in the Italian City-States.* International Library of Historical Studies, 4. London: I. B. Tauris, 1996.

Weinstein, Donald, and Rudolph M. Bell. *Saints and Society: The Two Worlds of Western Christendom, 1000–1700.* Chicago: University of Chicago Press, 1982.

White, T. H., ed. and trans. *The Bestiary: A Book of Beasts.* New York: G. P. Putnam's Sons, 1954.

Wilmott, Michael J., and Charles B. Schmitt. "Biobibliographies." In *The Cambridge History of Renaissance Philosophy,* Charles B. Schmitt and Quentin Skinner, eds., 805–41. Cambridge: Cambridge University Press, 1988.

Wisch, Barbara, and Diane Cole Ahl, eds. *Confraternities and the Visual Arts in Renaissance Italy: Ritual, Spectacle, Image.* Cambridge: Cambridge University Press, 2000.

Witherington, Ben, III. *The Acts of the Apostles: A Socio-Rhetorical Commentary.* Grand Rapids, Mich.: Eerdmans, 1998.

Woodbridge, Linda. "Renaissance Bogeymen." In *A Companion to the Worlds of the Renaissance,* Guido Ruggiero, ed., 444–59. Blackwell Companions to European History. Oxford: Blackwell, 2002.

Zacher, Christian K. *Curiosity and Pilgrimage: The Literature of Discovery in Fourteenth-Century England.* Baltimore: Johns Hopkins University Press, 1976.

Zanardi, Mario, ed. *I gesuiti e Venezia: Momenti e problemi di storia veneziana della Compagnia di Gesù (Atti del Convegno di Studi, Venezia, 2–5 ottobre 1990).* Padova: Gregoriana Libreria Editrice, 1994.

Zardin, Danilo. "Le confraternite in Italia settentrionale fra XV e XVIII secolo." In *Città italiane del '500 tra Riforma e Controriforma,* 165–80. Lucca: Maria Pacini Fazzi, 1988.

Zumthor, Paul. "The Medieval Travel Narrative." Catherine Peebles, trans. *New Literary History* 25 (1994): 809–24.

Index of Scriptural References

General Index